CHURCHILL
THE YOUNG WARRIOR

CHURCHILL
THE YOUNG WARRIOR

HOW HE HELPED WIN
THE FIRST WORLD WAR

JOHN HARTE

Skyhorse Publishing

Skyhorse Publishing books may be purchased in bulk at special discounts for sales promotion, corporate gifts, fund-raising, or educational purposes. Special editions can also be created to specifications. For details, contact the Special Sales Department, Skyhorse Publishing, 307 West 36th Street, 11th Floor, New York, NY 10018 or info@ skyhorsepublishing.com.

Skyhorse® and Skyhorse Publishing® are registered trademarks of Skyhorse Publishing, Inc.®, a Delaware corporation.

Visit our website at www.skyhorsepublishing.com.

10 9 8 7 6 5 4 3 2 1

Library of Congress Cataloging-in-Publication Data is available on file.

Cover design by Rain Saukas
Cover photo: Public domain

Print ISBN: 978-1-5107-1702-2
Ebook ISBN: 978-1-5107-1703-9

Permission from The Orion Publishing Group, London UK, to quote passages from Sir Basil Liddell Hart's HISTORY OF THE FIRST WORLD WAR, published first in 1930 as *The Real War 1914-1918* by Cassell & Company Ltd, London UK. Copyright 1930, 1934 © 1970 Lady Liddell Hart.
Permission also from Penguin Random House UK, London UK, to quote extracts from CHURCHILL: A LIFE by Sir Martin Gilbert, first published by Heinemann, London in 1991.

Printed in the United States of America

"History is the result of unintended consequences."

—*Attribution unknown*

CONTENTS

AUTHOR'S PREFACE

THERE HAVE BEEN ONLY TWO WORLD Wars until now. But many people believe that a Third World War is inevitable—partly because the Digital Age has placed our worst neighbors on our doorsteps, and partly because of the flaws in the human condition. And history demonstrates the problems they have already caused us for centuries. So it should pay us to explore why the First World War erupted and what could have been done to prevent it from happening, or halt it before it was too late.

Since one man played a pivotal role in both World Wars, this book describes what he learned about war and the flaws in human nature while fighting in several wars as a young soldier, as a war correspondent at the frontline, as an aspiring young politician, and also as First Lord of the Admiralty who contributed to the Allied victory in the First World War. (My previous book, *How Churchill Saved Civilization,* shows how he led the free world to victory as an older man of fifty-nine in the Second World War).

Seventy years after Winston Churchill led the Allied Forces of the free and democratic world to victory against fascism, a false mythology has grown about him, so that new generations are given a misleading image of a portly middle-aged and somewhat conservative statesman with old-fashioned sentiments. In fact, he was a thoroughly modern, imaginative, and adventurous young man, who fought coolly on several battlefronts as a professional army officer, where he learned that enemies have to be crushed instantly with even greater force and determination than before, until they can do no more harm. He never gave in, and argued that war is preferable to slavery. He possessed a killer instinct, which he sought from his generals in the Second World War.

He was a Liberal in politics, a champion of the marginalized, the poor and needy, the old and infirm, and the underdog.

The First World War still contains mysteries which have not been satisfactorily explained. They are described here for readers to understand the complexities that face historians. They reveal so many poor judgments, and so much irrational and self-destructive behavior on the part of leaders who influenced events, that it is hard for most historians to credit so many mistakes, so much incompetence, folly, and muddling through that led to one disaster after another and resulted in the gruesome deaths of millions.

In 2013, historian Margaret MacMillan—the great-granddaughter of David Lloyd George, Britain's Prime Minister during much of the First World War—wrote a new book on World War I in an attempt to discover why it began, because it is still so much of a mystery. Many historians agree, however, that the cause was the network of treaties and alliances that were set in motion when the heir to the Austro-Hungarian Empire was assassinated and Austria mobilized its troops for war against Serbia. But not everyone agrees. One of the most esteemed military historians, the late Captain Sir Basil Liddell Hart, who served in the First World War, attributed it to Pride, Fear and Hunger.[1]

Margaret Macmillan writes:

We also remember the Great War because it is such a puzzle. How could Europe have done this to itself and to the world? There are many possible explanations; indeed, so many that it is difficult to choose among them. For a start the arms race, rigid military plans, economic rivalry, trade wars, imperialism with its scramble for colonies, or the alliance systems dividing Europe into unfriendly camps . . .[2]

And there are other factors that could have triggered the eruption of the First World War. I have set out many of them for readers to examine like clues in a murder mystery: Who had the motive to start the war? And what did they expect to gain?

All histories and biographies are selective. This one is written for general readers in the digital age, instead of in the traditional formula for specialists, academics, or historians, in which every possible detail is meticulously recorded. Intelligent and busy readers today demand facts that are easy to read and about one-third of the traditional length of biographies or histories. Sir Winston Churchill's official biography, for example, is eight volumes long, or 25,000 pages. Its abridged version by the same biographer runs to a thousand pages.[3] This book is deliberately around only 300 pages, without excluding anything significant that might prevent readers from understanding the events and their consequences, and arriving at reasonable conclusions.

A reasonable prediction for the eruption of a possible Third World War was used as a title for a 1987 book by Robert McNamara (former US Secretary of Defense under Presidents John F. Kennedy and Lyndon B. Johnson). He called it *Blundering into Disaster*. When literary critic Martin Amis reviewed it, he wrote, "Our experience of World Wars is confined to just two models— Sarajevo and Munich, critical accident and unappeasable psychosis." World War III, he implied, "will more likely be some kind of mixture. The only thing that could precipitate general nuclear attack would be the fear of general nuclear attack. You would never go first unless the enemy looked like going first; and, in a crisis, he would look like going first, and so would you." In the meantime, as he observed, we continue living in a "dangerous dream," in which our political and military leaders continue to make much the same mistakes as before.

Perhaps the most powerful influence on Winston Churchill's worldview was what he learned as a young professional soldier, and what he drew from his studies of history and Social Darwinism. It was that, whatever the political or military, or cultural or social situation today, it had all happened many times before in one way or another. The key to the future could be found in what happened in the past. Powerful nations rose and fell, and crumbled into dust that was swept away by the winds of time, as we all are. There was nothing new in trivial human affairs. It was no use making a fuss about it - you had to stare reality in the face without blinking and outwit the challenges that life created.

—*John Harte, Ottawa, Canada, April 2017*

1

JENNIE

WHEN BABY JENNIE CRIED OUT WITH surprise and not a little dismay at her change of venue as she emerged into the world of 1854, she drew in her first breath of the exhilarating air of New York City and decided she loved it. She was named after the much beloved opera singer Jenny Lind, who was reputed to be one of her father's mistresses. Leonard Jerome had been well off financially, but invested a great deal of money in railroad stock, which fell sharply in value, leaving him penniless. He had no choice but to declare bankruptcy.

But the New York Stock Exchange was a handy bank to draw on for risk-takers of his flamboyant and fun-loving personality. So his investments soon did well again by buying short on the upward swing of the market before laying out any money, and becoming a new-rich millionaire. There were plenty of them about in America at the time, and Jennie was spoilt by easy money from the beginning. So were her two sisters.

Who could fail to spoil Jennie at fifteen? She was appealingly beautiful. Her eyes were warm as amber-colored honey, her hair dark brown. Her figure was alluring and graceful, with its tiny fashionable waistline and full bosom and hips—all calculated to initiate and maintain a full social life with society's trendsetters. She was always a spendthrift and wore the most fashionably seductive Paris gowns. Men turned their heads to watch her, and were drawn to her, not only for her beauty but also for her lust for life. They found her irresistible. Wherever she went, she attracted new lovers. Jennie was always the talk of the town.

All three sisters naturally learned the skills required of young ladies, like piano-playing, riding, and ice-skating, while their parents entertained extravagantly, and Leonard bought a large yacht. Their neighbors were billionaires, and included the Vanderbilts. Leonard Jerome even built a private theater in his mansion in order to parade his opera-singing mistresses. He also owned shares in an influential newspaper and supported President Abraham Lincoln in his efforts to free the slaves. So that with all the social and political activity, Jennie—who was his favorite daughter—became aware of current events and foreign affairs by the time she was sixteen.

With her father's interest in thoroughbreds and horse-racing, Jennie had been riding horseback since she was a child. The Jockey Club of America first met in her father's house, called Jerome Park. It was the social event of the year. So Jennie was accustomed to socializing with the smart and wealthy set. Leonard Jerome leased his home to the Jockey Club thereafter as a speculation. That was the point at which her mother tired of her *bon viveur* husband's lifestyle with his mistresses and took Jennie and her sisters away to Paris.

The women were excited to leave for Paris, which was the fashion center of the world. Although the move was partly to escape from her husband's garish lifestyle with his mistresses, it was also partly to find wealthy husbands for Clara's three marriageable daughters. Clara was evidently a self-confident and independent woman, and Leonard had no qualms at leaving them on their own there—the girls at a fashionable finishing school, to continue with their piano lessons and learn court etiquette and ceremony. Now Jennie rode on the Bois de Boulogne and mixed with French royalty and the aristocracy, and listened with fascination when her older sisters regaled her with their own glamorous experiences.

When German troops crossed the frontier into Alsace and also annexed Lorraine in August 1870, as part of the German Empire, France was diminished and dismayed. German Chancellor Bismarck intended to keep the French that way, to avoid another experience like the Napoleonic Wars which had torn their destructive way through Europe. A French attempt to save Bazaine resulted in their defeat at Sedan. The French Emperor was deposed and the Prussian Army marched through Paris to demonstrate who was in charge of Europe. It was time for the Jerome women to leave France.

They fled to London, where Leonard Jerome booked a suite for them in Brown's Hotel, that well-run and discreet establishment off of Piccadilly for the well-bred who dislike glitter and show and the new-rich. Leonard employed a governess to chaperone the girls in London's central parks. Since Jennie had always been surrounded by money and attention it was natural for her to assume she always would be. And, since she was a remarkable beauty at eighteen, her good fortune continued.

Cowes on the Isle of Wight, where Leonard Jerome settled them, was a small, exclusive world of its own, known mostly for the Royal Yacht Squadron and yacht racing with its attendant social life. Queen Victoria lived on her country estate on the island for the summer months at Osborne House. Visitors to Cowes included other royalty and the aristocracy. There was the fun-loving Prince of Wales—the future King Edward the Seventh—who enjoyed horse-racing, yachting, and a flutter at cards, as well as his favorite mistresses. Cowes was at the center of the social calendar each and every August.

It took no time for the three Jerome women to become a feature of the social scene. They were presented to the Prince and Princess of Wales. And the alluring Jennie was invited to meet the twenty-three-year-old Lord Randolph Churchill, who was one of the Duke of Marlborough's sons. His family was as dazzling socially as the Jerome family in America. They engendered a similar atmosphere of glamour and charm. With it came the usual attraction of arrogant power. The two young people fell in love instantly when she was eighteen and he twenty-three. Nevertheless, it took a settlement of a quarter of a million dollars for her father to win over the Marlboroughs to the marriage.*

Her wedding to Lord Randolph took place at the British Embassy in Paris, where they had already indulged in an amorous affair. So that, when their first child was born two months early, and far too soon for Victorian propriety, the event was brushed off as the result of a fall during a pheasant shooting party and then riding on horseback afterwards. Her son, whom they named Winston, showed none of the typical signs of a premature birth.

---

* A 2008 television documentary about Jennie (Winston Churchill's mother) was screened on Britain's Channel 4, on November 11, at 9 p.m. It hinted that she was known as "Lady Randy," because of hundreds of lovers whom she was alleged to have slept with. But who would know how many lovers she had! The allegation was simply a bitchy remark by author George Moore, who thought he was being witty.

The family name of the Dukes of Marlborough was Churchill. They lived at the huge Blenheim Palace in Oxfordshire, which was in a typical state of disrepair. Typical, because land, which had once been a good investment if used wisely, had fallen in value, and so had the finances of the English aristocracy. The Industrial Revolution had changed the economy and society, as new technologies always do, often with unfortunate consequences. So it had become an acceptable custom and a sign of the times for the aristocracy's young sons to marry wealthy American heiresses and restore their estates. Money changed hands, and a title was bestowed on the heiress, so that Jennie Jerome was transformed into Lady Randolph Churchill. Her son was Winston Churchill.

Randolph

Randolph was the third son of the seventh Duke of Marlborough and Lady Frances Vane. His full name was Lord Randolph Henry Spencer-Churchill. He had been born in one of the best streets in London and educated at Eton where, it was alleged, the future leaders of England were taught how to lead. He was described there as vivacious and unruly, but perhaps simply lively or high-spirited would have been a better description for the Churchillian form of energetic enthusiasm. Randolph went on to Merton College in Oxford. He possessed a reputation as a keen reader and took a degree in modern history and jurisprudence. He was also initiated in membership of the Freemasons, and would naturally have expected his son Winston to follow suit.

Lord Randolph was elected to Parliament as a Conservative in 1874, the year he married Jennie, on April 15, and in which his son Winston was born on November 30. Lord Randolph was complimented on his maiden speech in the House by Benjamin Disraeli, who became Conservative Prime Minister for the second time in that same year.

A year later, Lord Randolph visited his doctor several times for what was later alleged to be the most common venereal disease of the times, syphilis.[1] It was later claimed to have been nothing of the sort, and that neither his wife nor his sons were infected with it. It was far more likely to have been a brain tumor in the left side of the left lobe. Either would be consistent with the symptoms which would gradually become noticeable, particularly when he rose to speak in Parliament and showed a deficit of attention, sometimes forgetting by mid-sentence what he had begun to say. It has been attributed to the secondary or tertiary stages of syphilis, because the Harley Street doctor he visited was a leading specialist in treating that particular disease.

Either way, the symptoms of whatever he was suffering from were not observable for some time. Meanwhile, it took four years for his speeches in the House to be taken seriously, despite his fluency and audacity and the sting in his attacks on members of the Administration. By the time he was noticed as a serious politician, he had developed what became known as "Tory Democracy," or what later became Progressive Conservatism. After ten years of public service in Parliament, the Tories had become progressive and Randolph was now a leading figure in the Party.

The word democracy is significant in that it reflected a horde of people who made up Victorian Britain, particularly London and the industrial cities of the north. But, although London was the biggest metropolis in the world, it had not yet been subjected to an official census of all its inhabitants, who suddenly became entities when Prime Minister Benjamin Disraeli referred to the English as "Two Nations." There were those who were recognized by society, and a huge number of inhabitants who had so far been ignored as invisible or beneath society's notice. In short, there were the haves and the have-nots. The only individual who had taken the time and care to interview them had been Henry Mayhew in 1861. He had called the other half "London Labor and the London Poor."

As a result of Lord Randolph's recognition by the establishment, he was appointed Secretary of State for India in 1885 in Lord Salisbury's cabinet. It was in that capacity that he arranged for Viceroy Lord Dufferin to invade Upper Burma and then annex the remainder of that country so that it became a province of the British Raj in 1886 and increased the size of the British Empire for Queen Victoria, who enjoyed being its Empress. Lord Randolph was thought to be the best Secretary of State that Britain ever had.[2] When at his best, he was considered tactful and dependable, before he suddenly resigned on a matter of principle at the end of that year. It was thought to be the unfortunate result of a power play in which he had over-reached himself.

Lord Randolph failed to return to the front line of politics with his previous political attacks over the following years, while his health deteriorated seriously. He planned a trip around the world with Jennie, and wrote a book about South Africa after travelling there and to Rhodesia.[3] But the trip was not the cure he had hoped for. He was so fragile by the time they reached Cairo that he had to hurry back to England to die. He was buried at Bladon in Oxfordshire in 1895. Although he left a considerable fortune, his widow Jennie was still a spendthrift and as hard-up as ever, since money meant nothing to her.

Five years later, Jennie married again, and Winston Churchill's mother became known as Mrs. George Cornwallis-West. But her life was not to be suddenly devoted to domesticity or the mundane, or retirement, in 1900 or thereafter. Captain George Frederick Myddleton Cornwallis-West was twenty-six, and an officer in the Scots Guards. Jennie was forty-six. George was only a few days older than Winston.

Despite George's eye for pretty women, Jennie felt secure in her new marriage, since she and George were congenial by temperament and shared the same sense of humor. Salisbury Hall, their elegant country house, offered what each wished for; easy entertaining—an important matter then—and the popular pastime of their class, first-class shooting. "They came to London often and danced happily together at all the big balls." But they were forced to rent it, since they did not have enough capital to buy it. King Edward paid a number of informal visits to Salisbury Hall, although he stayed there only once. He was getting too heavy to walk upstairs.[4]

She was still strikingly beautiful, with her amber eyes, her dark brown hair, full breasts, and an irrepressible lust for life. Jennie was still irresistible to men. It was from her that Winston inherited his exuberance for life. And, since Jennie was always in full charge of her relationships, it is clear whom he inherited his leadership quality from, too. He was pushy and gifted, with an innate desire and ability to lead. Even more was her ability to get society to accept her on her own evaluation of herself—as Winston Churchill would. All those attributes would stand him in good stead when he rushed cheerfully onto the world stage and conquered everyone he encountered—or almost everyone, since he made a number of serious enemies too.

Winston

Winston lived in Dublin until the age of six, where his grandfather was the Viceroy and Lord Randolph was his secretary. Even then, the infant Winston would have been conscious of regular military parades passing to and from the Viceroy's impressive residence. It was customary then for upper class and aristocratic mothers to pass their newborn babies to a nanny. Then, as they grew up, to a governess. It was not a result of cold-heartedness—although there was plenty of that about in England—but more a recognition that they were experts in bringing up children, whereas young mothers were inexperienced. It also allowed parents to make full use of their time in service to the country, like Lord Randolph to the Viceroy, or the social life and admiration that Jennie enjoyed so much.

Babies and infants were considered poor company for adults, since they had nothing of value to say. Infants would frequently be warned, when on display to friends or guests, that they should be seen, but not heard. So communication between offspring and parents was stalled at the first hurdle. It may well have been the moment when children began to suffer from an inferiority complex. On the other hand, it was almost traditional for infants molded by their nannies to give them the kind of affection otherwise reserved for a mother. Since the opposite was true of the majority who were working class families, or lived on small farms in rural areas, this English custom also separated social classes from the beginning. So it is not surprising that Winston formed a special bond with his nanny. She taught him to read, write, and do his sums. And they played together in Dublin's beautiful Phoenix Park.

Winston's school was Harrow, which seems to have left no deep mark on his character except that he hated it. It is said that he remained close to the bottom of the lowest class for most of his time there. But far too much is made of such general observations at a time when a great deal of trust was placed in boarding schools by parents, but rarely fulfilled by the school. Teachers were more incompetent than not. Management of schools was generally poor, and so was the standard of teaching. In some schools, beating boys with a cane was such a regular occurrence that no great issue was made out of prefects' beatings, beatings by house masters, or by schoolmasters, and certainly not by the threatening figure of the headmaster, whose beatings were likely to leave a lifetime scar on the minds of his victims as well as on their posteriors.

Writing, later on, of his experiences of the prep school for entry to Harrow (St. James's School), Winston would explain:

Flogging with the birch in accordance with the Eton fashion was a great feature in its curriculum. But I am sure no Eton boy, and certainly no Harrow boy of my day, ever received such a cruel flogging as this Headmaster was accustomed to inflict upon the little boys who were in his care and power . . . My reading in later life has supplied me with some possible explanations for his temperament. Two or three times a month the whole school was marshalled in the library, and one or more delinquents were hauled off to an adjoining apartment by the two head boys, and flogged until they bled freely, while the rest sat quaking, listening to their screams.[5]

It would be easy to smile at what we might imagine was typical Churchillian hyperbole in his later style, to entertain and amuse, but that would be an erroneous assumption—for what he described was the norm at British boarding schools in Victorian times, and often right up until the 1940s, rather than the exception.

Many a house-master or a headmaster had lost sight of the fact that they were paid to educate. Poor administrators became so frustrated at their incompetence, or their overwhelming workload, that they took out their frustrations on the schoolboys. Sadism was rife, and so was homosexuality. Every strike of a cane on a boy's bare behind was an admission of the schoolmaster's incapability to teach or to keep schoolboys focused on their lessons, since they were generally incompetent at their jobs.

Prime Minister Lord Salisbury was just one other example of a dispirited and gloomy man who had observed as a child how evil others can be from his school, which was Eton, where he had been bullied mercilessly, and left because of it. He had suffered from a loveless childhood and received brutality at boarding school from the age of six. It produced in him a pessimistic outlook and he was often filled with depression and even feelings approaching paranoia.

Churchill's recounting of a conversation with his form master is, similarly, unlikely to be an exaggeration, but more likely to be repeated again and again throughout Britain's school system: it was the clash between a bright little boy (probably at the age of nine or ten) and a somewhat wooden-headed adult schoolmaster attempting to explain a Latin declension to him:

"O table,—you would use that in addressing a table." And then seeing he was not carrying me with him, "You would use it in speaking to a table."

"But I never do," I blurted out in honest amazement.

"If you are impertinent, you will be punished, and punished, let me tell you, very severely," was his conclusive rejoinder."[6]

It could mean a flogging, since schoolmasters of the time seldom missed an opportunity to regale the whole school with their power by thrashing a boy in front of them in order to warn any others not to be insolent.

Teachers were all male and poorly paid. For some it was a last-ditch attempt to find employment, since they were generally unemployable. Most did not enjoy their jobs and hated the boys. Those who had to take on extra work to pay their bills by also teaching at some other, commercial night-school, were too tired to teach in the morning. They created useful ways of fobbing off the children by telling them to read a textbook in class while they took the opportunity to recover their senses or quietly drop off to sleep in front of the class. Many were extraordinarily ignorant, despite their academic degree, and few knew the subject they had been hired to teach or how to teach it. It was commonplace that many had only been employed because of their ability at sports; so that all they could do was run around a muddy football field in their boots and blow a tin whistle.

Several books written by author and satirist Evelyn Waugh feature such incidents even later on, in the 1920s and 1930s. Waugh himself applied to teach after he left university: "That's what most of the gentlemen does, sir, that gets sent down for indecent behavior," says a college porter in one of his best-selling novels.[7] Waugh admitted freely that he wasn't any good at it, and nor was anyone else who came through the teacher employment agency, which took the dregs at the bottom of the employment market that no one else would hire. Winston's earlier life was, after all, almost concurrent with the novels of Charles Dickens, in which we are regaled with schools of ignorance and cruelty, greed, and cost-cutting at the expense of the pupils. There are only about sixty years between the barbarous times that Dickens wrote about and Churchill's school days, several of which describe the cruelty of school-masters that resulted in the pitiful mental or physical state of their pupils.

We have only to read *Nicholas Nickleby* with its sadistic fictional schoolmaster named Wackford Squeers, which was based on a real-life Yorkshire school-master whom Dickens knew named William Shaw. And there are also *David Copperfield* and *Oliver Twist,* where schoolmasters reach for a bundle of canes to release their frustration by thrashing another helpless childhood victim.

Unfortunately, respect for authority had been instilled as a priority into Victorian parents and boys. It would not be until the 1960s in Britain that people began to see through the pretense to their incompetence. Winston was ahead of his time in recognizing it at school, in the War Office and the Admiralty, and in Parliament.

Meanwhile, other intelligent boys who had previously shown promise found it easy to despise their teachers, and soon lost interest in studying. It is likely that Winston was one of them, and that was the reason he hated Harrow, which he entered when twelve and attended for four and a half years, three of which were in the Army Class. Although Churchill hastened to mention that boys were not thrashed there, like at the prep school where he studied, we should remember that the headmasters of such schools wielded total power over their charges, not only when small, but possibly for the rest of their lives. They were taught not to sneak when small—which effectively concealed any misdemeanors or abuse of the school staff. And after they left, a hesitant reference to a possible employer, or faint praise from the headmaster, could effectively have them turned down for a job in the civil service; so boys had little choice but to show loyalty to their school.

Perhaps most importantly, intelligent or intellectual boys had to keep quiet or risk showing up their class teacher in front of the other boys. That was why some of the more intelligent boys were given poor marks. So we should not attach too much importance to Winston's low grades, since the schools could not be trusted to provide a good education. No wonder it took him three attempts to pass his exams for Sandhurst. It was less likely to be a reflection on him than on the school.

What he loved was the English language. But he felt lonely. His father had been distant before he left for boarding school, and now Winston kept writing to his mother to visit him, or to come home. But there was no response to his entreaties to Jennie. Blame has been laid on Lord Randolph because of today's very different attitude. But this was a commonplace situation a hundred and fifty years ago, when it was thought that separating children from their family at the earliest age was good for them. Since they would not be spoilt later on by the world or the army, or employers, it was a rehearsal for when they'd be on their own. In one satirical book written by Waugh, the British Public Schoolboy hero finds it easy to settle down when sentenced to prison toward the end of his career, since he was already conditioned to its ghastliness by boarding school.

Strangely enough, most fathers had an erroneous idea of the value of teaching in such schools, despite the fact that they had endured the same indifference and ignorance from the same school, and the same thrashings when they were children. They thought there must be something in their nostalgia for their old school, but failed to understand it was really nostalgia for their youth. And mothers like Jennie were cautious about interfering between their husbands and their nostalgia for their schooldays.

What was more, Winston suffered from a lisp that he failed to eradicate entirely throughout his life. But he enjoyed the songs at Harrow. Perhaps that was because the massed chorus of schoolboys' innocent voices, filled with hope, instilled hope in all. He was dismissive of the one song he mentioned that was unique to Eton, perhaps because it equated rowing down a river to chaining him for life to the school and the woolly juvenile interests it conditioned boys to.

> *Jolly boating weather, And a hay-harvest breeze,*
> *Blade on the feather, Shade off the trees,*
> *Swing, swing together. With your bodies between your knees—*
> *Swing, swing together, With your bodies between your knees.*
> *Rugby may be more clever, Harrow may make more row,*
> *But we'll row for ever, Steady from stroke to bow,*
> *And nothing in life shall sever The chain that is round us now.*

Singing that song enough times together as a ritual in the Great Hall appeared to bond Old Etonians together for life. And Churchill would become very suspicious of that in later years when he saw them covering up each other's ineptitudes in politics and the army—for it was Rugby's famous headmaster Dr. Thomas Arnold who, in 1827–41, established a pattern for British public schools. "The public schools and, thereafter, Victorian Oxbridge, set out to produce Christian gentlemen, like knights in Burne-Jones stained-glass, to govern the empire, join the church or the law or the public service: not to produce hard-driving technologically aware leaders of an industrial nation in a tough, competitive world."[8]

After leaving Harrow in 1893, Winston entered the Royal Military College at Sandhurst. He applied to train in the cavalry because its grade was lower than for the infantry—although his father preferred the infantry. Winston obtained his commission as a subaltern, or second lieutenant, in the Hussars in 1895. The pay was poor and had to be augmented by another sum from Jennie. He was always behind on payment of his bills, as a consequence of the high cost of the lifestyle required of an officer. He needed more money, and thought of a way to obtain it. That and other events taking place in the world outside would shape his destiny.

CHAPTER TWO

THE SHOTS THAT ECHOED AROUND THE WORLD

WHAT SUDDENLY STOPPED EVERYTHING IN ITS tracks and changed the course of people's destinies, including Winston's, was an incident that took place in a backwater of the Balkans, an area that had so far managed to remain a dead end in European history. Although it is generally accepted by historians that the First World War arose as a consequence of treaties and alliances between the major superpowers in 1914, the incident that triggered it took place in the unlikely town of Sarajevo in Bosnia, a recently annexed territory of the Austro-Hungarian Empire.

Even when we have all the facts before us, some people are hesitant to credit the eruption of the Great War to the stubborn and rebellious act of one half-educated teenage rebel. And some British historians have shown themselves to be not entirely satisfied with such glib answers. They worry that there are so many other possible alternative causes, even though none seems to be entirely reasonable. But nations are led by people, and people have never been known to be entirely rational. Perhaps social psychologist Gustave Le Bon was the first intellectual to point out, long ago, that the same problem confused past historians into misunderstanding why the French Revolution erupted—because historians had not examined the minds of the leading figures.

To understand the full significance of all the possibilities, a little history helps to paint a more realistic picture of the Austro-Hungarian Empire than we are normally accustomed to, since it describes the assassination of a head of state that ultimately resulted in the loss of more than seventy million lives.

The dual monarchy of Austria-Hungary was the second largest country in Europe, after only Tsarist Russia. It consisted of Austria, Hungary, Bohemia,

Moravia, Galicia, Styria, Tyrol, Carinthia, Bosnia, and Herzegovina. Despite its huge territory and a population of close to 53 million by 1914, it was ruled by a dynastic family of Habsburgs, several of whom were considered to be mentally unstable due to interfamily marriage and inbreeding which kept money and power in the family.

Like most empires at some stage of their development, the Austro-Hungarian Empire suffered from economic and military problems. But its biggest problem by far was nationalism—which largely meant what to do about ethnic and religious minorities who always tended to be abrasive. One typical solution followed by authoritarian regimes was nationalism, for which it is necessary to create a fictional "enemy" from outside (or inside), to hold the population defiantly together against them. But the Emperor, "Franz Joseph stood above the interests and prejudices of his peoples." For example, "He abhorred the populist anti-Semitism of Karl Lueger . . ."[1] Lueger had gained followers from the illiterate and superstitious masses by slandering Jews as the imaginary enemies. But there was a wide choice of other identifiable people who would have been far more justified in being described as "enemies" in Austria-Hungary.

Most, if not all those others, with their different languages, religions, and cultures, wanted independence. But the views of most populations tend to swing like a pendulum between what is desired for the sake of liberty, and what is desirable for national security. Franz Joseph had compromised with the desires of the biggest and most militant language group by agreeing to equal rule with Hungary under a dual monarchy in 1867. But compromise had unintended consequences, because Hungarians were not the only aggressive ethnic group which was nationalistic. German was spoken by 24 percent of the population, Czech by 13 percent, and Polish by 10 percent. Other languages were Ruthenian, Romanian, Croatian, Serbian, Slovak, and Slovene. Although the Serbian language was spoken by only 4 percent, it didn't stop them from being carried away by a primitive culture of blood vengeance in order to "wash their national honor clean." They felt it had been tarnished on June 28 in 1389 when the kingdom of Serbia had been conquered by the Turks, who enslaved the Serbs. That particular anniversary date was deeply engraved in the heart of every Serb. They kept alive conflicts from the past, and learned nothing new, except for race and religious hatred towards everyone else. It would lead in the end to ethnic cleansing.

Magyarization

After Austria merged with Hungary in what was known as "The Compromise," the government encouraged *Magyarization* by language, culture, and even family names. Hungarian, which had been spoken by only 20 percent of the population before Magyarization, became used increasingly, so that 15 percent of non-Hungarians also spoke Hungarian as a second language by 1910. Twenty-three percent of the population of Budapest was Jewish, and most spoke Hungarian and supported Magyarization, even by agreeing to Magyarize their names in support of the government's nationalist policy. But others were not so accommodating.

Ethnicity identified itself with each traditional religion. It meant that the so-called "ethnic problem" not only involved confrontation between nationalists and not even in accordance with geographic borders—but also between religious cultures, from Roman Catholics to the Orthodox Church, Calvinists, Muslims, and Jews. It seems that nobody could get along with each other because of nationalist interests that encouraged religious hatreds, born out of envy or fear of the other "foreign" groups.

Since each church claimed to be the only true religion, other people's religious beliefs were viewed as a threat that diminished the value of their own identity. Language, culture, and religion fostered nationalism. It created a serious problem, since nationalism was triggered by a psychic epidemic that Jung and other Austrian psychoanalysts would describe years later as xenophobia or paranoia. Austria's ethnic groups could be likened to a squabbling family at the dinner table, each one watching the others' plates suspiciously to ensure that no one else was served a bigger helping than theirs.

Typical of the fragile line between reality and romantic illusions in the human condition, *The Times,* like most media, saw foreign politics through rose-colored spectacles. They knew it was how English readers preferred it. The Austro-Hungarian Empire was, after all, the inspiration for popular romantic novels like *The Prisoner of Zenda* and *Rupert of Hentzau,*[2] and comic operas like *The Merry Widow.* As *The Times* correspondent wrote in 1908:

> On June 12 there passed before the Emperor, in a procession which lasted more than three hours, 12,000 of his subjects, of all races and tongues, in costumes of historic periods, shouting their loyal greetings.

Nobles and warriors have assembled before the monarch before but never before has there been so complete a muster of the peoples of the empire. The Austrians, who are a nation without knowing it, found themselves that morning, and the people of Vienna cheered each race and clan, in the consciousness that not only common loyalty to a common dynasty personified in a venerable Sovereign, but also a common history, common interest, common enemies and a common destiny, all unite them.

It was all nonsense. In fact, "On December 2, 1908, the day of Franz Josef's anniversary, German students grabbed fellow students at the cafeteria of Vienna University and threw them out, because nationalistic German students didn't want to mix with Slavs, Jews, Italians, or any other group, and forced them to set up their own segregated cafeterias according to their own language and culture."[3] The Austro-Hungarian Empire would cease to exist only ten years later, after the heir to the throne, the Archduke Franz Ferdinand, was assassinated.

The Archduke

The Archduke was puffed up with even more vanity and ego than most privileged members of the Habsburg family, or the government, or the military. Even so, Austrians considered he had married a commoner, because she was a Slav. In fact, Sophie was a noble in her native Czechoslovakia, where she was the Duchess of Hohenberg. But Czechs were just another ethnic minority and not to be taken seriously by others. Racism was rife, and based—as is often the case—on myths and fantasies and libelous propaganda. Nevertheless, for marrying a commoner in a love match, the Archduke lost most of his privileges and was kept on a very tight budget—or so he endlessly complained to whoever would listen to him.

One of the privileges they both lost was that they could not appear in public gatherings together except at military parades. So she was thrilled to be able to accompany him on the military parade through the streets of Sarajevo on the Feast of St. Vitus, which fell annually on June 28—a date so incendiary that it had its own special name, the *Vidovdan*.

It was on that fateful day of *Vidovdan* in 1914 that the royal couple sat together in an open motor car, with the Governor of Sarajevo sitting in front of them—instead of in a traditional open carriage drawn by splendid horses—since it was the beginning of the modern era.

28 June, 1914: Sarajevo, Bosnia

They step into the third of six automobiles in the procession at 10:45 that morning. The Archduke is as pleased as Punch, whom he somewhat resembles. It is a grand opportunity to show off to his wife and posture to the public in his vainglorious uniform with its medals and a heavily plumed hat that resembles a miniature waterfall.

Crowds of holidaymakers gather in their Sunday-best suits or traditional peasant costumes on a typical blistering hot Balkan day, when bare feet could be burnt on hard earth walkways or cobblestones, and pedestrians withdrew to the shaded side of the street to shelter from the harsh midday sun. Despite being on the threshold of modern times, the royals are met by an enchanting display of cavalry in splendid colorful uniforms from the past, with rakish shakos on their proud military heads and sabers worn at muscular thighs clad in white tights, as their riders sit arrogantly erect on the polished leather saddles of well-groomed horses.

Seven men stroll in a casual group through the crowds in the street, toward one of the bridges that cross the River Miljacka. They all wear customary hats to keep off the heat of the sun. Some even wear three-piece suits, despite the heat, to show they are middle-class students. Danilo Ilic walks ahead of the others in the group of friends, accompanied by Trifko Grabezh, who is clean-shaven like Ilic and looks very smart in his Homburg hat and dark suit. Three more conspirators follow the pair at a reasonable distance from where they cannot lose sight of the others in the festive crowds. Gavrilo Princip keeps well behind them all, as if on his own. He is nineteen, but has grown a meager beginner's moustache to make him look older. Bringing up the rear is Muhamed Mehmedbasic. Several of them carry lunch bags.

The young revolutionaries settle themselves in unobtrusive positions by the embankment and wait patiently for something to happen that will signal the right opportunity to spring into action. They are part of a larger group of twenty-two assassins chosen and placed along the route at intervals of five hundred yards. They planned this dramatic response to the insult on their honor in a modest café named *Zeatna Maruana*. Bosnia-Herzegovina had only recently been annexed by the Habsburg Empire, and they were offended that the crown prince had arrogantly chosen to enter the Bosnian capital on *Vidovdan,* the day of shame and national celebration for Bosnian nationalists.

The First Bomb

The young men hear louder and louder cheers from the jovial crowd lining the street in a holiday mood, and cavalry hoof-beats accompanied by the jingle of harnesses, as an entourage of soldiers on horseback appears. The procession of soldiers is followed by several motor cars. Seated comfortably in one of them, which is open for their tour of the small town of Sarajevo, is the Archduke Ferdinand of Austria, with his shiny waxed moustache twisted at the ends into two triumphantly elevated points. By now, he has exchanged his ceremonial plumed hat for a more workaday glossy leather cylindrical shako. His wife Sophie sits eagerly beside him, intensely happy that he has brought her along. She holds up a bouquet of flowers with which she has just been presented, and sniffs at it with evident pleasure. Then she turns to her husband to remark happily on their favorable reception.

They are smiling intimately at each other and gazing into each other's eyes when the first bomb hits the rear of their car and glances off it without exploding. They barely notice a second bomb aimed at them from a different direction, because it too misses them and glances off of something or other that they can't quite see, to explode harmlessly in the road beyond their carriage, without harming anyone. But the explosion alerts them to danger, just before Princip rises from his momentary concealment and desperately fires two shots at each of them. The first hits the Archduke's jugular vein. The second strikes Sophie in her abdomen.

The Archduke and his wife collapse as Princip empties his revolver in their direction. Soldiers rush at him, and he tosses the firearm away and stands his ground defiantly in the face of the onslaught. It is his proud moment in the sight of history. As they grab hold of him roughly, he remembers to shout out the lines he'd prepared:

"I am not a criminal! I am a fighter for freedom. *Not* a criminal! Freedom for the Slavs! Freedom for Austria!"

A Fighter for Freedom

That, at least, is how the romance or mythology, or propaganda of history, was presented. And the bridge from where he fired his shots was named after him for fifty years, because Serbs continued to view him as a nationalist hero and not a murderer.[4] But romantic notions that historians have handed down to us were vehemently resisted by the down-to-earth and prescient investigative reporter Rebecca West, who seems to have been watching from every vantage point at the time.

"Dear God," she wrote, "is nothing ever what it seems?"

In fact, the Sarajevo police had been warned beforehand that attempts would be made on Franz Ferdinand's life. Notwithstanding the glowing report of the royals in *The Times,* many of the population were angry at Austro-Hungarian misrule, corruption, and despotic injustices. Many were racists or religious bigots, or both. So Princip brought a revolver with him from Belgrade. He justified the assassination in his own mind as an "honor killing."

As for the sentimental picture of the Archduke, Rebecca West's disgust is clearly evident from her description of him as a butcher, killing as many animals as he could when out hunting, to show off his double-barreled Mannlicher rifles. Shooting wild animals was considered to be a sport, a passing fashion of the times among aristocrats and landed gentry. Two thousand, one hundred and fifty pieces of small game in one day! In her opinion it sublimated "the hatred which he felt for nearly all the world." (With the exception only of his wife and three children.) His frustration and anger at life simmered because of his tuberculosis, and because he felt imprisoned by the Habsburg establishment—in spite of his whole life having been supported by "the privileges that were given to the members of the Habsburg family."[5] To his fury, he was restrained on all sides by government administrators who kept him short of money. Evidently he was not well-liked.

Treachery

Rebecca West suspected treachery in his entourage. But what in fact transpired could just as easily have resulted from typical Austrian sloppiness. There had already been an attempt on his life by another young bomb-thrower named

Cabrinovic, in which the Archduke's *aide-de-camp* had been bloodied. So the Archduke had asked the Military Governor of Sarajevo beforehand if he thought any bombs would be thrown at him during the drive. The Governor's reply was not reported, but evidently he thought it unlikely, since he chose to share the vehicle with them.

In the previous drama, one of the schoolboy would-be assassins—the reluctant Mehmedbasic—never threw his bomb at all. He just waited until the carriage had passed him by and hurried off to catch a train to Montenegro in order to escape from the scene as quickly as possible

His companion, young Popovitch, claimed he was too close to a policeman to risk throwing his bomb, so he too gave up. Grabezh assumed that Cabrinovic had already succeeded, and missed his own chance. And Princip, hearing a bomb explode, thought it had hit its intended target. But when he saw the royals still alive, he wandered off to a café in a daze of failure and despondency.

Cabrinovic came round for a second attempt, but threw his bomb far too wildly. Then he hurried off to swallow the prussic acid they had all been told to take, to avoid capture and torture—in fact, to avoid them giving the game away as to who was behind the plot and why. Cabrinovic's bomb failed to be effective, and he resisted taking the poison after all his heroic posturing, and was arrested.

> Franz Ferdinand would have gone from Sarajevo untouched had it not been for the actions of his staff, who by blunder after blunder contrived that his car should slow down and that he should be presented as a stationary target in front of Princip, the one conspirator of real and mature deliberation, who had finished his coffee and was walking back through the streets, aghast at his failure and the incompetence of his friends, which could expose the country to terrible punishment without having inflicted any loss on authority. At last the bullets had been coaxed out of the reluctant revolver to the bodies of the eager victims.[6]

Or, to put it more prosaically, Gavrilo Princip pumped all his bullets at the two figures who suddenly and unexpectedly appeared before him in their open car, as the moment he had planned for finally arrived as a consequence of sloppiness by the Austrian administration.

Tortured

The soldiers closed in on him immediately, and Princip was beaten viciously and bloodily. He and Grabezh were tortured in prison to make them condemn everyone who had helped them, but without success. The garrulous Cabrinovic, on the other hand, never stopped talking but invented fictions. It was Ilic who told everything under torture. So their associates and helpers were soon rounded up in jail to await trial. In the meantime, no connection was ever found to link the conspirators to the Serbian government.

Whoever attempts to make sense of what really happened, and why they did it, is in for disappointment, and must end by making conjectures of their own, since most terrorist episodes are senseless. But two significant clues help to clarify the background to the situation. One is that three of the conspirators—Princip, Grabecz, and Cabrinovic—knew their lives would be short anyway, because they suffered from tuberculosis, which was a death sentence in those days. And, like many suicide bombers and terrorists, they may have chosen to go out in a blaze of romantic glory, instead of being forgotten forever. The reluctant Cabrinovic expressed probably genuine regret at his trial, and received a letter of forgiveness from the three orphaned children of the assassinated Archduke and his wife.

There were two possible charges in Austro-Hungarian law: conspiracy to commit high treason by a Serbian official, for which the sentence was death by execution, or conspiracy to commit murder, for which the sentence was a maximum of twenty years in prison. All three conspirators died of tuberculosis while behind bars.

The other clue to the motivation of the conspirators came from the bearded Cabrinovic, who claimed he had only been persuaded by Princip because he realized that, if he didn't do what Princip told him, the organization behind Princip—the Black Hand gang—would destroy his house and his family. No doubt others were also coerced by threats. Mehmedbasic, for example, was also seen by the court to have been genuinely reluctant to take part, but had been blackmailed into the affair. He was sentenced to fifteen years in prison.

So it appears that Princip was the only one filled with eagerness to die for an imaginary cause, and completely unconcerned about his friends being tortured or killed, or any other deaths that might occur as a consequence of the assassination.

Just a Poor Boy from the Mountains

Like the other conspirators, Gavrilo Princip was a student, the grandson of a Slav immigrant; "just a poor boy come down from the mountains to get his education here in Sarajevo, and he knew nobody but his school fellows."[7] He appears to have been a teenage idealist hoping to find a perfect world. Disillusioned by what he saw, he turned to nationalism—one of three dominant factors in history, according to Dame Rebecca West: *Nationalism, Imperialism,* and *Love of slaughter for its own sake.*

He became weary of school life made chaotic by fellow students who were overcome by political discontent. Wanting to prove his worth as a hero in the Slav cause, he became friendly with a volatile nineteen-year-old printer named Nedeljko Cabrinovic, who was a persuasive talker who preached anarchism—one of those who is happy to get things going and then let others take all the risks. Other friends included the angry young schoolteacher, Danilo Ilic, whom they met in cafés as well as at school. Ilic was attempting to form a terrorist organization to commit what he romantically called *desperate deeds.*

It was a youngster named Pushora who showed Princip a newspaper announcing the proposed visit to Bosnia by the Archduke. Princip informed Cabrinovic by sending him the press cutting. With only a few enquiries, they found they could obtain bombs from the leader of "The Black Hand" society of assassins, led by a man known as "Apis," whose real name was Dragutin Dimitrijevic. It was a Serbian revolutionary organization which had either been infiltrated by Serbian military intelligence or set up by them from the start. So-called "secret" societies were notoriously deceitful, complex, fickle, and not to be trusted because of their double agendas. For example, it was the same year that Russia's Chief of Secret Police, Feliks Dzerzhinsky, set up a similar trap as a counter-revolutionary society in Moscow, called "The Trust," to attract dissidents who wanted to join, and then murder them on arrival. One of his victims was the British spy Sidney Reilly, who disappeared when he arrived in Moscow soon after the Russian Revolution began.

Apis was the epitome of those "who love slaughter for its own sake." After their meeting, their training, although limited, was carefully planned and organized by The Black Hand. Apis would be tried and shot to death by a firing squad in 1917, with two other conspirators.

The Trial

During the trial of the student conspirators, one was asked, "Don't you realize that your religion [Orthodox Church] forbids the killing of a man?" What he meant was, did his traditional faith play any role in the assassination? For example, had anyone's religious susceptibilities been offended? The boy stated that there was no religious motive for the crime.

Once in court, Princip showed more common sense and wisdom than most of his co-conspirators. He claimed he represented the tragedy of the peasants who "resented the poverty that Austrians had brought to his kind." Cabrinovic apparently enjoyed all the attention and muddied the waters by continuing to spread fictional stories of mysterious plots by Freemasons (a useful myth that Adolf Hitler would borrow for his own use later on in Austria and Germany when inventing so-called enemies from outside). In a more serious mood, Cabrinovic blamed his act on the oppression of minority populations in some ethnic provinces—which was true. He claimed it turned honest men into rebels, in which "assassination became a display of virtue."

As far as Princip was concerned, there were no outside plots, either by Freemasons or Serbs. "We originated the idea," he insisted. "[A]nd we carried it out. We loved the people." That action by one teenager precipitated the first ever World War which, in turn, resulted in the Second World War.

Princip, Cabrinovic, and Grabezh were each sentenced to twenty years in prison, since they were under twenty-one. Two of them were dead by 1917. And Princip—who was kept in irons—suffered horribly and attempted suicide three times. One of his arms had to be amputated. He died in 1918, the year the Great War he had triggered finally ended, leaving millions dead.

Squandered Lives

If we hope to find common factors among the seven conspirators, we know they were all young. Rebels and revolutionaries nearly always are. Freud's contention that all revolutionaries are rebelling against their father was very likely in this case. We can also observe that whereas assassins, like Luccheni, had nothing to lose but a miserable life of poverty, humiliation, and despair, the Sarajevo students were provided with an education intended to lead to a better life, but they chose to squander it.*

We can touch all the bases: uncontrolled hormones at pubescence, inexperience, lack of parental guidance, ignorance of the world, a little knowledge from a little formal education but not enough, their lives dominated by political unrest and ethnic persecution, and coercion. Added to that were frustration and all the uncertain tremors that arise, grow, and accelerate toward the end of an era, or on the edge of war. But didn't their own personality characteristics play a part?

What about Princip's total unconcern that the bullet with which he killed the Archduke ricocheted and resounded all over the world and murdered millions of innocent people? World War I would have been unlikely to have happened without Princip deliberately firing wildly into the open automobile at point-blank range and not caring about anyone else. And the Second World War would have been unlikely to have broken out without the first one. For every action there is a reaction. It is part of the law of unintended consequences—a fact that most adolescents appear to be ignorant of when they are focused solely on pleasing themselves.

The Protagonists

If we consider that Princip suffered from a personality disorder that either motivated or resulted in antisocial or psychopathic actions, he would probably be described by psychologists as *erratic* and *emotional.* In which case, they would classify him as "histrionic." The symptoms of that disorder are "pervasive and excessive emotionality and attention-seeking behavior." Such individuals *feel unappreciated when they are not the center of attention. Often lively and dramatic,*

---

* Luigi Luccheni was a poor and jobless Italian laborer who assassinated the Austrian Empress Elizabeth on September 10, 1898 in Switzerland. He harbored a grievance against society and swore to kill a royal for it. He was thought to be mentally defective.

they tend to draw attention to themselves. And, if not the center of attention, may do something dramatic, like making up stories or creating a scene.[8] Environmental factors are opportunities for a histrionic individual to exploit by making a scene in which he plays the central role.

The most significant act that defines his real motive is the consistent factor in all other assassinations. The assassin make no plans to escape. None attempts to run away after achieving what he set out to achieve, because of a delusion of martyrdom and the primary aim, which is suicide. The *real* motive of the assassin is *not* the kill, but the preparation for his own melodramatic death. Every assassin who managed to murder a head of state was triumphant at what he had achieved for himself, which was a form of suicide in which someone else could be relied on to end his life and also be blamed for the incident, while feeling relieved at avoiding any disgrace, or sin, of self-murder. It could be described as peevish juvenile spite that says, "Now look what you made me do!"

The Bungler

Whom he kills is almost immaterial because it is only the means to that end. But the advantage of murdering a celebrity is that he transfers the celebrity to himself.[9] So the success of the theatrical performance is important to the entire ritual, since the murder is only the assassin's secondary goal. The identity of his target is merely the third factor in importance, because whoever he targeted was only a figurehead, most probably an ineffectual bungler who only got in people's way.[10]

Perhaps we should leave the last word on the conspirators to author Joseph Conrad, who was more mature, unromantic, and wiser than Princip or any of the other assassins. As a former merchant sea captain who knew the bare-knuckle truths of the world, he wrote in his best-selling novel about anarchists in England, "These people are unable to see that all they can effect is merely a change of names."[11]

What the conspirators were up against was an indifferent and uncaring society, represented—not so much by the unimaginative and well-intentioned, hardworking, bureaucratic Emperor Franz Joseph—but rather the heir to the Habsburg throne.

The Archduke was as indifferent and insensitive as the assassins to the entire population of the Austro-Hungarian Empire, except only for his wife and children. He was entirely self-absorbed with his own vanity and privileges, and inflated by his own perceived self-importance. He lived in a fantasy world, which was more like a silent movie directed by Erich von Stroheim than reality. Von Stroheim remembered from his own youth in Austria the overweening vanity, ambition, vainglorious posturing, and extraordinary ignorance of powerful men and woman like the Archduke and his wife, senior government officials, and military officers—anyone, in fact, with a little power to exploit to his or her own advantage. Only their own personal splendor and egotistical fantasies and follies concerned them. As for their questionable ability to lead a nation, or organize, or administer it—although Austro-Hungary should otherwise have been a model multicultural society—it was carried on in the typical sloppy Austrian manner, long described as *shlamperie*. The job was far too big for them. And they were far too little for the job.

CHAPTER THREE

PRELUDE TO WAR

————

ALTHOUGH THE ASSASSINATION OF THE ARCHDUKE at Sarajevo is generally accepted as the trigger which launched the First World War, it is clear that there were other longer-term factors involved which had been simmering for some time. Princip was not the first partisan, or rebel, or terrorist to protest Austrian rule over Bosnia. Franz Ferdinand had been warned that his visit could spark riots, but he stubbornly disregarded the advice and toured the city in an open car, in the customary way. His choice of bravado might even have been deliberately prepared as a show of strength in front of his dear wife. Pride, vanity, and ego were hallmarks not only of the Habsburgs in Austria and elsewhere, but also of the Romanov dynasty in Tsarist Russia and the Hohenzollerns in Germany. Ego can act on the senses like an intoxicating drug that makes people act irrationally.

While the heir to the Habsburg throne intended to demonstrate that the Habsburg dynasty was in control, the Bosnian rebels decided to show him that he was not. Ego played a crucial role in starting the First World War. But there was also the usual incompetence when the Archduke decided to change the route, and the driver didn't understand; so he drove them to the most danger-ous point where he lost his way, then tried to reverse the car directly in front of the most dangerous revolutionary, Princip, who happened to come out of a café and see them appear before his startled eyes. The war which followed was caused by a bizarre accident.

Another factor that stirred up ripples which would move out in all direc-tions across the world was a photographer who happened to be nearby and took a picture of Princip at the moment he was grabbed by soldiers and arrested after the shots rang out. His photo appeared in newspapers everywhere. This clear evidence of a political assassination ensured that something would have to be done, if only out of national pride. But what would assuage injured pride? By whom? Where? And for what specific purpose?

Austria instantly blamed Serbia for the murders, since it seemed to make sense at the time, in terms of motive. And the Austrian Emperor decided the whole nation should be punished by invading Serbia. It was now that the alliances between nations came into play. Serbia was too small to resist Austria, so its government called for help from Tsarist Russia. Austria was too small to overwhelm the armed forces of Russia with double its population, so the Emperor called on Germany for help.

Now the German "Schlieffen Plan" came into its own. Von Schlieffen had designed his military strategic plan with suitable tactics, out of fear of encirclement on the continent of Europe by the two strongest military powers—France and Russia—based on his conviction, and that of the German chiefs of staff, that they could not fight a war on two fronts. This third alternative cause for making war involved fear and anxiety to a very high degree, even though it may have been completely imaginary.

Two out of those possible reasons for the war are ones chosen as part of three by military historian Liddell Hart—pride and fear.[1] And there was a possibility that timing might be made to be on their side. They estimated that Russian troops could not arrive for six weeks, because they would be slow and ponderous in mobilizing. Meanwhile, the Germans could attack and beat the French quickly, to provide time to turn on the Russians. But that simplification relied on being in complete control of the situation, whereas no one could forecast what the French or the Russians might decide to do. And the German army always liked to be in complete control. Instead, it might be compelled to react to unforeseen events, instead of taking the initiative.

Nevertheless, they prepared to put the plan into action. And the moment France mobilised its army, Germany was left with no choice but to initiate the Schlieffen Plan, which was to attack France through Belgium. Since Britain had an alliance with Belgium, to protect it by declaring war on its enemy, the question uppermost in the minds of the German General Staff was, would Britain honor its guarantee?

Now, within only a matter of weeks after the assassination in Sarajevo, five of the six nations involved had signed treaties and were about to erupt in war. Since speed was of the essence, Germany invaded Belgium on August 4, 1914. Britain duly declared war on Germany. And France and Russia became Britain's allies. Germany's sole ally was Austria, since Italy had not yet revealed its hand. Each of them was certain that—to judge from previous European wars—this one would be all over by Christmas.

Kaiser Wilhelm

Few people in England expected war, except for Winston Churchill and the War Cabinet. But Kaiser Wilhelm cast envious eyes on the naval superiority of the British fleet that ruled the waves around which its empire sat complacently. Germany didn't require a huge fleet because it had no empire spread across the world, as Britain did. Nevertheless, the Kaiser had directed German industry to swiftly organize itself to produce modern battleships with the speed and fire-power to compete with Britain's dreadnought class that made all other navies obsolete. What began as a deterrent to war initiated an arms race between the two nations that would end in one. In some people's minds, it was the arms race that caused the war, providing a fourth possible reason.

Winston Churchill had already become Home Secretary in Asquith's Liberal government, and was far too deeply absorbed in other challenges of his job to take the possibility of war seriously enough. Despite accusations by political opponents that Winston Churchill was a "warmonger," he had actu-ally been lulled into similar complacency as Asquith had about Germany, by his invitation from the Kaiser to inspect German military exercises in 1906. It seemed to him then that the German army was designed more for pageantry than war, with cavalry squadrons charging imaginary enemies with their lances and obsolete tactics more suited to the 1870s than a modern army. He gave them full marks for their numbers, their discipline and organization, but failed to take the Kaiser seriously because he sometimes acted like a buffoon.

What woke Churchill and the British government up was the Agadir Crisis in 1911, when Germany apparently felt powerful enough for aggression. First they gauged the mood for war of the French and the British by persuading a Hamburg merchant to lodge a complaint about a fictitious incident in French Morocco in April. It created international tension and triggered the deploy-ment of an unusually large force of French troops in Morocco. Germany took the opportunity to send a gunboat, the SMS *Panther,* to the Moroccan port of Agadir on July 1. Until that moment, Churchill had believed Germany would avoid war.[2] But they were apparently testing the water before taking the plunge.

Now Germany, France, and England had another three years to increase production of war materials. Germany was mechanized by that time. Its lances and its ten-shot Mannlichers with their swift reloading mechanism had been replaced by machine guns, and its cavalry by armored cars. And they had embarked on a program to match and even overtake England in the number of modern dreadnoughts in their fleet. But who was their intended target? Would it be France, Russia, or England—the three allies whose military strength made the German High Command nervous?

Until then, Britain's naval fleet was aimed largely at defense in case of attack, or to prevent a blockade by France or Russia.

By the time 1914 began, the Chancellor of the Exchequer, Lloyd George, announced there was little chance of a naval war between the two powers since Germany knew they couldn't win. He wrote a letter to Winston Churchill— who was now First Lord of the Admiralty—in which he claimed that Britain could not afford the four new dreadnoughts already agreed on to assure superior naval strength. But Churchill knew by now that they were necessary, because war was certain—it was only a question of when and how it might start. He believed that Germany intended to attack France, and England would have to go to the aid of the French.

The German Admiral Turpitz's "Risk Theory" considered that Britain would never risk taking them on if the German navy was big enough. He planned five squadrons with eight battleships in each. But the ratio of dreadnoughts was 20:13 in Britain's favor when war broke out.

As a fairly recent biographer of Winston Churchill wrote, "Lusting for conquest and nursing obscure grievances, Germany had been looking for an excuse to fight and now had found it, supporting Austria against the Russian czar and his ally in the west, the French."[3] So here we have yet another possible reason for war. The excuse that Germany had been searching for was the welcome assassination of the heir to the Austrian throne in Sarajevo by a Serbian nationalist.

If we still wish to find a "rational" reason for the First World War, and examine the minds of the movers and shakers of the time, we could make a judgment that it was triggered by Kaiser Wilhelm's delusions of military encirclement. But it is hard to tell even now whether the deluded Kaiser caught this psychic epidemic from the tensions of his Military Chief of Staff, von Moltke, or the other way round. It certainly seems that von Moltke caught the emotional disease from his predecessor, the late von Schlieffen, who wrote "The Schlieffen Plan." Moltke, then, was another alternative cause of the war. And, as we shall see, he had become emotionally involved in the German obsession.

The Schlieffen Plan was a blueprint for war which reflected its author's paranoia about the military might of France. He had a long memory and still feared the shadows of Napoleon Bonaparte's almost invincible *Grand Armée*. Despite the fact that Napoleon and his armies were long since dead, von Moltke was afraid of military encirclement by the French. And since he also respected British military and naval might, he was certain that Germany would be hugely outnumbered if those two nations became allies—or France and Russia, because of Russia's enormous population that might eventually overwhelm Germany.

The Schlieffen Plan was constantly on von Moltke's mind, so that it became his Bible. The plan depended for its success on a pre-emptive strike on France at the outset. Invading France meant taking a shortcut through Belgium. And Britain had a treaty to go to Belgium's aid if they were ever attacked. Since Moltke was certain the British would honor their treaty, it was vitally important to strike fast and hard to conquer France before a British force could cross the channel and arrive on the Continent of Europe.

The German staff were eager for war—it was what they had been trained for. Their enthusiasm for battle took even the bombastic Kaiser by surprise, despite all the threats he made as a matter of habit, without necessarily intending to fulfill them. This time he caught their enthusiasm and went along with it. It was his big chance to show his royal British cousins that Germany was their equal—perhaps even the first among equals, since it was now stronger militarily. Willy had long been touchy and angry at their personal dismissal of him as an irresponsible upstart; now he was compelled to show them what he was really made of.

Frustration and Fury

So meticulously detailed was von Schlieffen's plan that he had even measured the steps of German troops in order to determine the exact time it would take to march on Belgium before invading France. That was where their problems and the German atrocities began. Because, in the event, their army included conscripts who couldn't march as fast as regular troops and had shorter paces. Frustration and fury enraged the Chiefs of Staff and the invasion forces at the delays, for fear that Britain might move fast to intervene and wreck the Schlieffen Plan. It was a typical fixed obsession for a plan or an idea, instead of basing actions on the capacities of the people involved. Sacrifices had to be made for the sake of the plan. So that, when German armies finally arrived in Belgian villages or towns, German troops took out their frustration and impatience on civilians by shooting them dead whenever they were too slow to obey their commands.

Nobel prize-winner for literature Elias Canetti believed firmly in the power of symbols to identify a nation's culture—the sea for England, the mountains for Switzerland, the dykes for Holland, and the forests for Germany. For out of the forests came the German tribes who had been happy there. They are jubilant with joy whenever they return to the rows and lanes of tall, stiff and disciplined trees that appear like so many marching troops, among whom Germans feel at home. It is like a marching forest.[4] And it has been said that "War is the National Industry of Prussia."[5]

Arrogance, frustration, and stupidity ruled as German officers grew anxious at delays and feared they would be blamed for the failure of the plan. At first, news of German atrocities to the civilian population in Belgium were discounted, because there was no tangible evidence, since they buried the bodies. Even so, the remains would turn up many years afterwards.

When Britain honored her agreement with the Belgians by declaring war on Germany, the Great War was underway in earnest. And what the opposing armies faced for the first time was a new form of trench warfare that bogged troops down in mud and caused more deaths by machine-gun fire than ever before, whenever they clambered out of their trenches from behind barbed wire and advanced courageously under witless orders into murderous enemy fire that cut them down. It was a war of attrition with little territory won or lost, and the sheer volume of deaths was far greater than in any previous war.

It took four years before the guns were finally silenced, and the slaughter ceased, when German, French, and British armies fought each other to a standstill. Exhausted and disillusioned French and German and Russian troops rebelled at the harshness and purposelessness of the war. In Tsarist

Russia, it led to troops shooting their officers to escape, and the beginning of the Russian Revolution, when Russian forces ceased fire and withdrew from the war. Only the entry of fresh American troops tipped the scales in favor of the Allies at the very end. There were no real winners except for the United States. The puzzle at the end was how had it all come about—how had the young men of Germany, France, Britain, Austria, and Russia been drawn so blindly to their deaths?

CHAPTER FOUR

THE YOUNG WINSTON

A GREAT DEAL HAD HAPPENED SINCE Winston left home to become a boarder in Harrow. When Lord Randolph came to visit his son there, he would take Winston and his older school friend to lunch at the King's Head Hotel, where Winston watched them talk easily as equals. "How I should have loved to have that sort of relationship with my father!" he would write longingly later on. But he was only an awkward schoolboy and his intermittent remarks made him look foolish.[1] Despite his dislike of Harrow, he got on rather well and was liked for his personal magnetism, his "commanding intelligence, his bravery and charm."

He wrote to an aunt when he was fourteen, that he would like to join a regiment but, since there was no likelihood of a war in his time, he would have to be a politician. He was reading Carlyle's *French Revolution*. He wrote that he was being taught by a master who took the greatest interest in him. And Jennie wrote him a letter containing sound advice.

There is a general impression that both his parents were distant and cold, but clearly that was not the case; they behaved towards their two sons in the normal manner of the times. In fact, their letter writing was unusually thoughtful, and came about because they were both literary and imaginative. But what he was seeking was affection and admiration—evidently he was very possessive of his mother and needed an audience—whereas all he received was stern advice and reproof. And Jennie would not regard clinging possessiveness as a virtue, and discouraged it.

Despite his poor grades at Harrow, he was evidently reading a great deal on his own and educating himself, since he appears to have had deep insights into what was happening in different parts of the world. Even so, he was required to attend a crammers school in London during the holidays, to pass his exams. Nevertheless, somehow he also managed to spend time on holidays in France, Switzerland, Italy, and other countries on the Continent of Europe—far more so than most English schoolboys. But if he expected congratulations from his father for his progress at Harrow, he was disappointed.

He had no way of knowing that Lord Randolph was seriously ill, with a condition that had begun to affect his sanity. Instead of fatherly praise when he was eighteen, Winston received a letter scolding him for not applying himself to enter an infantry regiment, but choosing the cavalry because it required lower marks. "Never," his father wrote, "have I received a really good report of your conduct in your work from any master or tutor you had from time to time to do with."[2]

Lord Randolph went even further in his long and rambling letter.

> With all the advantages you had, with all the abilities which you foolishly think yourself to possess & which some of your relations claim for you, with all the efforts that have been made to make your life easy & agreeable & your work neither oppressive nor distasteful, this is the grand result that you come up among the 2nd rate & 3rd rate class who are only good for commissions in a cavalry regiment. Do not think I am going to take the trouble of writing you long letters after every folly and failure you commit and undergo. I shall not write again on these matters & you need not trouble to write any answer to this part of my letter, because I no longer attach the slightest weight to anything you may say about your achievements and exploits.

As if the knife he had thrust into his son's heart had not possessed the required effect, he warned Winston that if his future conduct continued to be similar to that in his previous establishments, "then my responsibility for you is over."

Those threats from a father he admired and wished to emulate were the unkindest thing that could have happened to Winston as he was about to embark on his career. He would ruminate hurtfully on the rebukes for the rest of his life. At the same time, the letter was an indication of Lord Randolph's state of mind: he appeared to be so despondent and furious at his own condition that he had apparently given up all hope of recovery, and lost sight of reality.

Winston was crushed. But when he returned from his holiday abroad, he found that his father had obtained a special commission for him in the infantry. Jennie wrote to him: "The future is in your hands. I trust in you to make it a success." And we sense that she had quietly intervened on his behalf.

When Winston took his Sandhurst examination in all the five categories, he did well, particularly in tactics. Perhaps his father's stern attitude had applied a much-needed shock to his senses. And their relationship continued and reverted to what it had been before. But Randolph's illness grew worse. He was described as "bowed down with physical and mental suffering." His speech was slurred and he often lost the trend of his thoughts, sometimes failing to finish his speeches in Parliament, while his audience waited uncomfortably during the long pauses before he sat down in bewilderment and confusion.

Lord Randolph left England with Jennie and his doctor to travel round the world, haggard and worn with pain, but ready for what he knew was inevitable. When the time came, he was strapped into a straitjacket. His condition was described as general paralysis. It was thought that such symptoms indicated syphilis, which could appear ten to twenty years after a infection.[3]

Winston never saw him again—except, he wrote, as a shadow.

Early Life in an Army Barracks

What he enjoyed about Sandhurst at first was leaving his boarding schools behind him and having a new start. Everything was new and everyone started equally with tactics, fortification, mapmaking, military law, and military administration. Apart from that there was the physical side with drill, gym, and horse riding. Discipline was strict and the lessons were long. In addition, Winston acquired books on the operations of war, infantry, cavalry, artillery, and infantry fire tactics, as well as histories dealing with those subjects in the American Civil War and the Franco-German and Russo-Turkish Wars.

They learned how to dig trenches, construct breastworks, "revetted parapets with sandbags, with heather, with fascines, or with 'Jones' iron band gabion. We put up *chevaux de frises* and made *fougasses* [a kind of primitive land mine]. We cut railway lines with slabs of guncotton, and learned how to blow up masonry bridges, or make substitutes out of pontoons or timber. We drew contoured maps of all the hills round Camberley, made road reconnaissances in every direction, and set out picket lines and paper plans for advance guards or rear guards, and even did some very simple tactical schemes." All of it was very elementary, but he found it thrilling, to a point where he remarked, if only he had been in the army a hundred years sooner, "what splendid times we should have had! Fancy being nineteen in 1793 with more than twenty years of war against Napoleon in front of one!"

But the last war against sophisticated troops had been the awful failure of the Crimean War. Now that "the world was growing so sensible and pacific— and so democratic too—the great days were over." It was a disappointment for him to miss such opportunities as he had been trained for. But he thoroughly enjoyed riding school. At that time, it appeared to be one of the most important skills in the world, since engine-driven vehicles had not yet been invented, other than with steam.

"There is a thrill and a charm of its own in the glittering jingle of a cavalry squadron manoeuvring at the trot; and this deepens into joyous excitement when the same evolutions are performed at a gallop . . . the sense of incorporation in a living machine, the suave dignity of the uniform—all combine to make cavalry drill a fine thing in itself." None of the horrors of the machine world had yet been introduced into battle. Until then he thought more of the pageantry and color of the cavalry, and blamed the very idea of mechanized war on democracy and science, with not a little impish glitter and challenge in his words. Until then, war consisted largely of individual battles between small groups of professional soldiers in far-flung places, and not entire populations including women and children, pitted against each other in extermination. Meddlers and muddlers would irritate him all his life.

But when he thought about it more seriously, he was obliged to recognize that Germany possessed twenty cavalry divisions, just as imposing as Britain's. His imagination dwelt on what might happen if half a dozen men concealed themselves in a hole with a Maxim gun and kept their heads. No more cavalry! Meanwhile, there were splendid parades with Queen Victoria in her carriage. Would all the posturing that went with the jingle of cavalry on parades disappear with the hard reality of mechanized warfare?

He did well at Sandhurst, as if to demonstrate that his miserable and generally useless years at boarding school had not been his fault but theirs. He returned home at the end of 1894, fully qualified to receive an army commission from Queen Victoria. From then, until the moment he wrote his book on his early years, he confessed that he was constantly occupied; or, as he put it, never had time to turn round. The world, for him, was like an Aladdin's cave. "All the days were good and each day better than the other."[4]

Life in an Army Barracks

He was now a junior officer, being paid enough money to meet the needs that regimental standards set for British officers in the imperial army. It was not enough. One traditionally popular way to augment it was gambling. It was true of many young officers, whether in the French, German, or Russian army. It sometimes resulted in a court martial or suicide.[5] But that was not Churchill's way.

If we pause to consider the emphasis on an army career in the Victorian age, we need to be reminded that industrialization was still relatively new and did not yet provide many regular or well-paid jobs. The British Isles were still composed mostly of small rural and agricultural communities with, as yet, only a few industrial cities with manufactories. So the British Empire was a boon to ambitious young men seeking adventure in foreign parts, either in the civil service, or as traders, or in the imperial army. Serving overseas in the army provided a glamorous uniform and exciting opportunities in exotic countries with possibilities of awards and medals. In those days few, except the moneyed classes, had been overseas. Most had never left the village in which they had been born. Visitors arriving by the new railways would poke fun at the simpleminded village inhabitants.

The job of the British Army was to maintain law and order in regions which had been left in chaos by previous rulers who had been overthrown or who had pillaged and destroyed the economies of their own country. British colonies also provided markets to export goods beginning to be made in industrial cities like Sheffield, Birmingham, and Manchester, which would soon become over-productive and need more consumers. Their economies required stability and their labor and trade needed protecting, which increased the living standards of local populations. But Winston experienced none of that, isolated at he was in the boring atmosphere of the army barracks.

His military life seemed to have started well at first. He wrote an article for the *Pall Mall Magazine* claiming that life at Sandhurst was "a pleasing emancipation" for those who enter from Eton or Harrow. It drew a rebuke from his former headmaster at Harrow who was evidently concerned for its reputation. Then, soon after he had begun his training at Aldershot—in charge of thirty men and horses—his old nanny Mrs. Everest died. He and his brother Jack were shocked. Winston became sad and depressed, as if she had been his mother; which is largely what she had been, since Jennie was absorbed in socializing.

Mrs. Everest had been a link with the past which he felt slipping away. Perhaps her passing made him realize he was grown up and on his own after his father and she had gone. All his dreams of comradeship with his father and entering Parliament at his side had vanished. His depression now began to include the army, which he felt was in a state of mental stagnation, and so was he. Army life in barracks narrowed the mind, whereas he wanted to study economics and modern history. He was restless, and tried to raise his spirits by studying his father's speeches to Parliament. He was searching for something more literary and less material; but perhaps he also drew some comfort in recollecting his father's greatness as a politician, even if somewhat exaggerated in his imagination.

He could no longer visit his mother at their old home because she was now living with relatives or in hotels. His home was now Aldershot, where the Duke and Duchess of York (the future King George the Fifth and Queen Mary) attended their field day. He met them at dinner. His life in the cavalry regiment naturally required a great deal of riding—eight hours a day in the saddle—and maneuvers, two hours of stabling, and then polo. He admitted to Jennie that he was already becoming seduced by politics. But at the same time he often thought of taking a degree in history, philosophy, and economics. But it still required knowing Latin and Greek to read classics which had not yet been translated into English.

Those were the interests that began to occupy his mind. And he began to realize, as most intelligent people do, that education starts after you leave school. So he began a course of private study, choosing Fawcett's *Manual of*

Political Economy. He planned to follow on with Gibbon's *Decline and Fall of the Roman Empire* and Lecky's *European Morals from Augustus to Charlemagne.*[6]

Jennie was still young and beautiful at forty, and soon became more than a friend, more of an ardent comrade who guarded his interests and helped to further his plans with her influence and energy. He felt they were more like brother and sister.

Soon afterwards, when he was twenty-one, he heard that Spanish forces were attempting to put down a rebellion in Cuba, which was a Spanish colony. He visited the Commander-in-Chief of the British Army for permission to travel to Cuba, and was given maps and information. Then he made his first transatlantic crossing by sea with a friend. They were met with effusive hospitality in New York, where they contacted Jennie's cousins. "What an extraordinary people the Americans are!" he wrote enthusiastically to his mother; "they make you feel at home and at ease." To his brother Jack, he wrote; "This is a very great country my dear Jack . . . . There seems to be no such thing as reverence or tradition."[7]

They took a ship to Havana, and then by train to join the Spanish troops on November 21. Afterwards, he proceeded to send five dispatches to the *Daily Graphic,* as if they were "letters from the front." He had contrived suddenly to become a war correspondent. Returning to New York, he was interviewed by a reporter from the *New York World.* When asked about the Spanish troops, he remarked, "They are well versed in the art of retreat." The United States went to war with Spain soon afterwards, and defeated the Spanish forces in Cuba. He returned to England with fine Cuban cigars, Cuban coffee, and guava jelly.

Social and Political Life

Due to sail for India in the autumn and given a few idle months beforehand, Winston gave himself over to the amusements of the London Season. English society still existed in its traditional form then. Everyone knew everyone else, and for very good reason, since most of the few hundred leading families who had ruled England for generations were interrelated through marriages. They were leading statesmen or leading sportsmen. In 1896, all their minds were caught up with Queen Victoria's Diamond Jubilee in the following year. And, of course, the Duchess of Devonshire's Fancy Dress Ball—since the English have always loved dressing up, almost as much as the Austro-Hungarians loved showing off their glittering uniforms.

Meanwhile, Winston's newspaper articles had attracted the attention of politicians. And his social life blossomed at Lord Rothschild's home, where the guests included Balfour (who would be elected conservative Prime Minister the following year) and Asquith (who would become liberal Prime Minister thereafter). *The Saturday Review* had published one of Churchill's articles on Cuba, and Joseph Chamberlain considered it the best account he had read of Cuba's problems. (Chamberlain would soon lead the opposition party in the House of Commons). Meanwhile, the United States was applying pressure on Spain to grant Cuba independence (which they would in 1901). And it was remarked that young Winston kept his eyes open. There was also a great deal of talk about what was going on in South Africa.

It was in December of 1895 that an event occurred in South Africa that Churchill considered afterwards to be "a fountain of ill." Lord Salisbury had just been returned to office and now carefully encouraged peace in Europe, ensuring that everything at home was peaceful too. He limited his actions to the British Empire and turned away from all kinds of provocations in Europe, the Americas, and the East. Moving toward the challenge of the Khalifa at Khartoum, and President Kruger in Pretoria, he found that the pressures of events in South Africa were about to explode into a crisis.

Johannesburg had become a dangerous element in the world of finance, as the formerly rural Boer farmers found that they possessed vast fortunes from the gold mines in the Transvaal. All that wealth now enabled the Boers to reach out to Holland and Germany for political support against the British. And the powerful fighting force of the religious zealots with their fifty to sixty thousand fierce and valiant Boer horsemen formed what Churchill would describe as "the most capable mounted warriors since the Mongols."[8]

Opposing them were the "Outlanders," as they were called, in Johannesburg. They were mostly British, and becoming another significant force in the country. They had become disenchanted with the Boers and their heavy taxes (or so they claimed). It was a case of "No taxation without representation," in the language of the Boston Tea Party. But there was no way the Boers would recognize them as vote-carrying citizens of the Boer Republic, or the Boers would become outnumbered and overwhelmed. Lord Salisbury and Joseph Chamberlain championed the cause of the British, but naturally, the Boers were unwilling to give up their rule and be outnumbered.

Chamberlain's case was that Kruger was refusing to give civil rights to the British, who were contributing 90 percent of the wealth of the country, because the Boer farmers were afraid they'd have to free the black slaves on their farms.

The wealth of the country was largely controlled by the Chairman and founder of the Chartered Company, Mr. Cecil Rhodes, who was also Prime Minister of the Cape Colony. The administrator of his company was Dr. Jameson. Jameson was known to be an impulsive frontiersman who would not be reluctant to use his force of 700 men to rebel against the Boer Republic. He threatened to march 150 miles from Mafeking to Johannesburg if Rhodes and the British government agreed. They had ample money to back them, since Rhodes was the major stockholder of the gold mines.

One April morning, after a provisional government had been formed in Johannesburg, Jameson and 700 horsemen, wheeling two guns, headed out across the veldt to the city. The incident became the focus of the world. And the German Kaiser took the opportunity to send a telegram encouraging the Boer President Kruger to take on the British. He even went as far as to order German marines to disembark at Delagoa Bay. Great Britain was blamed by all for the fiasco, as Boer commandos surrounded Jameson's raiders and forced them to surrender.

The British government hurriedly disembarrassed themselves of the whole ill-managed affair, and Cecil Rhodes blamed Jameson for being a hot-headed independent rebel. The ringleaders were allowed to ransom themselves out of trouble and, after being sentenced to death, Jameson was given a two-year prison sentence instead.

The whole affair faded as new problems took its place. But the British had been involved, and their reputation was besmirched. In addition, the British government recognized the Kaiser's ill-will and suspected his intentions. They never forgot his hostility from then on. The problems in South Africa were not over yet—there were too many unscrupulous, stubborn, and impulsive players involved, and too much mineral wealth for the country to be ignored.

India

For his next trip overseas, Winston planned to travel to Egypt, where General Kitchener was endeavoring, with great difficulty, to retake the Sudan. When his journey couldn't be managed, Winston turned to Crete, where the Greeks were fighting for independence from Turkish Rule. Then there were British forces suppressing an uprising in Matabeleland, and Winston attempted to join them. The 9th Lancers were scheduled to take ship to Matabeleland in August, but his own regiment was bound for India. He was unenthusiastic and considered Matabeleland was the best opportunity for exciting adventures, awards, and glory. He urged Jennie to use her influence on his behalf, and told her he was impatient to leave. Notwithstanding her efforts, he sailed with the 4th Hussars for India on September 11.

They arrived in Bombay on October 1. He was encamped in Poona three days later. Then they left for Bangalore. But India, he decided after several months, was a land of snobs and bores. Now he regretted being away from England during the East Bradford election, which he would have liked to contest. He was almost twenty-two, restless and eager to demonstrate his worth. But each time he met the British residents of India at social events, like the balls at the Viceregal Lodge in Calcutta, he felt nostalgic for England, and ballroom dancing was not one of his skills.

What suddenly overcame him was a desire for learning the types of subjects not taught at school, like ethics, and history which had been badly taught.

By the time Jennie sent him Macaulay's works in twelve volumes, he was already on to Plato's *Republic* and Winwood Reade's *Martyrdom of Man*, Hallam's *Constitutional History*, and Adam Smith's *Wealth of Nations*. "From November to May I read four or five hours every day history and philosophy;" Schopenhauer on Pessimism; Malthus on Population; Darwin's *Origin of Species*; "all interspersed with other books of lesser standing."

His readings in the following years raised questions for him about religion. Until then he had blindly accepted whatever he was told about it. At Harrow there had been three services each Sunday, as well as morning and evening prayers every weekday. In the army they questioned whether there was another world in the hereafter and whether we had lived before. Christianity "made people want to be respectable, to keep up appearances, and so saved lots of scandal!" So that when he read *The Martyrdom of Man* and learned that "we simply go out like candles," he was offended. After reading much the same elsewhere, he felt indignant at having been told so many untruths. Then, when he prayed at the front line and returned home safe for tea, he was comforted to realize that he always got what he wanted if he prayed, whereas reasoning "led nowhere." Some of his cousins who'd been to university teased him with arguments that nothing has any existence but what we think.

But Churchill was also a tease, and as an author, felt obliged to entertain his readers by continually reminding them how absurd life is. With his command of the English language, he was very witty. Since entertainers feel they are always on display, one can see how easily he might be misunderstood if his audience did not possess that mocking sense of upper-class humor which laughs heartily at its own sense of self-importance and rarely takes itself seriously.

His range of interests included journalism as a war correspondent, the army, and politics. He longed to be a politician like his father. But what was he really? What he needed, in order to establish his credentials, was influence. Meanwhile, he was promoted to brigade major in February 1897. He had become full of zeal, he wrote to Jennie.

That same February, Britain supported the Turks in the Greek revolt on Crete, whereas Winston's sympathies lay with the Cretans. He always sympathised with the underdogs, and viewed the conflict as a matter of right or wrong, whereas he considered Prime Minister Lord Salisbury viewed it from a point of view of profit and loss. Salisbury's purpose, he told Jennie, was to sustain the Turkish Empire in order to prevent Russia from invading Constantinople. He was becoming more enthusiastic than ever to oppose Salisbury's government, and was suddenly keen to take a month's leave in England. But Jennie upbraided him—everyone would say he couldn't stick to anything. Six months with his regiment was not enough, particularly as his regiment might be called to Egypt at any time. "You seem to have no purpose in life," she wrote.

The truth was that Jennie was now as strapped for cash as he was. "I will only repeat that I cannot help you any more . . ." He must try to live within his income and cut his expenses to do it. The advice was sound, but he took as little notice of it as she did. As usual, he was restless and impatient for success.

He read the *Annual Register of World Events* and made his own notes in the margins of the summaries of Parliamentary debates, where he expressed his own ideas. One of them was a plea for equal education for everyone.

He remained in India during the spring, when Turkey declared war on Greece. It presented him with an opportunity to travel to the battlefront as a war correspondent. He trusted in Jennie's influence to find a newspaper to commission him. He reminded her that Lord Rothschild knew everyone—and left for Bombay, fully expecting to find Jennie had arranged everything by the time he arrived in Italy.

But he arrived too late—the Turks had already defeated the Greeks. So he proceeded on to London. There he made his first political speech to the Primrose League, which Lord Randolph had founded to carry on Disraeli's memory and Randolph's Tory Democracy values. He praised the Government Workmen's Compensation Bill to protect them from the costs of injury at work, and from poverty.

The *Morning Post* gave a good report of his speech. After which he returned to Bangalore and began work writing a new novel, a political romance, as Disraeli had done to achieve popularity.

Soon afterwards, Jennie received a letter from his commanding officer to let her know that Winston was heading for the war on the North-West Frontier at Malakand, where Afridis and Orakzais and other tribes from Afghanistan had violated the peace. Once there, he heard that Jennie had persuaded the *Daily Telegraph* to publish his letters from the battlefront.

Under Fire at the Frontline

He reached the North-West Frontier at Malakand in the first week of September. The first of the letters he sent to the *Daily Telegraph*—without a byline but recorded as by "a young officer"—described a confrontation by civilization, "face to face with the militant Mohamedans." He rode ahead of a cavalry detachment through the valley to Nawagai, hoping to arrive in time for the action. He was met by about fifty armed tribesmen who, fortunately, turned out to be friendly.

They are very cruel people, he wrote home to a friend: they need a lesson. He explained that their own Sikhs put a wounded man into an incinerator and burnt him alive. "This was hushed up," he added. Now he was attached to the second brigade of the Malakand Field Force, which was ordered to take action. Winston switched back from a part-time journalist to a serving officer and experienced action for the first time on a battlefront. He rode forward with the 35th Sikh infantry. The firing was so hot that he had to continue on foot, since his pony was not accustomed to the noise of battle. When they retreated, the wounded were left to be cut up by the enemy.

Lieutenants Cassells and Hughes, who were standing beside him, were struck by Afridi rifle fire. And another Afridi tribesman attempted to cut up Lieutenant Hughes. Winston fired, and the Afridi dropped, but came on again. Hughes was killed. Winston and another officer carried a wounded Sikh back towards the retreating Sikh infantry, leaving his blood on Winston's uniform. The Afridis came as close as forty yards, and Winston and another officer fired at them—to be pelted with stones in return. They fired again. All the excitement of adventure dissipated when the affair became deadly, and the Afridis continued their attacks for over an hour. Winston defended himself with his service revolver, until he found a rifle and fired forty rounds at close quarters. Four of the enemy fell.

As soon as the action ended, skirmishing continued. It was considered a great escape after being under fire from 7:30 in the morning to 8:30 at night. Winston considered he had acquitted himself quite well, although fifty British and Sikh soldiers were killed and a hundred wounded.

"I rode on my grey pony," he wrote to Jennie, "all along the skirmish line when everyone else was lying down in cover. Foolish perhaps, but I play for high stakes and given an audience there is no act too daring or too noble." An officer commanding the Sikhs recommended that he should be mentioned in dispatches. "I shall get a medal," he crowed, "and perhaps a couple of clasps," he added.

The action had come about because the British had held the Malakand Pass for three years. It ran to Chitral, which was considered to be strategically important. But the Pathan tribes in the Swat Valley lost their patience with troops passing through their territory, and attacked the garrisons holding the pass. They killed a number of people, including women and children. Lancers and cavalry had chased them away. But there were a whole series of violent incidents subsequently, followed by the necessity of British expeditions that had to return to scold the tribesmen and fine them for any damage. Then the tribesmen began to make roads through the valley and interfere with the strategic route to Chitral.

Now a British punitive expedition was planned to subdue the Mahmands—as well as the Bunerwals whom Sir Bindon Blood had already reasoned with successfully, without having to kill anyone. Both were Pathan tribes, and he liked them.

The life of the Pathans was full of interest, according to Winston when they campaigned on the Indian frontier. The sun-filled valleys with their abundant water were fertile enough for a sparse population. But the nineteenth century brought the breech-loading rifle and the British. The rifle was a great advantage in the highlands, where it could kill a neighbor accurately at 1,500 yards, while remaining in the comfort of one's own home and firing through a window, or strike a horseman in the valley below. Rifle-theft became a new and rewarding occupation, and admiration for Christian civilization flourished in India. But the British were a nuisance because they objected. Worse, they retaliated.

Consequently, Winston found the kind of adventure he had been looking for at the frontier, after a punitive attack on the Pathans, when he and the Sikhs had begun to retreat. It suddenly occurred to him then that they were only a very small party—five British officers including himself and about eighty-five Sikhs. They were scrambling up the Mamund Valley to punish a further village. When they reached its mud huts, they found them deserted. He lay down with another officer and eight Sikhs while the others searched the huts, then sat down to rest out of the heat.

After about a quarter of an hour, their captain arrived and told them to withdraw and take a fresh position below. Suddenly the whole mountain came alive with flags waving and swords flashing. Intermittent shot-fire broke in white puffs from place to place. Loud explosions burst out. Then white and blue figures appeared several thousand feet above them, dropping down towards them from ledge to ledge, like monkeys flying down branches. Shouting arose with the explosions of the rifle shots, and the figures came closer. Their Sikhs opened fire, which became more and more rapid. But the figures continued to scramble down the mountainside towards them, to a position among the rocks only about a hundred yards away.

He borrowed the rifle of the Sikh beside him, who passed over a handful of cartridges. There was an untidy volley from the rocks, with shouts, exclamations, and a scream. The others got up and turned to retreat. He wondered why half a dozen of their men had lain down, until he realized they had dropped dead. One had blood pouring out from his breast, another was kicking and twisting on his back in pain. The British officer's face was covered in blood, his right eye missing.

Since no wounded man could be left behind on the frontier, to be tortured or cut to pieces by Pathan tribesmen, they began to drag the wounded away or carry them downhill. But there was no sign of the supporting party who should have been down there. They wrestled the wounded down without a rearguard, when twenty or thirty figures appeared, firing furiously down at them from between the mud huts. They dragged the protesting wounded further downhill, stumbling and hopping and staggering and crawling. He looked to his left, where the Adjutant had been shot and four of his men were carrying him. Half a dozen Pathans, with swords flashing, leapt out of the houses. The soldiers carrying the officer dropped him and fled. The closest Pathan leapt at the body of the officer and cut it in pieces. When Winston took out his revolver to shoot the tribesman, he scuttled behind a rock and fire broke out from all over. That was the moment Winston discovered he was alone with the Pathans. He ran to a knoll as fast as he could. The Sikhs were holding the knoll further down, and he bounded towards it.

They all ran down towards the plain, followed by their pursuers trying to cut them off and firing on both flanks. When they finally got away they left one officer dead and a dozen wounded men to be cut to pieces by the pursuing Pathans.

Winston was in action twice more that week, at Domadola and at Zagai. He felt lucky, which was a good sign in a soldier. All the time, of course, the heat was unrelentingly harsh. And he had begun to understand why whisky was such a popular tipple with India hands.

Sixty more men were killed or wounded on September 30, when the 31st Punjabi Regiment was in action at Agrah. "I cried," he wrote to Jennie, "when I met the Royal Wests and saw the men really unsteady under fire and tired of the game, and that poor young Browne-Clayton, literally cut in pieces on a stretcher . . ." He was only a year older than Winston. It may have been the first time he wept with emotion and sentiment, but it would not be the last. (Forty years later, he would weep to see working-class women lining up to buy birdseed for their pet budgerigars during the shortages with German bombing raids on London). Despite his tears at the deaths of boys so young, there was no doubt that Winston loved every minute of the adventure and the danger.

"The tribesmen torture the wounded and mutilate the dead," Winston wrote to his grandmother. As a consequence, the British and Sikh troops never spared a single man of the enemy who falls into their hands. "Nature sets little store by life."

Jennie chided him for boasting. And he replied that he only did so to close friends who already knew how conceited he was; and having an audience was half the fun. Anyway, he joked, being under fire was good experience for a political life. He had been under fire now on fifteen occasions since his first encounter on the frontier, and was satisfied with his coolness in dangerous situations.

In fact, his exuberance at the sight of gruesome deaths and deadly dangers to come was probably a need to talk about the shock of new experiences that could turn one's life upside-down and linger in the mind forever, rather than being boasting. Far better to talk than bottle up all the images for future recall, as any psychiatrist would advise. (It was not until 1917 that bottling up grim memories for repeated recall later on would be named shell-shock.) The experience of lethal danger and death and grief required an outlet. What was important was that he had found himself cool and ruthless under fire and also a way to assuage any irrational feelings of guilt that frontline soldiers frequently suffer from. For others who become mentally blocked and can't communicate their shock or grief, there is only crippling pain. Winston had tested himself under fire and passed the test. He was now a hardened soldier.

CHAPTER FIVE

THE CAVALRY CHARGE

WINSTON WISHED HE COULD COME TO the conclusion that the barbarity and losses, and the expenditure, resulted in a permanent settlement of the frontier, but he doubted it: "I do not think however that anything has been done that could not have to be done again." He gave his opinion in the *Daily Telegraph* that it was folly to allow the tribesmen to be in control of the buffer zone between British India and Afghanistan. That opinion made him set aside writing a novel in favor of a true account of the Malakand field force.

He sent his manuscript to Jennie in England. He preferred histories that conjured up the past, since many traditional ones did not bring it alive. He'd previously mentioned his book to Balfour and now Balfour recommended his own literary agent, who found a publisher for it within a week. Winston still wished to leave for Egypt, but his mind had hardened to the challenge of winning an election and being esteemed in the House of Commons, as his father had been. He was now twenty-three.

In response to Jennie's remarks about persisting with the army to demonstrate that he could, in effect, hold down a job, he wrote to remind her it was a pushy age and we must shove with the rest of them. After Egypt, he would turn from war to politics. The link between the two vocations was the switch from showing his mettle under attack on the frontier, to showing it under fire from the opposition in Parliament. He stayed with Lord Elgin the viceroy in Calcutta in 1898. It was an influential move into circles that could facilitate his career either way—eight years hence he would work for Lord Elgin at the Colonial Office. He had already discovered that promotion was based not on what one does but on what he is; not a matter of brains so much as character

and originality. Introductions only admit a person onto the scales where everyone has to be weighed.

Meanwhile, he was short of cash again. He grew annoyed at what he considered Jennie's extravagance with her fashionable clothes, her travelling and
entertaining: she had spent a quarter of their fortune in the three years since
Lord Randolph's death. Fortunately, he received an advance from his book on
Malakand, and good sales resulted in a reprint.

Jennie and her influential friends now thought he was wasted in the
army—that was a turn of events!—and could do much better at his writing.
The Prince of Wales confirmed her remark about his writing, but perhaps he
had written to Winston more to caution him about being tactless in what he
wrote, which—as he said—"would be resented by the authorities."

On the other hand, it seemed that everyone was looking for someone to
blame for the failure to suppress the attacks of the tribes on the frontier. But
Winston had noted before that there are no great victories or magnificent
successes, and no surrenders; soldiering was just a persistently grim and gru-
eling job of work, and very repetitive. And if ever there are successes, "we are
assailed by the taunts and reproaches of our countrymen at home." He wrote
about the ethics of policy on the frontier, and then a couple of feature articles,
and a short story, then pressed on again with his novel. He felt he was on a roll,
and his income grew.

Nevertheless, he still wanted to be elected in Bradford and travelled to
London on July 2, to speak to an audience there. He found they listened to what
he said and liked it, and applauded him several times. That was encouraging.
Lord Salisbury read his book about Malakand, and invited him to the Foreign
Office for a meeting soon afterwards. Winston was greeted with old-world courtesy by the Prime Minister, who went on to tell him that his book had provided
him with more information than any other report of the affair, and offered to
help Winston—who was the son of his old colleague—in any way he could.

Winston felt encouraged to send a telegram to General Kitchener asking
to be considered for the expeditionary force. The General thought otherwise.
Even so, Winston seldom took no for an answer and had an informal message
sent to him through Jennie, mentioning the Prime Minister's interest in him.
It took only forty-eight hours for instructions to arrive for him to leave for
the 21st Lancers in Egypt. He contacted the *Morning Post* successfully before

leaving. He was in Marseilles three days later. He took ship to Egypt from there, where he met old friends from Harrow.

He'd longed for a political career when in England, but now he was close to the front again, he found he was excited with another adventure in view. He became focused on battle and now thought only of arms and ammunition and the Dervish army.

The Lancers were sixty miles from Omdurman by August 24. He wrote to Jennie not to be anxious, since he didn't think he'd be killed, but that she should rather be consoled by the thought that all human beings are insignificant. Perhaps his mind was on *The Martyrdom of Man* again, or Darwin's *The Origin of Species*. Or perhaps it was because of writing objectively and philosophically—as if viewing the event from a huge historic distance. Because of his reading and writing histories, he could view most incidents with detachment, as if they were happening to someone else. He was like an artist painting a huge panoramic picture with a few tiny dots on a seashore to represent the insignificance of mankind.

As he closed in on Omdurman two days later, General Kitchener's forces of 25,000 men also drew closer to the chosen battlefield beside the waters of the Nile.

Omdurman

He soon learned on arrival that Kitchener had been reluctant to take him because he knew that Winston was only in the army for his own temporary convenience, so Kitchener didn't want to meet him.

The Dervishes chose to attack Kitchener's forces at Omdurman, across the river from Khartoum. It appeared that their army would clash with British troops before dark. Winston was instructed by the cavalry commander to move in order to find a clearer view and judge the enemy's size and movements, and report to Kitchener. He climbed a hill to get a better look. Once there, he saw the Dervish army was enormous, but dwarfed even so by the immense desert landscape. Glancing to the east, he saw the British and Egyptian troops, but neither of them could see the Dervishes for the hill between them. The enemy forces were broadly spread out and deeper than the Allies, and were slowly advancing.

Winston hastened back down to his gray pony and saw Kitchener together with the Sirdar and a dozen staff officers riding towards him. The imposing, upright general, and the insignificant junior officer advanced towards each other, the hooves of their mounts crunching gently on the firm sand and somebody's horse gently whinnying.

Kitchener asked him to describe what he'd seen and listened thoughtfully to what Winston had to say, while they rode beside each other. "How long d'you think I've got?" Kitchener asked him.

"At least half an hour," Winston informed him. "Probably an hour and a half," he added.

"They may as well come today as tomorrow," was the offhand retort.

The goal was to liberate large regions from the tyranny of the Dervishes in the Sudan. Kitchener had already destroyed the army of Mahmoud, who was the captain of the Khalifa. His final action would be against the capital city.

The Dervishes came to a halt on one side of Surgham Hill, with the British and the Sirdar's Egyptian army on the other side. Winston would recall many years later, in a more technical and mechanical age, that these battles were not real battles, but only actions. "In those lighthearted days, in Britain's little colonial wars, death in action then, was a splendid game with a sporting element. It was," he wrote, "very different in the First World War, where death was expected, and severe wounds were counted as lucky escapes."

A unit of the Egyptian cavalry climbed on to Surgham Hill for the night, while cavalry patrols rode out to have a look at the enemy forces for themselves. Winston joined one of them. He was awed by the sight of 40,000 men laid out ahead of them. Their lines were five miles long and broken up by squares. They were shouting war songs. The immensity of their size made the little British patrol feel lonely and vulnerable, so that they shivered in the dark.

He scrawled a message in pencil for Kitchener. There were no Dervishes within three miles of the British camp. But as the sky grew lighter, he could see the mass of figures was still advancing. Winston reported their movements. Then he waited. Soon, a force of 2,000 men drew within 400 yards of them. Until then, Winston had thought they were spearmen, but now he saw that the force also included riflemen. Although they saw Winston's cavalry before them, they ignored them as if they were not there.

"Foolishly," he said later on, "I fired and shot down four of them," Then he squeezed a whole magazine into the crowd. The Dervishes sent twenty riflemen forward, who took target practice on the British army. Winston's cavalry galloped off as the enemy bullets whined towards them. But no one was hit. He sent seven of his lancers behind the hill and climbed to the top on his pony, where he dismounted.

The Khalifa's entire army of almost 60,000 Dervishes advanced in disciplined order towards them, wrote Winston; rising up on the rolling land between them and the British troops, then gradually descending on the gentle slope towards the battlefield, with the Nile beside them, as the British infantry stood shoulder to shoulder to bar their way. When the Dervish army came close enough for rifle fire, Kitchener ordered the infantry forward and left the cavalry at the camp. Winston was startlingly aware of gazing at the zealous fanaticism of a past age, faced with British state-of-the-arts weaponry. The enemy also possessed about 20,000 rifles as well as spearmen. But the British Army of two and a half trained infantry divisions, standing waiting in two lines, were supported by more than seventy guns on the river bank and in gunboats on the Nile, all of them firing with calm discipline. The Dervish attack was stopped in its tracks as six or seven thousand of the enemy fell where they stood.

When their spearmen could advance no further, their riflemen lay down on the desert floor and aimed a fusillade in Winston's direction, causing about two hundred British and Egyptian casualties.

Kitchener now wheeled his troops into his customary echelon formation and proceeded to march south to the city with his left flank alongside the river. His intention was to separate the Dervish army from the capital city and bar them from food, water, and sanctuary. But the enemy reserves of about 15,000 were untouched and began their advance on the British forces, which continued to march across the desert. British military precision and guns increased the numbers of dead Dervishes, which were now in excess of 20,000 men who lay in scattered heaps as the mass of their army disintegrated into bits and pieces of flesh that merged with the low-lying layer of a shimmering mirage like a wave of sea across the desert floor.

As Winston told it later, the next hour was filled with the noise of 20,000 rifles firing, with sixty guns and twelve Maxims—although they saw little from their camp, where the cavalry fed and watered their horses. But when the attack slowed, they came out to take positions on the left flank of the British line and rode forward slowly toward the massed Dervish reserves. It was Winston's first cavalry charge, and he was prepared to use his lance to spear the enemy.

Meanwhile, a line of a hundred and fifty men stood between them and the mass of Dervishes behind them. They allowed the British cavalry to move forward to about 250 yards from them. The cavalry rode across the front of the Dervish line, scanning them for a point of entry to wheel and spear them. But Winston soon discovered they were riflemen who kneeled and opened fire at them close up.

A trumpet call marked the advance, and each cavalry officer took his chance whether to wheel away left and gallop off, or right-wheel to charge the enemy. Winston spurred his horse into a cavalry charge against riflemen who had no intention of yielding. When he next looked to his front and drew his Mauser pistol, instead of a thin line of riflemen, the unyielding line of men was now twelve deep in some places, where reserves of Dervish soldiers had climbed out of concealment from a trench, which he now saw was a ravine with steps carved in it where they had climbed up out of hiding.

The British cavalry, 310 officers and men, galloped through them with surprisingly few casualties, although he saw one soldier cut up. Winston had already emptied his pistol into the enemy. The charge had lasted only two minutes. An officer and twenty men had been killed.

He said at the time that it was probably the most dangerous two minutes he'd live to see. Then he noticed some of the British infantry were scattered and in individual combat with the enemy. He spurred his horse into a trot and rode up, firing his reloaded pistol into the enemy's faces, and killed some of them—three for certain, he said; two doubtful, and one very doubtful.

But when he looked round him, he saw the Dervishes reforming and regrouping only twenty yards away. He glanced at them without comprehension for a moment, and saw the men kneel and take aim with their rifles. Then he realized the danger he was in for the first time. He wheeled his horse away and galloped back to his troop as the riflemen fired at him. He reined into a canter to rejoin his men, when he saw a Dervish suddenly rise up in the middle of the troop. They turned their lances at him. Although wounded in several places, he ran towards Winston with spear raised, and Winston shot him at less than a yard away. He dropped and lay dead.

Winston recalled his troop of fifteen men in case they had to make another charge, asking a sergeant if he'd enjoyed himself. "Well, I don't exactly say I enjoyed it, Sir, but I think I'll get more used to it next time."

Meanwhile, the Dervishes were retreating. "I never saw soldiers more willing," he wrote to Jennie a few weeks later. But before they left the field, he saw the carnage of horses and men returning from the charge, some with fish-hook spears protruding from them, and faces and limbs cut to pieces. He no longer felt so heroic. He had been about to suggest another charge, but the gasping vision and the expiring victims discouraged it.

"We all get a little cold an hour afterwards," he admitted.

An officer who was a friend of Jennie's telegraphed her to say, "Big fight. Fine sight. Winston well." More than 10,000 Dervishes had been slain, and 15,000 wounded.

Winston's criticisms of some of the vengeful barbarity of officers and troops earned him enemies in the army, but his cheerful demeanor was liked by others.

Even so, he was in a unique position whereby, as a war correspondent, he could write about whatever he saw with impunity. But he was only a junior officer, and his superior officers would be bound to object to a subaltern criticizing them in the newspapers. One of them was General Kitchener, whom he considered was a barbarian for preserving the Mahdi's head in kerosene as a souvenir of the battle. It was, perhaps, a metaphor for the time when Britain had progressed as a civilized world power with recognition of human rights and the abolishment of slavery, whereas not everyone was rising with the tide of nineteenth-century culture. Many were still dragging their feet, since civilization never advances in a clear straight line, and can fall back to barbarism very fast, to take us all back to the primitive slime from which life was born.

As he left Khartoum to return home, he heard from a doctor that a fellow officer named Richard Molyneux had been wounded and needed a skin graft. Winston offered some of his own skin, which was cut out from his forearm. It was a knightly gesture.

The Seven Knightly Virtues

Winston's unusually close yet distant relationship with Jennie, and his courting danger on the front line, on one hand, and seeking the life of the mind on the other, is reminiscent of the courtly life of a medieval knight in armor, who was trained to be a well-rounded man. For some deeply-hidden reason in the unconscious mind, the Victorian Era in England during the reign of a queen brought back into custom the chivalrous attitude towards women which had once been so prominent during the earlier reign of Queen Elizabeth the First. It had existed even earlier than that, in the romantic but still brutal time of Queen Eleanor of Aquitaine. She too became queen of England, in the twelfth century, when the beautiful and cruel stories of Camelot and *Le Morte d'Arthur* emerged in songs by troubadours.[1] And there was the epic and allegorical poem of *Sir Gawain and the Greene Knight* in the fourteenth-century Arthurian legend.[2]

The Elizabethan Renaissance and the rebirth of Florence had been times when men and women of character, education, and nobility could turn their hands to soldiering and statesmanship, painting, poetry, and alchemy, and also be swashbuckling pirates at the same time, like Sir Walter Raleigh and Sir Francis Drake. So it should come as no surprise that the romantic young Winston—born in Queen Victoria's reign—would have liked to be a Renaissance man. In many ways, he already was. He had switched with ease from the tedium and sweat of army barracks, with its stamping of metal-studded boots and coarse shouting of orders in the infantry, and the jingle of harnesses and smell of horse dung and leather in the cavalry, to more intellectual pursuits. With his sensitively romantic nature, coupled with his dedication to the vocation of soldiery, and his love of good English literature, he would have been bound to read about the mythology of the knight in shining armor, with its attributes of the Seven Virtues of a Knight, and the grit to go out and put them into action.

If the Seven Deadly Sins in Christendom were lust, gluttony, greed, sloth, wrath, envy, and pride, then the opposites would feature as virtues of the ideal human being. Certainly, they appear to have become Winston's own ideal models of knightly behavior. The five virtues emblazoned across the allegorical Sir Gawain's shield are friendship, generosity, chastity, courtesy, and faith. Courage and prowess complete the seven. A knight is armed with those virtues to keep him focused on chivalry. Winston would very likely have read the Arthurian legends that resulted in his own worldview and personal attitudes, as we can see from the declaration in the famous legend.

This is the oath of a Knight of King Arthur's Round Table and should be for all of us to take to heart. I will develop my life for the greater good. I will place character above riches, and concern for others above personal wealth, I will never boast, but cherish humility instead, I will speak the truth at all times, and forever keep my word, I will defend those who cannot defend themselves, I will honor and respect women, and refute sexism in all its guises, I will uphold justice by being fair to all, I will be faithful in love and loyal in friendship, I will abhor scandals and gossip—neither partake nor delight in them, I will be generous to the poor and to those who need help, I will forgive when asked, that my own mistakes will be forgiven, I will live my life with courtesy and honor from this day forward.[3]

There are two other attributes of a knight which appear to be more clearly evident in Japan, which is still a far more formalized society, with its virtues of *Bushido*. "The Way of the Samurai" embraces frugality, loyalty, prowess in the martial arts, honor, wisdom, and serenity. And yet, loyalty and honor were certainly much respected virtues of English knighthood, which involved a socioeconomic class that spread across national boundaries from Europe to the Saracens in North Africa, who were linked to the Middle East by Islam.

Thomas Malory describes the death of the legendary King Arthur of Camelot in the days when, supposedly, knighthood still existed, before honor and virtue became tarnished by treachery and cities began to hire more ruthless mercenary armies who were loyal only to princes who could afford to pay their price, instead of persuading knights to become followers. The knighthood of Arthur was very likely where Winston learned that the purpose of war is not to play frivolous or inept games with their unintended consequences, but single-mindedly to persist in order to crush the enemy before it is too late. His framework is clearly shown in the legend of the fight for good or evil as portrayed by King Arthur and the treacherous Mordred—his villainous nephew whose name describes the dreaded alternative to victory—murder by means of "A Terrible Death."[4]

"Alas for this fateful day!" exclaimed King Arthur, as both he and Sir Mordred hastily mounted and galloped back to their armies. There followed one of those rare and heartless battles in which both armies fought until they were destroyed. King Arthur, with his customary valor, led squadron after squadron of cavalry into the attack, and Sir Mordred encountered him unflinchingly. As the number of dead and wounded mounted on both sides, the active combatants continued dauntless until nightfall, when four men alone survived. King Arthur wept with dismay to see his beloved followers fallen; then, struggling toward him, unhorsed and badly wounded, he saw Sir Lucas the Butler and his brother, Sir Bedivere.

"Alas!" said the king, "that the day should come when I see all my noble knights destroyed! I would prefer that I myself had fallen. But what has become of the traitor Sir Mordred, whose evil ambition was responsible for this carnage?" Looking about him King Arthur then noticed Sir Modred leaning with his sword on a heap of the dead.

"Sir Lucas, I pray you give me my spear, for I have seen Sir Mordred."

"Sire, I entreat you, remember your vision—how Sir Gawain appeared with a heaven-sent message to dissuade you from fighting Sir Modred. Allow this fateful day to pass; it is ours, for we three hold the field, while the enemy is broken."

"My lords, I care nothing for my life now! And while Sir Mordred is at large I must kill him: there may not be another chance."

"God speed you, then!" said Sir Bedivere.

When Sir Mordred saw King Arthur advance with his spear, he rushed to meet him with drawn sword. Arthur caught Sir Mordred below the shield and drove his spear through his body; Sir Mordred, knowing that the wound was mortal, thrust himself up to the handle of the spear, and then, brandishing his sword in both hands, struck Arthur on the side of the helmet, cutting through it and into the skull beneath; then he crashed to the ground, gruesome and dead.

Like those ancient heroes of mythology, Winston Churchill's compassion for the pain of others would sometimes make itself evident, and he would weep quietly at unexpected times for the frailty of human nature, and attribute it to the martyrdom of man, which is part of the unfortunate human tragedy.

Today, the West has become accustomed to constitutional monarchy with the royals as ordinary working people. But when there was only butchery and bravery, the earliest monarchs were soldiers like Winston, who knew that either you stand up and fight right away, or you perish horribly—and that, once war begins, you must continue to the very end, in order to crush tyranny.

The Martyrdom of Man

Evidently Wynwood Reade's book made another deep impression on the young Winston. Its author described it as a commentary on "Savage Africa"—which he had travelled to and explored in 1862, 1865, and 1868. *The Martyrdom of Man* was published in 1872. Reade had made another voyage to Africa as a *Times* correspondent in the Ashanti War in 1873. Reade began writing the book that Winston read with wonder and interest, intending it to show that the inner regions of the African continent were not cut off from the mainstream of events, as previous historians had declared, but were connected through Islam with the East, and through the Islamic slave trade. He claimed that both elements strongly influenced the moral history of Europe and the political history of the United States. But the explorer and author had been gradually diverted from his intentions by writing a history of the world. That was because he could not write a true history of Africa without describing Egypt and Carthage. From Egypt, he was drawn to Asia and to Greece; and from Carthage he was drawn to Rome.

He found he could not describe Muslim progress in Central Africa without explaining the nature and origin of Islam which, he claimed, cannot be understood without previously studying Christianity and Judaism, on which it is based. And none of them can be understood "without a study of religion among the savages." Although Winston's leanings were towards rationalism and secularism, this book evidently set his mind churning in different directions to numerous subjects which laid the foundation for his interest in the origins and trends of cultures and their histories.

"I sketched the history of the slave-trade," declared Wynwood Reade, "which took me back to the discoveries of the Portuguese, the glories of Venetian commerce, the revival of the arts, the Dark Ages, and the invasion of the Germans. Thus finding that my outline of universal history was almost complete, I determined in the last chapter to give a brief summary of the whole, filling up the parts omitted, and adding to it the materials of another work suggested several years ago by *The Origin of Species.*"

Like that explorer of geography and the mind, Winston would enjoy similar challenges and discover that whenever one door of discovery is opened, it leads to another one. And, in the case of joyful autodidacts like Winston, entering through one of those doors leads to lifelong learning that never ends. He would find as many fantasies and grotesqueries on the way as Alice found in her own odyssey in a Victorian Wonderland, and through the Looking-Glass World that was a metaphor for Victorian England, which was as full of contradictions, ambiguities, and paradoxes as human nature itself.

The Origin of Species

When we consider Winston Churchill's life and times, we tend to forget that they changed in his lifetime from Victorian England to Edwardian England, and then to a post-Edwardian age; so that England and the world made him and remade him several times over. The foundation of his character and attitudes was formed at the peak of the British Empire in Queen Victoria's younger days when her Prince Consort, Albert, still lived. Although most people would scorn imperialism a century later, it came as a means of stability at a time of chaos nearly everywhere else. And just as Imperial Rome was obliged to survive against hardy and ruthless barbarians who continually attempted to plunder and destroy it out of envy for its magnificence, Britain found itself in a similar position when rogues and fanatics, scheming foreign leaders, and zealous religious fundamentalists created rebellions all over the world. When they made mischief in the British Empire, it was often alluded to as "twisting the British lion's tail." Troublemakers simply couldn't resist seeing how far they could go before being stopped. Britain's expedient response was invariably to send a battleship to the trouble spot as a show of strength. It generally worked. But sometimes it required a demonstration of strength by the marines as well.

The *Pax Britannica* kept the world more or less safe, in the same way that the *Pax Romana* had done for the Roman Empire, until the collapse of the two superpowers of that time—Persia and Byzantium—which crumbled from fatigue after fighting each other for almost a century.[5] Then, poor and hungry Arab tribesmen galloped or ran across the deserts for food and plunder, and gradually established the Ottoman Empire under the Turks.

But there was another attribute which the British Empire possessed, beyond the military side of imperialism, or the commercial side of the great trading companies. Peace, tranquility, human rights, and the self-confidence that the Empire instilled also inspired intellectual challenges which initiated scientific discoveries, triggered industrial inventions, and opened up innovations that brought the West into the modern era almost as we recognize it today.

In the meantime, young Winston Churchill benefited from his firsthand experience of the comparative stability of the imperial age, as well as his own personal voyage from boyhood to manhood. He shared in the ways and means by which law and order and peace and economic viability were established and maintained with the imperial tools or weapons of the British Empire; politically, militarily, judicially, and administratively. But that peace of mind and tranquility all but vanished in the Edwardian Era before the outbreak of the First World War.

CHAPTER SIX

THE VICTORIANS

———

DESPITE BEING BORN IN THE STAID Victorian Era, neither the impish image of the young Winston nor the somewhat more dignified one of the older statesman, Mr. Winston Churchill of World War II, appear to root him in Queen Victoria's reign, among the heavily bearded and rather pompous-looking gentlemen of that self-satisfied and complacent imperial age of mutton-chop whiskers. So it is a credit to young Winston that he had already overcome the obstacles of Victorian self-righteousness, with its fixed and narrow mindset and attitudes, by his early twenties. He believed in rational questions and answers and results, instead of traditional or supernatural ones. He was already a modern man who asked blunt questions that were directly to the point, and expected sensible answers instead of vague generalities that missed it.

The male-dominated Victorian society, with its solemn Church rituals, would face its first shock of truth about real life when the eminent naturalist Charles Darwin published his *The Origin of Species* on November 24, 1859. In it he demonstrated that all species of life evolved over time from common animal ancestors.

After his famous and historic voyage on the *Beagle* to acquire botanical specimens of plants, birds, animals, and insects, Darwin retired to his country home in rural Kent for twenty years before daring to reveal to the world what he had discovered. His wife was an ardently regular churchgoer who would be greatly upset at his revelations, and he knew he would be reviled by churchmen and other Christians who believed that everything in the old and new scriptures was entirely true as written, and that the world was only six thousand years old. In short, his theory "opposed sacred scripture and the faith." Its publication drew considerable woolly criticism from the church, despite twenty years of thorough scholarship that demonstrated it was true. It resulted in many rational and intelligent clergymen losing their faith and feeling their lives had been a hollow mockery. Some Victorian novelists depict them wandering aimlessly through their romantic or comic literature, tormented with the knowledge that they were now an obsolete species.

In 1871 Darwin published *The Descent of Man,* which investigated human evolution by natural selection. It demonstrated that instead of a divinely planned world with all life put into place exactly as it is today, and remaining unchanging, in fact all life continually changes according to daily challenges over time and in influential places, in accordance with the powerful predatory characteristics and skills of its enemies—or complacency that allows them to be destroyed by more aggressive species. The certainty of earlier Victorian life was gone by the time that the young Winston grew up.

There can be no doubt that Darwin shaped Winston's worldview about human beings. What young Winston was confronted with was the evolutionary imperative—eat or be eaten. Social Darwinism divided the world into two camps. There was the age-old and primitive worldview that the strong are born to overpower and exploit the weak. And there was the Judeo-Christian attitude represented by the Ten Commandments or the "Golden Rule," which is the compassionate alternative. There was no doubt which side Winston was on. Nor was he merely a passive observer—he was an ardent crusader for what had become his steady beliefs. And he would never falter in those beliefs; they were bigger than anything else in his life.

Naturalist Alfred Russel Wallace also famously discovered the Origin of Species and shared his excitement with the acclaimed Charles Darwin. The incident shocked Darwin, after he had cautiously refrained from publishing his own discoveries for twenty years. It forced him, reluctantly, to reveal his own studies of the flaws in human nature. *The Origin of Species* was published in conjunction with Wallace's findings, and the public was confronted with its wild animal origins for the very first time. The bizarre idea that we are all descended from some hairy wild primate that walked on four legs was ridiculed by their opponents and vigorously lampooned by newspapers and magazines. Nevertheless, it provided psychological explanations by Sigmund Freud for man's irrationality and his other flaws, like continuing to behave like a voracious wild animal that only takes what it wants to eat, rapes randomly, and has no concern for anyone else.

Winston was a teenager when all that occurred, and read Darwin and Freud then and later on, as a matter of normal self-education when he was searching eagerly for the works of modern rational thinkers who would direct him in the course his life would take.

Patriotism

Another great Victorian—not a scientist, but a literary giant whose writing and attitudes would certainly have influenced Winston—was Rudyard Kipling. His unusual gifts and work tend to be neglected today, as a consequence of smear campaigns against the British Empire and Victorian "jingoism." It was a Victorian word that Winston used himself when he went to British India and deplored the snobbery among the imperial officers and civil servants and their frivolous and narrow-minded socialite wives with racist prejudices.

Jingoism is defined as flag-waving or extreme patriotism, and even nationalism of an "us-and-them" type of arrogance. It certainly existed in the British Empire, and post-Edwardian authors criticized it—like E. M. Forster in his famous novel, *A Passage to India,* in 1924.[1] Kipling was certainly a flag-waving patriot. But through his keen and shrewd observation and his ear for sounds, his novel *Kim* brought alive all the colors and clamor and spicy smells of India during the British Raj, with the swirl of colorful saris and the traditional robes worn at the time by Punjabis and Pathans, Sikhs and Kashmiris, Muslims and Hindus.

Despite the modern misconception of Rudyard Kipling's racist views, his 1892 ballad—which depicts the time at which the twenty-year-old Winston became a junior cavalry officer—is a testimony to the courage of a dark-skinned Indian who carried water to the dry-throated and thirsty British and Indian troops fighting on the front lines in the intense Indian heat. The water carrier he immortalized was named Gunga Din.[2] The ballad depicts the adventurous age in the British Raj, when the young Winston grew up and became a hardened soldier under fire. These are things that the young Winston did not write about in Kipling's way because, no doubt, he took them for granted as typical background to his early life.

In a tribute to India and the Indians, as well as the British "Tommies," Kipling's lines, written in the coarse slang and bigoted phrases of Britain's imperial soldiery, describe with crude gallantry something of what the young Winston would have experienced as an officer serving in British India at that time.

You may talk o' gin and beer
When you're quartered safe out 'ere,
An' you're sent to penny-fights an' Aldershot it;
But when it comes to slaughter
You will do your work on water,
An' you'll lick the bloomin' boots of 'im that's got it.
Now in Injia's sunny clime,
Where I used to spend my time
A-servin' of 'Er Majesty the Queen,
Of all them blackfaced crew
The finest man I knew
Was our regimental bhisti, Gunga Din.

He was 'Din! Din! Din!
You limping lump o' brick-dust, Gunga Din!
Hi! Slippery hitherao!
Water, get it!
Panee lao!
You squidgy-nosed old idol, Gunga Din.'

'E would dot an' carry one
Till the longest day was done;
An' 'e didn't seem to know the use o' fear.
If we charged or broke or cut,
You could bet your bloomin' nut,
'E'd be waitin' fifty paces right flank rear.
With 'is mussick* on 'is back,

---

* mussick: a goatskin water bag slung across his back

'E would skip with our attack,
An' watch us till the bugles made 'Retire,'

It was 'Din! Din! Din!'
With the bullets kickin' dust-spots on the green.
When the cartridges ran out,
You could hear the front-files shout,
'Hi! Ammunition-mules an' Gunga Din!'

I sha'n't forgit the night
When I dropped be'ind the fight
With a bullet where my belt-plate should 'a' been.
I was chokin' mad with thirst,
An' the man that spied me first
Was our good old grinnin', gruntin' Gunga Din.
'E lifted up my 'ead,
An' he plugged me where I bled,
An' 'e guv me 'arf-a-pint o' water-green:
It was crawlin' and it stunk,
But of all the drinks I've drunk,
I'm gratefullest to one from Gunga Din.

It was 'Din! Din! Din!'
'Ere's a beggar with a bullet through 'is spleen;
'E's chawin' up the ground,
An' 'e's kickin' all around:
For Gawd's sake git the water, Gunga Din!

'E carried me away
To where a dooli lay,
An' a bullet come an' drilled the beggar clean.
'E put me safe inside,
An' just before 'e died:
'I 'ope you liked your drink,' sez Gunga Din.
Yes, Din! Din! Din!

You Lazarushian-leather Gunga Din!
Though I've belted you and flayed you,
By the living Gawd that made you,
You're a better man than I am, Gunga Din!

Kipling was good at catching the rough, sentimental phrases of the common soldier of the times, despite the buttoned-up mouths of the British officers who were afraid to reveal their emotions except in cool camaraderie. His barroom ballads thrilled Victorians, but it was his novel *Kim* that revealed his deep love of India. This was the real earthy and sweaty, wounded and bleeding life and death of the semi-literate British soldier in the colonial empire that Winston came to know.[3] He loved it because it was real—he abhorred insincerity and pretenses.

Barroom Ballads

When we think of barroom ballads in the Victorian days of Empire, we usually think of Robert Service or Bret Harte and the pioneering days in the Wild West, of lonely cowboys plucking a stringed instrument and singing nostalgically, *"I dream of Jeannie with the light brown hair,"* while recalling a sweetheart they'd brushed with for an instant who would never be forgotten. The pioneering days on the Indian frontier in the British Empire were little different from the Wild West. They drew similar people—soldiers, adventurers, prospectors or explorers, gamblers, thieves, killers, and gentlemen. Isolated in vast and lonely desert plains in the heat, they either drew together for company, or edged away from society if they had something to hide from the old country. Welcoming tearooms and barrooms were some of the first of the dreary little commercial establishments to open, set up by someone with a few greasy banknotes or a little pile of gold-dust.

Brothels came next, as female company trickled cautiously to the frontier from the slums of London, Glasgow, and Dublin, as a result of overcrowding and competition. The trickle turned into a stream as favorable reports crept back to relatives and girlfriends escaping from the new and squalid industrial cities of Sheffield, Manchester, Nottingham, and Birmingham. But it was a brutal all-male society at the beginning, and they had to find ways to entertain themselves.

The harmonica of the lonely cowboy was one way, but not enough to relieve the emptiness and boredom of each and every day that stretched out into an unknown future. Nor was the ukulele. Emboldened by the drink, some sentimental character would inevitably get up in a tavern and bawl out an easy-to-remember song that brought back war and nostalgic memories of home and an imagined sweetheart. People would applaud and urge him on for another chorus. Or someone would explode at an imagined insult when on edge and ready to fight with bare fists. Bare-fisted fighting was a commonplace entertainment that thrilled Victorian senses, like bear-baiting or cockfighting, or watching dogs tear each other to pieces in a pit. It sent the adrenaline surging with primeval memories of the hunt and the chase and the kill. Men fought each other to a standstill, in and out of bars, and down the primitive streets, until they lay bloodied and senseless in the dust. There was often nothing else to do, and it invariably drew an audience of bored men.

Lonely men in bar rooms which became more and more familiar could imagine they were among friends, and perk up at the sound of a rich baritone voice singing *"When Irish eyes are smiling"* from a shadowy corner of a saloon. The singer would be urged on in the dearth of entertainment, since singing reminded audiences of home. Even a false memory was better than the strangeness and loneliness of a new life in a foreign and threatening country, as they'd wonder again and again if they'd done the right thing to come out here to this wilderness with dark-skinned tribesmen who might kill and rob you at any moment. But the fact that you could get up and stand on a chair or a table and bellow your heart out with *"On the Road to Mandalay"* was reassuring, since the laughter and applause came spontaneously. In reality, it was more likely that you'd be beaten over the head and robbed the moment you got outside.

"Gunga Din" would also be sung back home in the old country by Victorian ex-soldiers from the colonies, or older gentlemen with mutton-chop whiskers and fruity voices. It was still an age when you had to think up ways to entertain yourself and each other, since there were few entertainments available except for the music halls. But you could imitate them by dressing up in fancy clothes, or putting on a funny hat and getting up to sing. Alcohol helped. If you wanted to socialize, you had to learn to play a musical instrument or sing a parlor song in front of a crackling coal-fire. Then, with a glass of beer in one hand, it was "Din, Din, Din!/ with the bullets kickin' dust-spots on the green/ When the cartridges ran out/ You could hear the front files shout/ Hi! Ammunition mules an' Gunga Din!"

Life and Death

Gambling with life and death was a continuous challenge in Victorian England and its Empire, when men had no choice but to joke about it, as if it were a game. But it was no joke for women, since childbirth was the most common cause of death. The medical profession had no idea why, although one doctor named Semmelweis thought that bacteria were the cause of it. Ignaz Semmelweis was a Hungarian physician who realized that doctors and surgeons must be carrying germs to their patients on their hands, or from the bloodstains of previous patients on their clothing. But he had no proof to support his claims, which doctors took as an accusation and wouldn't listen to him. He was sure that puerperal fever was contagious, and that deaths could be greatly reduced if doctors and caregivers would only wash their hands. But they shunned the idea that they were deadly carriers, and drove Semmelweis out of town into a lunatic asylum for harming their professional reputations.

Germs had first been seen through a microscope as early as 1675. Semmelweis had his revelation in 1847 in the maternity ward of a hospital in Vienna. But the medical profession still involved butchery, and the general run of doctors didn't understand what he was saying, and didn't take any initiative to investigate his claim. The truth took about 170 years to penetrate scientific minds, when Louis Pasteur came up with his theory of germs in 1872. Even then, the medical profession ridiculed him for another twenty-five years before attempting to do something about it.

Meanwhile, women and men died by the thousands. The average number of children in a family in those days was seven, but they were lucky if two were left alive after stillborn deaths, deaths at birth, and deaths in infancy. Men often remarried several times to maintain a family after their first or second wife died. It was a common sight to hear the hoof-beats of horses on cobblestones, and look out of an upstairs window to see another black hearse drawn by a another gleaming black horse with a black plume waving from between its ears, and a line of mourners in black following on from behind. The profession of undertaker was a busy one, and cemeteries were filled with gravestones standing like a theater audience reminding visitors that their turn was next.

Winston was thirteen before the Pasteur Institute was established, so he would have grown up knowing something about the dangers and treatment of germs. Even so, medicine had not advanced all that much to treat wounds at the battlefront and prevent soldiers from dying from infection. So it was probable that more soldiers were killed at the front line from bacterial infection than from lances, sabers, bullets, or shells. The hardiness and courage of British soldiers in those conditions in Victorian times was extraordinary. But they had no choice— they were caught between the uncertain authority of doctors and surgeons who didn't know what they were doing, and generals who didn't know much more.

It was not only at Omdurman with Winston that British soldiers were game for another charge at the enemy—something similar occurred earlier on, in the blundering Charge of the Light Brigade in 1854. That foolhardy charge in the Crimean War made history out of the stupidity of its commanding officers—particularly the wooden-headed Lord Raglan—and the courage of the British troops. Raglan gave the wrong order and they carried it out without a murmur. The British cavalry famously charged through a valley, straight towards the barrels of the waiting Russian guns, with other cannons lined up and ready, facing them from both sides. Out of the 600 men who made the charge, only 500 came back. And apparently they were game for all the excitement of another charge immediately afterwards.

Was it courage or stupidity on the part of the cavalry? Or did they—like Winston—really enjoy it as a death-defying game? If it was the excitement of adventure that drew them into the army, as it had done with Winston—or glory, which had also contributed to his enlistment in the cavalry—it must have set their adrenaline rushing. They were glorified in Tennyson's popular poem, which describes what is now viewed as the greatest ever military blunder in British history.

The cavalrymen turned the disaster into a legend of bravery which was extolled by the popular English poet, Alfred, Lord Tennyson.

> Flash'd all their sabres bare,
> Flash'd as they turn'd in air,

> Sabring the gunners there,
> Charging an army, while
> All the world wonder'd:
> Plunged in the battery-smoke
> Right thro' the line they broke
> Cossacks and Russian
> Reel'd from the sabre stroke,
> Shattered and sunder'd.
> Then they rode back, but not
> Not the six hundred.

The truth of the catastrophe had been hinted at for years after Raglan died, soon after, of dysentery and depression. Recently, in 2014, letters turned up which were written by some of the men who had charged on their horses with their comrades—some scribbled in pencil and sent home to their families only hours after they left the battlefield. They said they all knew that the order to charge was "perfect madness." One referred to the action more cautiously as "some unfortunate mistake." Some praised the gallantry displayed by the men in the carnage as "a scene . . . unparalleled in history."

Private Thomas Dudley (17th Lancers): "When we received the order, not a man could seem to believe it . . . Oh! If you could have seen the faces of that doomed 600 men at that moment, every man's features fixed, his teeth clenched, and as rigid as death, still it was on—on!" He felt as strong as six men. But he would not attempt to tell what they did to the enemy.

Private Thomas William (11th Hussars): "I could see what would be the result of it, and so could all of us; but of course, as we had got the order, it was our duty to obey. I do not wish to boast too much; but I can safely say that there was not a man in the Light Brigade that day but what did his duty to his Queen and Country."

Captain William Morgan (17th Lancers): "Gallant, brilliant, and useless . . . On we went—astonished but unshaken in nerve—over half a mile of rough ground, losing dozens of men and horses at every stride, to attack horse artillery in our front, supported by three times our number of cavalry, heavy batteries on our right and left flanks, backed by infantry, riflemen &c."

Anonymous Officer (17th Lancers): "We all knew the thing was desperate before we started, and it was even worse than we thought . . . However, there was no hesitation, down our fellows went at a gallop—through a fire in front and on both flanks, which emptied our saddles and knocked over horses by scores. I do not think that one man flinched in the whole Brigade . . . I never saw men behave as well as our men did. As we could not hold our ground, all our dead and badly wounded were left behind, and know not who are dead or are taken prisoner."

Private William Pearson (4th Light Dragoons): "Dear Mother, every time I think of my poor comrades it makes my blood run cold, to think how we had to gallop over the poor wounded fellows lying on the field of battle with anxious looks for assistance—what a sickening scene!" He fell off his horse while charging, as it stumbled when another horse was shot in front of it. Seizing the mount of a dead comrade, he continued to charge.

Private William Henry Pennington (11th Hussars): On his return ride he had to pass Russian cavalry attempting to cut them off. "Of course, with our handful it was life or death; so we rushed at them to break through them . . . I galloped on, parrying with the determination of one who would not lose his life, breaking the lances of the cowards who attacked us in the proportion of three or four to one, occasionally catching one a slap with the sword across his teeth, and giving another the point in his arm or breast."[4]

CHAPTER SEVEN

THE LADY WITH THE LAMP

———

HEROINES OF THE VICTORIAN AGE THAT Winston would have known about were Florence Nightingale and Nurse Edith Cavell. Their lives paralleled each other at some time in Winston's earlier years. Florence Nightingale initiated and influenced the development of modern nursing, which was accelerated during the early years of the First World War. She was employed as a nurse in the Crimea at the time of the historic Charge of the Light Brigade into the trap set by the Russian gunners, with their cannons at the end of a valley and on both sides, which their victims had fallen into. The role of nursing badly injured soldiers, and its education, were first described and defined by her. Before that there was no hope for the badly wounded.

Nor was there even a clean uniform for nurses when she began—not surprising when even established professional medical doctors had no idea of sterilization of infection, or infection control. Most surgeons had not yet reached a stage of wearing clean overalls over their frock-coats, which were often stained with blood and pus from hospital surgery or their patients at home. For some it was even a badge of office. Nor did most wash their hands before or after attending to patients.

With filth and germs infecting battlefield injuries, it was evidently time for more fastidious women to take the lead in implementing cleaner and more sanitary surroundings and hospital clothing, and sterilization from regular, automatic hand-washing. So the training of new nurses was rigorous. It was a new vocation that required floors to be scrubbed regularly with disinfectant to prevent contamination by germs brought in from the street, and microorganisms from infected patients that spread throughout. It had come into use only very recently in 1854.

Nurses complained at the hard work that never stopped from dawn to dusk and made their hands red from the buckets of hot water when they were told to kneel down and use a hard scrubbing brush. Many of the younger nurses had volunteered largely because of the opportunity for socializing with wounded officers and men. Florence Nightingale established high standards for her nurses and managed to achieve a flawless reputation for them, in the face of ribald innuendoes that they were more like prostitutes. She became known as "The Lady with the Lamp" from her regular nightly visits to patients when she would walk the dark corridors holding up her lantern to examine the more seriously wounded patients.

She passed on her experience and knowledge by writing tracts which could easily be read and understood by nurses with limited education. She herself came from a wealthy upper-class English family who lived in Florence before the First World War and then moved to Hampshire and Derbyshire in England.

She was an attractive woman, although sometimes thought to be severe. But after several long-term relationships with men, she decided she was not suited to the constraints of marriage, and preferred to continue her nursing vocation. After visiting Greece and Egypt, she felt "called to God." Her turning point into full-time nursing came after visiting a Lutheran community in Germany which helped the sick and poor. The first book she wrote was about training according to their methods. In 1853 she became superintendent of a similar institute in London. But she became known largely because of her work with the wounded in the Crimean War, when she wrote home about the appalling condition of British troops who had been in battle.

She arrived at the military barracks in Scutari, where she found the medical staff overworked with far too many patients, so that many of the wounded were being overlooked and poorly cared for. There was a shortage of medicines and a spread of infections from which many failed to recover. As a result of official indifference, she wrote to the *Times* with success. It was an influential newspaper, read by government officials. It was said that Miss Nightingale reduced the death rate in her hospital from 42 percent to 2 percent, largely by introducing hand-washing. Queen Victoria awarded her a specially inscribed medal to commemorate her work in the Crimea.

The "lady with the lamp" symbolized the onset of modern science in the nineteenth century. Whereas we tend to believe that change has never moved so fast as today with our new technologies, we forget that the Industrial Revolution in that century involved far greater changes because of the inventions of the telephone, the wireless, the railways, and the internal combustion engine. Although Winston Churchill was rooted in the beginning of the Victorian Era, it was being rapidly transformed into "modern times." Nineteenth-century men and women like him became twentieth-century giants.

The Bourgeoisie

The Victorian Era in England was a morally uplifting and inspiring time in which most people wanted to aspire to something higher than the dull bourgeois style of life that had now been achieved, with its abundance of material possessions. There seemed hardly enough room in the cluttered Victorian home to put anything down or place another picture on the highly-patterned wallpaper. Its overstuffed sofas were protected at the head by antimacassars to prevent men's brilliantine from soiling it. The same thing applied to armrests and unwashed hands. Tabletops were often covered with colorful Turkey rugs that were so cheap you could place them also on the floors of the lavatories. Wax fruit decorations stood in bell-like glass jars to keep the dust off them. Vases as tall as a man often stood in the corners of rooms and on landings, as if Ali Baba and the forty thieves, or an oriental djinn, might jump out of a vase in the shadows at any minute. And there would often be a large Chinese brass gong standing vertically in a prominent position so that everyone could hear it struck for dinner by a butler or parlor maid.

Not an inch of space must be left uncovered in the Victorian home. In less luxurious or tasteful homes for the times, or country cottages, there would be an abundance of curios picked up in oriental bazaars from wherever the Sahib had been sent by his regiment and been under fire at the battlefront. There were ivory carvings and coffee tables with black lacquered bamboo legs surmounted by huge worked brass trays, and folding screens from the Orient. Wherever the Memsahib had travelled with the major or the colonel, she would have brought back silks, shawls, curtains, or floor coverings. Or he would have brought back elephant tusks, or—even more hideous—their feet to use as umbrella stands.

It was unclear when the point would be reached where they had enough possessions on display, since the palaces of the Romanovs, the Hohenzollerns, the Habsburgs, and even Queen Victoria herself were little different in their reach for bourgeois comforts. They only differed in size and magnificence to fill more palatial surroundings. In Germany, it would be big, heavy, and tasteless Biedermeier furniture that symbolized wealth and respectability and filled larger room better than anything else.

For Victorians of the middling sort, we can see the confused and bewildered state they were in by a famous painting that immortalizes the *petit bourgeoisie*. It was considered such an extraordinarily outstanding painting at the time that it was bought for the nation by a trust, since it was considered priceless. The framed oil painting by Walter Richard Sickert now hangs in London's Tate Gallery. It is not so very large—we might call it middling, to match its subjects. He entitled it *Ennui*.

It depicts a middle-aged couple who linger in their claustrophobic sitting room, with averted eyes. Evidently they are tired of being in such close proximity with each other for so long that it seems like an eternity. She gazes unseeingly at a framed painting on the wall above a sideboard, with her back to him and shoulders slumped. He sits at the table with a glass of beer in front of him and a cigarette held in his mouth. We can see he doesn't really want it but doesn't know what else to do but smoke it. There are their possessions around them—not a great deal, but they wouldn't know what to do with anything more, or where to put it. They are listless and don't know what to do next. They aspired to possessions and found themselves still joyless, spiritless, and entirely devoid of inspiration or motivation. It is not long before the First World War. Look—there is the date at the bottom of the painting. It says 1914.

Perhaps the American poet W. H. Auden gazed at it as well as us, and paused to study it thoughtfully for a while before he wrote the following poem years later, to sum up what it meant to him.

Here am I, here are you:
But what does it mean? What are we going to do?
A long time ago I told my mother
I was leaving home to find another:

I never answered her letter
But I never found a better.
Here am I, here are you:
But what does it mean? What are we going to do?[1]

That question was struck the moment that Darwin published his theories of
Evolution and our human origins. We are all on our own, without benefit of
our self-created mythologies and our imaginary gods; so what do our lives mean
and what are we going to do with them?

The Statue of Liberty

Wystan Hugh Auden would write another minimalist poem many years later
in a bar in New York City, where he fled at the outbreak of the Second World
War. It is entitled "September 1, 1939," and begins with him analyzing the
present situation as he attempts to describe the personal and social consequences of a historical event. It was another case of what does it mean and
what are we going to do about it?

I sit in one of the dives
On Fifty-second street
Uncertain and afraid
As the clever hopes expire
Of a low dishonest decade:

But we have jumped time and space to arrive a generation ahead of the story—
although still in Winston Churchill's life span—to demonstrate that there was
and is always a link between the two countries, Britain and the United States
of America. They were both originally Anglo-Saxon nations that then opened
their doors to refugees and immigrants from all over the world, who proceeded
to change the cultures while absorbing the residue of the democratic heritage of
the "Rights of Man" from their new surroundings. It is a similar link as between
Florence Nightingale with her oil lantern held high in the Old World, to find
her way through the corridors of the military hospital, with serious concern for
her patients—and the other lady with her torch held high at the entrance to

New York Harbor. She leads to Ellis Island, where immigrants arrived after the "Spring of Nations" swept across Europe in an upheaval that tore people from their homes in search of liberty. Some only got as far as England, where they were dumped by unscrupulous smugglers after paying for the whole trip to the United States. At the base of the Statue of Liberty are the words of another poet, Emma Lazarus.

> *Give me your tired, your poor,*
> *Your huddled masses yearning to breathe free.*

Great cities like London and New York were filled with those huddled masses. But many older Americans were uneasy with the new ones, with their strangely different ways, although they were invisible to the "quality" for a long time, who passed swiftly by in their horse-drawn carriages— despite the fact that Victorian novelists like Charles Dickens and Elizabeth Gaskell had written about them in England. They were the other half of the "Two Nations." Perhaps it was because novelists are only tellers of fiction, who entertain readers with an idle hour or two to relax in, that the other half of the population were not considered to be real people. Henry Mayhew, on the other hand, knew more about the street people in London than anyone else as a result of his personal studies and interviews, where he made almost endless notes, and even photographed particular ones individually, so that their pictures became converted to line drawings for his books. He wrote so much, so obsessively, that his three volumes are packed with enough small print to put off all but serious students. It was far too much to reach the hands of influential politicians, who are rarely serious book readers. The young Winston Churchill was an exception, because he was imbued with curiosity and motivated by compassion.

It would be only after the turn of the century that Maxim Gorki in Russia wrote *The Lower Depths*.[2] Most people had not yet heard of Dostoyevsky's vagrants and terrorists, "living in a corner" of a room shared with three other families. Dickens was popular reading in Russia because he knew how most people lived, whereas others barely recognized these poor creatures as human beings at all. It is remarkable that Winston Churchill did so, and sympathized with them in their appalling conditions.

The Victorian novelist Charles Dickens was also motivated by curiosity when he took a year off from writing popular novels to visit America, "the land of the free," and see everything he had heard about for himself. The New World was well known as a modern haven for the oppressed of Europe; and it purposefully decided to right the gruesome wrongs of the Old World. Dickens was at the peak of his international fame when he toured the White House and attended sessions of Congress. But his first impressions were marred by his discovery of the American male's passion for what he considered to be two disgusting habits—chewing tobacco and spitting great gobs onto the floor. Dickens wrote:

> Both Houses are handsomely carpeted, but the state to which these carpets are reduced by the universal disregard of the spittoon with which every honorable member is accommodated, and the extraordinary improvements on the pattern which are squirted and dabbled upon it in every direction, do not admit of being described. I will merely observe, that I strongly recommend all strangers not to look at the floor; and if they happen to drop anything, though it be their purse, not to pick it up with an ungloved hand on any account.
>
> It is somewhat remarkable too, at first, to say the least, to see so many honorable members with swelled faces; and it is scarcely less remarkable to discover that this appearance is caused by the quantity of tobacco they contrive to stow within the hollow of the cheek. It is strange enough, too, to see an honorable gentleman leaning back in his tilted chair, with his legs on the desk before him, shaping a convenient "plug" with his penknife, and, when it is quite ready for use, shooting the old one from his mouth as from a pop-gun, and clapping the new one in its place.

Naturally, he planned to see for himself the conditions of slavery in the South—since it had been made illegal in England. He found Charleston too far away in his limited time, and far too hot, and visited Richmond in Virginia instead. He was shocked and revolted at what he encountered of the condition of the slaves and the attitude towards them of their white overseers and owners. When he returned to England, he wrote his *American Notes*, attacking the institution of slavery and repeating accounts from newspapers of runaway slaves who had been disfigured by their cruel and sadistic owners.

Dickens travelled across America by stagecoach and riverboat with his wife Kate and her maid, as well as his secretary, at about the time when Winston Churchill was born into Britain's Victorian world. Dickens found it both enlightening and entertaining. But he was disappointed that it was not the republic of his imagination. He blamed American newspapers for not inform-ing readers what was happening in the outside world. And in the next novel he wrote, he described a fictional young Martin Chuzzlewit's trip to America, to regale English readers with his discontents. Naturally, Americans didn't like being described as primitives.

Discovering that Americans loved celebrity lecture tours, and that he could make a great deal of money by returning on a reading tour, he planned his next trip around 1860, but his plans were interrupted by the American Civil War of 1861. Money lured him back there in 1867, despite his poor health. He was mobbed by an adoring American public on his return. But he suffered throughout the trip and his ill health caused him to limit his read-ing performances to the Atlantic states. Mark Twain was in the audience at Steinway Hall in New York in 1868. And at a dinner in his honor, Dickens remarked on the great changes and improvements that had taken place since his previous visit.

Despite the generational gap that separated Dickens's society from the society that the young Winston was born into, they shared profound simi-larities. Charles Dickens's novels have been described as featuring conflicts between two different types of people—family-oriented groups of congenial societies, and more institutional and obstructing groups of hidebound and corrupt people; phonies, hypocrites, and parasites.[3] Winston's sympathies always lay with the congenial societies. Some critics of Dickens's novels claim that the novelist exaggerated and was overly sentimental, but those similari-ties are evident even in twenty-first century New York City or London, with their conflicts between the top socioeconomic group of one percent and the majority who feel manipulated and devalued, even robbed, by the big estab-lishment institutions.

If Florence Nightingale's lantern symbolizes the new discovery of bacteria, which were invisible unless seen through the lens of a microscope, the Lady with the Lamp held high at the mouth of New York Harbor symbolizes the discovery of a part of humanity which had been virtually invisible to society until they fled from oppression and persecution in the Spring of Nations in Europe. They needed a helping hand. And Winston Churchill was one of the first leaders to recognize it, as a consequence of his personal acquaintance with history, when he rubbed shoulders with the poverty-stricken Boer farmers in South Africa and discovered that almost half of the population in Britain were no better off.

CHAPTER EIGHT

THE FLAWED HUMAN CONDITION

DESPITE THE DANGERS FROM ALMOST EVERY corner of the world during Britain's reign as the only superpower, the status of empire empowered the British people and gave them extraordinary confidence, which stimulated physical and intellectual exploration of unknown parts of the world—huge continents like Africa and India, the American West, and even the icebound parts of the Antarctic and small islands in the South Seas like Tahiti and the Pitcairn Islands. And there was the continued search for the North-West Passage to China. Winston's times on the frontiers of the empire coexisted with the Klondike gold rush of 1896. Diamonds had already been discovered near the Vaal River in South Africa in 1867. They would bring Britain to compete for the rich minerals with the Boers in Natal and the Transvaal.

The ill-fated expedition of Scott to the Antarctic took place not so very long afterwards. Other explorers, like John Hanning Speke, had already discovered Lake Victoria in East Africa and named it after the queen. He died in 1864. American adventurer Henry Morton Stanley became an explorer of Central Africa after finding the "lost" Dr. Livingston on the shores of Lake Tanganyika in 1871. Livingston was a medical missionary who had been scandalized by the Arab slave trade in Africa, which he strongly opposed and sent back reports about to England, until he had disappeared from the sight of civilization.

Richard Burton was an adventurer of another kind—more like Winston Churchill in his fondness for literature and philosophy—a cerebral man, an adventurer of the mind. He was also an Arabist who translated the *Arabian Nights* (or the "Thousand and One Nights") into English. Sir Richard Francis

Burton was an eccentric Englishman of the type who felt more comfortable in the regions he became familiar with during his explorations, and its clothes and food and customs. He was a geographer for the British Army, a writer and soldier who always had something interesting to say and write about. He became a Muslim and a haji while researching the Middle East for the British Government. He also persisted in attempting to find the source of the Nile in North-East Africa with Speke. They famously had a falling out, and Speke made the discovery of the Nile after Burton had, so to speak, turned his back on him after a quarrel.

The restless urge to be constantly on the go and explore the unknown places of the world and the mind was typical of Winston Churchill, too. He was a man of his age and also above it, always changing and becoming a modern man. Whether it was the environment and spirit of empire, or from his own personal instincts, we will never know. But it was in this area of the physical and mental challenges of exploration that Winston showed his Victorian roots.

The Deeper Recesses of the Mind

At much the same time, psychologist Sigmund Freud's father died in 1896, and young Sigmund began to refer to the Oedipus relationship between men and their mothers. He learned of the theme from the famous stage play by Sophocles in which King Oedipus marries his mother unknowingly and provokes the Greek Chorus to condemn him for concealing the truth from the city which is cursed by his incest. The idea simmered for a while in Freud's imaginative mind. Perhaps he'd had similar instincts about his own mother in his youth that he had brushed aside until he saw the tantalizing significance.

It would have been about the same time that Winston served under fire at the front in Malakand. And Winston would, no doubt, have picked up on Freud and Carl Jung's studies of the unconscious mind, psychology and psychoanalysis, and at least some of the major discoveries of Freud, such as his diagnosis of the so-called "Oedipus Complex," in which he claimed that it was commonplace for sons to be in love with their mother and become jealous of, and antagonistic toward, their father, and even wish to kill him. Rebels, Freud would note sometime later, first rebel against their father. And so, it seems, everything came down to sex in the end.[1]

Although the idea was unlikely to have entered Winston's mind as a young man—or he would most probably have been in denial, like most other people—he may have wondered about his own powerful relationship with Jennie later on, as he matured, and as he learned more about the revelations of the Austrian psychoanalysts.

Freud lived at a time when Vienna was still at the center of the Austro-Hungarian Empire. He was in charge of the public Polyclinic in Vienna, where he had ample opportunity to study the workings of the human mind when it malfunctioned—as in the case of the vagrants and agitators whom he, and the brilliant twenty-three-year-old clinical psychologist Wilhelm Reich, diagnosed and attempted to heal. He also had his own private psychiatric practice at home, where his patients were mostly frustrated and neurotic middle-class women.

The Habsburg Emperor Franz Joseph was now an elderly and ailing man. His fragility and his conservatism—he had always tried to hold back time, because he didn't like change—seemed to have affected Vienna's entire population, which appeared to be as sick and inert as he was. Whether or not it was the result of intellectual and artistic stagnation, several symptoms of a particularly Viennese mental illness became manifest. One was the rebellion of artists and writers and composers, who felt compelled to say something about what was happening but became confused and dysfunctional when they tried. Another was the abundance of prostitutes in Vienna at that time.

The significance of the obsession with sex would be seen fifteen or more years later in Germany, which suffered from similar sexual symptoms that seemed to presage another war. Instead of an abundance of psychiatrists, as in Vienna, six hundred nightclubs in Berlin alone provided sexual services of every description as an outlet. As the poet Auden exclaimed after his own visit, "Berlin is a bugger's daydream. There are 170 male brothels under police control."[2] Those in the Tor district offered boys in lederhosen. "Berlin boasted an erotic demimonde consisting of an estimated one hundred thousand women and thirty-five thousand men who regularly prostituted themselves . . . It also became the world's premier tourist destination for sexual predilections of all kinds."[3] Such mass production lines for fornication almost suggests that nature was desperate to produce huge amounts of sperm before another world war could kill off millions of young and adventurous men. Was the abundance of testosterone a sign that those fit and restless young men were ready to volunteer to throw away their lives on the battlefields once again?

A third symptom in Austria was a revolutionary air of thought which pervaded the numerous cafés in Vienna, where psychiatrists like Alfred Adler would sit at their own familiar tables with their colleagues; only rarely with the more solitary Sigmund Freud, who preferred to think alone. Freud found Vienna to be an unhappy city. It was narrowly provincial and bigoted. But he shrugged it off, with its anti-Semitism, because of his low expectations of human nature. He chose to live within his own intellect and imagination, scorning the fashionable cafés off the *Ringstrasse*, more intent on solving the problems of society and writing about the flawed human condition.

Munich had more character, intellect, and sophistication than the city of Vienna, which seemed isolated from reality. Vienna's provincial insularity and its state of paralysis was illustrated by two jokes that floated around the tables of intellectual cafés. A popular one-liner that provided an inkling to its dark social undercurrent was: *"Suicide is a way of life in Vienna."* Another was: *"Vienna is like being in an isolation cell—you can scream all you like but nobody hears."*[4]

The fourth symptom was one that tended toward a political revolution, which was forming even before the First World War, also in intellectual cafés in Munich's Schwabing District in Germany, which was full of restless young male students. For example, the "Cosmic Circle" (*die Kosmische Runde)* met in popular local cafés in that famous (and sometimes infamous) district from 1897 to 1908, to discuss a proposed social revolution. It was not to be a violent insurrection but a revolution in ideas aimed at overthrowing the values of the older patriarchal and authoritarian institutions, like the Junkers and their Teutonic death-wish military culture.

Most of its founding members have long since been forgotten. But those whom they influenced, like D. H. Lawrence, Frieda von Richthofen, and Otto Gross—and those who influenced them, like Max Weber—are still remembered. They discussed world-changing forces like anthropology, cultural history, and mythology, out of which they developed a startlingly original worldview, quite different from that of the long-established patriarchal society that crushed young men and women, and against which they angrily rebelled. Their informal meetings were taking place while young Winston Churchill was still fighting as a soldier for the British Empire.

Freud's Wednesday Group met regularly in Freud's apartment and would become and was the nucleus of the Vienna Psychoanalytical Society, with members or guests like Adler, Stekel, Jung, Ferenczi, Karl Abraham, Hanns Sachs, Otto Gross, Wilhelm Reich, and Otto Rank—all of them unique and original thinkers, looking for ways to understand the German-speaking nightmare that Reich would call an "emotional plague," and heal the dysfunctional Viennese.

The Viennese seemed to be unable to communicate their feelings or thoughts—either to receive information from the fast-changing outside world, or to impart information about the strange things that were going on in Vienna, although they tried. Their mental condition was exemplified by the artist Egon Schiele's famous painting of a naked man—himself—with all his limbs chopped off. It was one of the intimations that something awful was about to happen there, and in Germany.

Moral Indignation

Victorian England, on the other hand, is frequently depicted as a straitlaced and sexually repressed society, even suggesting that sex crimes would increase as a consequence of repressing natural sexual desires. But in reality, Victorians appear to have been as passionate and sexually active, beneath their staid exteriors and women's voluminous crinolines, as today. And the rate of violent sex crimes did not appear to have increased. What did happen at this time in England was the discovery of a brutal murder of a prostitute in the East End of London in 1888. It was the first of Jack the Ripper's crimes of unusual mutilations. And, perhaps as a consequence of Freud's Viennese psychiatry, the previously unimaginative British police began to consider what they called "motiveless murders," as opposed to traditional ones of theft, jealousy, rape, or fraud.

Churchill couldn't have avoided hearing about it when he was fourteen. But it was only one set of crimes, and most probably committed by an American from New York State.[5]

A serious sense of respect for the bereaved queen was right and proper too, since she was the imperial role model of prim and proper family values, and even women's fashions. And she was now wearing a black hooped skirt. But sex was a powerful motive from which huge families were bred, and thousands of unwanted children roamed the streets and filled orphanages in Victorian England.

It seems that women were better at controlling their desires in those days, by sublimating them in harmless dreams of romance. It was the male of the species who was the predator. Freud's previous colleague, Dr. Josef Breuer, may have been the first psychologist to recognize men's diffidence at having their sexual performance disclosed or their sexual peccadilloes laughed at. Fortunately for the English, even mentioning sex was taboo. So that, when Dr. Breuer cautioned Freud to desist from discussing sex openly, it was not that he himself was a prude, but he knew the defensive posture of denial that his patients adopted to conceal their own sexual desires or practices. Breuer chided his young colleague for talking too much about sex because of people's moral indignation.

Daydreams and Fantasies

Back in the 1860s when London had become a modern metropolis and the cultural center of the world, it provided a mass market for all sorts of merchandise. Among them were indecent books and images. "Young working-class men were believed to be particularly vulnerable to the appeal of penny fiction and the crude performances played out in cheap theaters throughout the metropolis. However, of all classes, it was women who were seen to be particularly susceptible to the appeals of the *visual* image . . . women easily entered a state of heightened daydream and fantasy, which utterly compromised the codes of respectable behavior advocated for women on the streets of the city."[6]

If some women were shocked by their own prurient thoughts, Victorian men were not. Many kept a secret collection of erotic literature and took laudanum—a narcotic concoction of alcohol and opium, which was supposed to bring on thoughts of erotic love—perhaps aided by Aubrey Beardsley's naughty erotic illustrations, with their mocking suggestion that a little flagellation of women's bare bottoms might help to stimulate both sexes. Sadism by caning boys' naked posteriors at boarding school was extraordinarily popular, and persisted in the education of privileged British schoolboys right up until this time, and even beyond it.

As Freud knew very well from spontaneous confessions of his women patients, propriety was made manifest in order to conceal the sexual reality beneath a woman's skirts. The respectable public face of society and law and order depended on not being reminded of passions seething beneath the skin, or on the flimsy faithfulness of wives, or the fragile virginity of daughters. But sex was the source of the evolutionary process. And many of Freud's patients who concealed their thoughts in public obsessed about it in private. It may have been this duality that caused Freud to come up with his theory of the conscious and the unconscious mind. And it would be a natural step for the pioneer in psychoanalysis to believe that sexual anxiety was the cause of all kinds of problems, described first as hysteria, and then as neuroses. But was he just talking about Viennese society, where he diagnosed his patients, or could his theories be applied to other cultures, like Victorian England, which appeared to be so cool and calm and orderly on the surface?

But those adjectives were more suitable for the smaller number of aristocrats and landed gentry who kept to themselves in their country mansions, where they were isolated from reality by squadrons of male and female domestic servants. Those servants too were comfortably separated from their own families and the rest of Britain's population by the good fortune of their privileged employment, compared with the lesser fortunes of either the average rural population or those who sought other means of survival in the burgeoning industrial cities, like Birmingham and Manchester, Bradford and Sheffield, where many boys and girls still went barefoot like peasants, and it was a great advance when young women employed in the mills graduated to wearing wooden clogs on their feet.

Although we tend to think of Churchill in a different time and a different category, he lived in close proximity to the same grim and grisly period as Charles Dickens wrote about in his novels. And equally compassionate Victorian novelists, like Elizabeth Gaskell, wrote about workers in the cotton mills in the Industrial Revolution. George Eliot wrote about the cottage industry of weaving at home. Winston Churchill's lifetime encompassed that great age of novel-writing which has never been bettered. George Eliot's *Middlemarch* has recently been described as the greatest novel in the English language.[7] The people who live in the pages of their novels were the masses; what another Victorian writer, Bulwer-Lytton, called "the great unwashed." And Conan Doyle, the popular creator of Sherlock Holmes, referred to the mass of stray boys and girls who swarmed in London's streets as his "Street Arabs."

Elizabeth Gaskell's *Mary Barton* and *North and South* provide far more typical descriptions of how most of Britain's industrial population lived than any of Churchill's books. And yet, ironically, he would find himself organizing factories to supply munitions to the armed forces in the First World War.

Joseph Conrad described the lives of those who made their living in merchant ships that traded in far-flung places which we will never see again with the same eyes. Robert Louis Stevenson gives us some idea of bandits and piracy in those days, who have long since become even more violent as terrorists. Thomas Hardy's stories still lingered longingly on village life and the sweet innocence of teenage girls obliged to seek work in domestic service among the landed gentry when their own homes and villages could not support them. Arnold Bennet wrote of a similar life for women in the Potteries. And H. Rider Haggard gave us a more adventurous idea of the imagined continent of Africa than Conrad's gruesome *Heart of Darkness,* with its manacles, chains, and mutilated black slaves desperately trying to escape from captivity by white mine-owners. Seldom, if ever, do we associate the life and times of Winston Churchill with any of that. Yet all of it was going on at the same time as when he was a young officer in the army and a young member of Parliament just beginning to read about poverty in his own country, and of how the other half of the population lived.

It was some time later, when he became Home Secretary, that Winston encountered armed and desperate anarchists living in the East End of London. And other refugees from some of the more oppressive police states of Europe, like Poland and Russia, lived in the same metropolis as he did. Count Peter Kropotkin arrived in Britain in 1876, after escaping from the hospital of Russia's most infamous prison. Like Voltaire and other free-thinkers, he settled in London because it was an intellectual hub for refugees, anarchists and revolutionaries, and counter-revolutionaries.

Although young Winston was fortunate to live much of his life in the sheltered societies of the army, the job of war correspondent, and the vocation of a member of Parliament, those worlds were relatively small in comparison with the grittier and more hectic lives of, for example, the chimney sweep and his black-faced young assistants, the sewer-hunter or cleaner, or the rat-catcher who inhabited the sewers of London for much of his life. Those were the anonymous inhabitants of the capital city. So were the street crossing sweepers—generally

Irish immigrants—who cleared the horse dung from the busier London roads. One of them was the old man with reddish hair from County Cork, who had been in England for only two and a half years. Henry Mayhew immortalized him and them, even pictorializing some from photographs he took, in his *London Labour and the London Poor.* He included, for example, the one-legged crossing sweeper at Chancery Lane, who paid one and nine pence a week for his lodgings, and lived on crusts of sandwiches and the remains of cheese scrounged from a local public house on the corner of the street, since he had no money left for food.

Those are only a few of the thousands of street people who barely managed to survive the times. Many of them didn't. And since none of them had the vote, and few were able-bodied enough to serve in the armed forces, they were of little interest to politicians or recruiting sergeants. And "the Quality," who lived in so-called "Quality Streets," would not even have noticed that they existed.

Even though the notoriously violent criminal nicknamed by newspapers as "Jack the Ripper" appeared in the East End of London in Winston's time, we are unlikely to find any mention of him in any reports about Churchill, who was only fourteen then. And yet, the murderer was part of the social changes taking place in Victorian England that would influence the thinking of the growing boy. Police were confounded when they discovered torn body parts of several prostitutes scattered around their rooms and in the cobbled alleyways outside. His apparently motiveless murders caused police to puzzle why some people committed violent murders repeatedly and what motivated their violence. It was partly about an awareness of irrational behavior, and partly about the possible motives for it. When a surgeon examined the ripped-open corpses, he found that at least one of the women's uteruses had been stolen. Those thefts turned out to be the clue to the murderer's mental condition. One of the possible causes attributed to such murders was the greater density of populations living far too closely with each other in a great metropolis like London or Paris. They were all signs of the times that the young Winston grew up in.

The murderer's grisly and incomprehensible acts took place during the very earliest experiments with gas lighting in London's more sinister streets, when lamp-posts or iron brackets on brick walls were positioned so far apart from each other that dense pools of darkness remained in between them. Even the illuminated sections of the street were barely visible during the infamous London fogs that gathered in the cold, damp weather, from the chimneys of coal fires in the grates of thousands of homes. If you stretched out your arm in front of you, it was often impossible to see your fingertips through the fog—which was why it was known as a "pea-souper."

Jennie and Winston Churchill would have experienced those changes in urban density and the transformation from romantic Victorian gaslight to the stark reality of post-Edwardian electric lighting and all its other features. Meanwhile, the new technology of the outdoor gas lamps brought pedestrians out into the street when they would otherwise have remained at home at night. Now some people loitered in the narrow cobblestone alleyways that were shrouded in darkness at night—except when moving closer to the gas lamps. And there was the poisonous yellow fog which cast sinister shadows on the walls of the buildings. Horse-drawn hansom cabs and carriages seemed menacing and dangerous as they noisily clip-clopped or raced their way through the London streets with the clatter of wheels on cobblestones.

Victorian police constables, who were few and unsophisticated, were also ill-prepared and unaccustomed to prevent the more morbid and violent types of crimes. Their normal affairs were drunkenness and petty thievery or burglary, and arguments between spouses that led to someone being roughed up. Crimes like theft, and violence arising out of jealousy or revenge, were commonplace and understandable. But these new crimes were beyond belief and—as far as the Metropolitan Police were concerned—entirely without motives.

CHAPTER NINE

WINSTON UNDER FIRE

———

WINSTON'S FINANCES BEGAN TO IMPROVE WHEN the *Morning Post* paid him for his letters from the Sudan and he benefited from serialization rights of his novel. On the other hand, he'd had to reject two offers from newspapers asking to report from two different war fronts on their behalf. But it was a good sign of his popularity as a military and political journalist. Having his name in the eyes of the public spread rumors that he was about to enter politics, and many people said he'd be sure to do well, since he had his father's ability. But now he had to return to his regiment in India.

Before leaving, he socialized with a young woman whom he'd met before, but he was not a regular socializer, except among politicians with whom he felt the air was buzzing with opportunities. Nor was he a womanizer. He was a cerebral man and too full of ambition for frivolity. Although he didn't imagine he'd be like Jennie, keeping one man after another on tenterhooks for her favors, nor could he imagine being tied to one woman for life.

He left for India soon after he turned twenty-four, having now decided he'd retire from the army in a matter of months and enter a life of politics. He debated with Jennie from Bangalore on where he would stand for election. Whether he was musing on his own future or simply trying out a few new lines for his novel, he described the Mahdi, who was an orphan, and wrote in his letter to her; *solitary trees grow strong, and a boy deprived of his father's care often develops a vigor of thought which may restore in later years the heavier loss of earlier ones.*

It was unusual for mother and son to exchange intellectual ideas, particularly as they related to psychology. There was something almost Freudian in his relationship with his mother, who appears to be more like his lady friend. Their relationship has been described as infatuation. But infatuations are generally considered to be short-lived, whereas their relationship lasted a lifetime. They adored each other. And he wished to share every thought with her and whatever he wrote. He never stopped writing to her, wherever he happened to be. They were mutual admirers.

Freud was bound to be another influence in understanding the motives and quirks of people he would have to get along with, influence their thinking, and sometimes even manipulate them. Like him, the young Freud was a modern man, an iconoclast who broke traditional customs and attitudes, particularly where open discussion about sex was concerned. Freud was not a typical Victorian. He was a neurologist studying the nervous system of lobsters in order to understand how human beings worked. His old colleague, Dr. Breuer, had tried to hush him up whenever he talked about sex, because he said people were touchy and would be offended. But Freud realized that sexual instincts were fundamental to life and could not be ignored, since there'd be no life without them. Winston was not a typical Victorian either; he possessed the facility of absorbing what was useful to his career and rejecting anything that was surplus to it.

Winston left India for London towards the end of March, deciding he could earn more as a writer, whereas being an officer in the army cost him money in keeping up appearances. He thought of adapting his book into a history of the war in the Sudan and, on the way back home, spoke with Lord Cromer in Cairo. Cromer directed him on the major events leading up to the loss of the Sudan and the heroic death of General Gordon, who was beginning to be viewed as a martyr to savagery. Cromer introduced him to the Khedive of Egypt, and the two young men behaved together like a couple of schoolboys at Harrow.

He was in London when a by-election was called in Oldham, and he delivered his election speech as a Tory Democrat, as his father had been. He promised to legislate on behalf of the aged poor as generously as possible. He opposed Home Rule in Ireland because he knew it would end in violent conflicts. He was opposed to compulsory restrictions on alcohol but supported voluntary temperance. And he followed Prime Minister Lord Salisbury in maintaining superiority of naval power, as well as protecting imperial frontiers from mischief-making and violent aggression.

He was received with enthusiasm by the constituents, but felt that public opinion was against the Conservatives, and so they would be unlikely to be *his* constituents. He spoke eight times a day as the election built up to its finale. The Conservatives were defeated, as he'd expected. Nevertheless, Salisbury was encouraging about his performance, and the experience earned him his spurs.

The question of what to do now filled his mind. He need not have worried; there was always a war somewhere in the Empire that required reporting on or leadership. To a politician who asked him to speak in Birmingham, he wrote of possible war in the Transvaal in November, where he planned to go as a special correspondent.

Ever since the Jameson Raid, the wary relationship between Britain and the Boer Republics was discussed keenly across the world, with all its misunderstandings. The dispute was also vigilantly watched and debated by the opposition party in Parliament, where there was division between those who felt that war would be necessary and those who attempted to prevent it.

Authorities in the Transvaal had been heavily rearming for three years, while the well-armed police kept watch on the Outlanders, and German engineers busily built a fortress to dominate the city of Johannesburg. Supplies of ammunition arrived from Germany and Holland to arm the Transvaal, the Orange Free State, and the Cape Dutch. Consequently, the British Government increased its Natal and Cape garrisons.

When an ultimatum came from Pretoria on October 8 for the withdrawal of British forces from the frontiers of the Boer Republics, it gave Britain only three days to complete its withdrawal. The issue had finally come to a head. And the Boers took the initiative by advancing their forces towards the Cape and Natal.

The British General Sir Redvers Buller had been named Commander-in-Chief of the Army Corps, and had orders to proceed to Table Bay in the Cape. "Buller," the British Colonial Secretary Chamberlain said to Winston, "may be too late . . . Mafeking may be besieged."

According to Churchill in later life, the British War Office was underfunded and isolated from reality. Nevertheless, their intelligence report was sent to General Buller, who replied that he "knew everything about South Africa."[1]

"Never, never, never believe any war will be smooth and easy," Churchill wrote in later life, "or that anyone who embarks on the strange voyage can measure the tides and hurricanes he will encounter." Once the signal for war is given, the Statesman becomes the slave of unforeseeable and uncontrollable events. "Antiquated War Offices, weak, incompetent or arrogant Commanders, untrustworthy allies, hostile neutrals, malignant Fortune, ugly surprises, awful miscalculations . . ." All play their role as soon as war is declared. He cautioned readers to bear in mind that however sure we are that we can easily win, there would be no war if the enemy did not think the same thing of his own chances.

Buller was an interesting choice of Commander and a fairly typical British officer. According to Churchill, he looked stolid, said little, and whatever he did say was incomprehensible. Since he couldn't explain things, he didn't attempt to. He grunted or nodded instead, or shook his head. He had displayed bravery and skill in his youth and filled sedentary administrative positions in Whitehall ever since. With his name known to the public, they had confidence in him.

"My confidence in the British soldier is only equalled by my confidence in Sir Redvers Buller," said Prime Minister Lord Salisbury on November 9, 1899.

Churchill explained the phenomenon like this: "He plodded on from blunder to blunder and from one disaster to another without losing either the regard of his country or the trust of his troops . . ."

Winston Churchill duly received a request from the *Daily Mail* to leave for South Africa as their war correspondent. Not content with one fee, he also offered his services to the *Morning Post* to travel from east to west and sell them another series of articles.

Chamberlain gave Winston an introduction to the British High Commissioner in Cape Town, Sir Alfred Milner, who was thought highly of by some, but as a bit of a manipulator by others. Milner was intriguing in South Africa to prevent the two Boer Republics—the Orange Free State and the Transvaal—from remaining independent of the Crown. As negotiations continued with President Kruger, war with the Boers seemed inevitable. Winston decided to take a cine-camera and film the war, but was outdone by an American film company with professional equipment. Feeling it would be advantageous to have officer status before the war started, he decided to apply to a British Yeomanry Regiment. Then he recalled a friend of his father who was Adjutant of the 9th Yeomanry Brigade in South Africa.

He hurriedly bought a new compass and had his telescope and field glasses repaired. Then he took a train to Southampton and sailed to Cape Town with his father's former manservant, as the war was about to begin.

South Africa

Immediately on arrival, Sir Alfred Milner told him the Boers had mobilized a far greater number of men than he had expected, and the town of Ladysmith was now threatened. Winston and a fellow reporter learned next day that 1,200 British soldiers had already surrendered. This was not a popular war with the British public, who sympathized with the poor Afrikaans-speaking farmers who were fighting for independence from the British Empire. They were descended from Dutch colonists who had fled from the Netherlands because of religious persecution. Most were Huguenots who also came from France and Germany during Catholic persecution. And here they followed the Dutch Reform Church. They had since become hardy pioneers who knew the habits of all the animal life in Southern Africa, as hunters, which meant they were fine sharp-shooters or snipers who knew how to make every bullet count. They also knew how to appear as if from nowhere, and strike. Then they'd wheel in an instant and ride their small ponies swiftly away, to disappear into the bushes or vanish into the open landscape.

Naturally enough, they resented the British "rednecks" who wanted to take their land away from them, with all the possible wealth from the diamond and gold mines, which was really all the political clash was about. Without minerals the territory was uninteresting to the British, but the mines now made it valuable. And the richest places to find them were at Kimberley in Bloemfontein in the Free State, and on the Reef of the Transvaal.

Their train brought them to East London, and they hurried to Durban on a small coastal vessel, with the intention of reaching Ladysmith by rail. On arrival in Durban at midnight, Winston found his close friend, Barnes, on a hospital ship bound for home after being shot in battle, and learned that Ladysmith was now isolated. General Buller had been sent from England under orders to relieve Ladysmith, but was unlikely to arrive for at least three days.

And there were no certainties in war. It would take Buller's army several more days while waiting for his stores to arrive for transportation to the battlefront.

They left for Pietermaritzburg, the provincial capital in the heartland of rural Natal. But they found the line went no further north. Winston hired a special train. When they reached Colenso on the other side of the Tugela River, the Boer Army was spread across the track to prevent further access north.

Cornered by a heavy enemy gun they couldn't argue with, they joined the battalions of British troops. This was hilly inland country, not far from mountains. They found a good cook and some good wine, pitched their tent at Estcourt railway yard, and entertained friends. Winston thought the British military in South Africa had underestimated the situation, and he was critical of the authorities and the British fighting men who had surrendered.

They took a Colenso train as soon as they could, and followed an officer to the trenches on the edge of town, which were now deserted. The Boers had vanished. It was something they were adept at from their experience as hunters of shrewd wild animals. They had extraordinary patience to wait until exactly the right time to strike. They had no respect for the formal ways with which British troops were ordered into line and regimented so that they were sitting targets for Boer sharpshooters.

Winston and Atkinson—the other journalist—rode with the British troops close to Colenso, then mounted a steep hill that gave them a view of the Tugela River. They were suddenly surrounded by armed British horsemen, but they had no difficulty in convincing them they were not the enemy. They learned that Ladysmith was blocked with the British cavalry inside. They discussed their best move and agreed to withdraw if General Joubert of the Boers decided to advance on the town. Winston was sure it would be unnecessary. Their armored train left Estcourt early in the morning with them and a hundred and fifty men on board, heading for Colenso. When the train arrived at Chieveley they heard that the Boers had stayed there overnight.

A messenger now warned them that some fifty Boers had been spotted by the railway. Then they rounded a hill that overlooked the railroad and were fired on by artillery which struck one of their trucks. The engine driver put on full steam to run at top speed down the line, intending to bypass the ambush. But a heavy stone deliberately placed on the line derailed a breakdown truck and two armored trucks in front. Winston ran out of the stationary train to organize men to dislodge the truck straddling the line.

A British naval gun opened fire, but was struck by a shell and ceased. The British gun crew opened fire from the protection of one of the armored trucks, and killed two Boers. Rifle fire and a Maxim-gun were aimed at them, with the pounding of artillery shells. It continued for an hour. Four British soldiers were killed and thirty wounded.

Winston sauntered around the train to study the situation and see what he could do about it, as cool as ever under fire—he simply ignored it. Then he helped the engine driver carry twenty wounded men and place them in the tender. They picked up more men as they managed to drive the engine very slowly in the direction of Frere.

The British commander attempted to get his men to a farmhouse nearby and fought the Boers from cover. But two British soldiers by the train held up white handkerchiefs for a ceasefire and surrendered. The commander had no alternative but to join them. Their hearts weren't in it. But Winston was still walking along the line, and ran into two Boers who raised their rifles. He turned swiftly and ran back to the engine along the track, with bullets cracking behind him, missing him by inches. He headed for an embankment to find shelter, but found no cover, so he kept running. Nothing struck him. He clambered up a bank and crawled on hands and knees beneath a fence at the summit. He found a small hollow there and took cover in it.

Sitting down, panting, and looking round him, he found himself about two hundred yards from a river where there was cover. He was about to leap up and make a dash for it, when a Boer horseman galloped straight at him, then reined in his pony and shouted. Winston realized he'd left his pistol behind on the train as the Boer raised his rifle and sighted it to aim at him. Winston instantly raised both hands, and was taken prisoner by the Boers.

CHAPTER TEN

A PRISONER OF WAR

WINSTON'S INITIATIVES AT THE DERAILMENT OF the train and his imprisonment by the Boers captured the newspaper headlines, since the British public was keenly interested in what was happening in South Africa, without clearly understanding the motives of either side. His manservant, Walden, went to Pietermaritzburg to take care of Winston's kit, and wrote to inform Jennie that her son was unlikely to have been wounded. He added that all the officers he spoke to believed that Winston and the engine driver would be awarded with a medal for their bravery.

Winston would write later on to a newspaper that he'd had to be patient while the Boers treated their prisoners like cattle when they rounded them up and marched them across the countryside for two days. After showing his press credentials, he was locked up in the ticket office of a tiny rural railway station at a *dorp* named Modderspruit, from where a train eventually took them to Pretoria. There they were escorted to a State school in the center of the capital city, which had been requisitioned for prisoners of war. As a result of the press publicity, General Joubert treated Winston's account that he was an unarmed newspaper correspondent with skepticism, and instructed that he must be kept under lock and key for the rest of the war because of the damage he could do.

Winston wrote directly to the Boer Secretary for War while he spent weeks in prison, to deny that he had taken any part in the military action. But a Boer officer who had been there said he'd led volunteers when the British officers were in a state of confusion. He also wrote to Jennie. He spent his twenty-fifth birthday writing letters in prison. One was to the Prince of Wales, in which he informed him that prisoners were now members of the Transvaal State Library, so he was improving his education. He also wrote to an American friend as a result of borrowing library books, that he had been studying financial combines in the United States and their enormous power horrified him—the merchant princes of the empire were one thing, but this form of capitalism, with its trusts, monopolies, and cartels was overstepping the boundaries of power. He shared his thoughts that there would be a great war in the next century for the existence of the individual in the face of the conglomerates.

He felt somewhat depressed because it was his birthday and he was trapped behind lock and key while affairs continued without him in the outside world. And time suddenly seemed to be running short. His father had died nearly five years previously and he had developed a fear of dying young, possibly through a hereditary condition suffered by Lord Randolph. He wrote again, more anxiously, to Souza, the Secretary for War, insisting that he had done no more in the train derailment than the driver and the railway staff had done, and they had been released while he was still locked up.

After receiving no reply to his letters he decided to escape. He asked Aylmer Haldane, who was a prisoner with him—since he had been in charge of the train—and Sergeant-Major Brockie if they would join him. Although the Sergeant came from Johannesburg, he spoke Afrikaans. They would simply climb over a wall near the latrine which they used every day, and drop into the garden of a private house. Then they would head out of Pretoria and travel only at night, with the intention of walking three hundred miles northeast to Mozambique, which was a Portuguese colony across the border.

His plan became more urgent as news seeped in of several British military defeats, and Winston became excited at the prospect of being free of the POW camp. But Haldane urged patience—it was better to choose the right moment to escape than rush it. Winston was so tensed up at the idea of his plan that he could no longer concentrate on reading while the three waited for the best opportunity. He played chess but was easily beaten. He watched anxiously as it grew dark at close to seven in the evening. As soon as it was dark enough, Haldane and he went to the latrine. The sergeant-major followed. But they found the Boer sentries standing and watching them instead of patrolling the grounds. They waited nervously for two hours before deciding it wasn't the right time to attempt an escape.

More news arrived from the front on December 12. It was rumored that the British forces had been beaten again by the Boers. Winston remarked that he'd thought he had a chance to drop over the wall into the garden the other night, but the risk had been too great that the others might have been stopped by a guard afterwards, and he would have found himself isolated and alone on the far side of the wall. But he was determined to leave that night, and his anxious pacing conveyed his intention to the other prisoners. Then he decided to write another letter to Souza, to explain the reason for his escape.

He and Aylmer Haldane took another stroll to the latrine that night before moonrise. But when they reached it they could not be sure their timing was right, and hesitated. Instead, they returned to the verandah for Brockie, who told them they were too scared to make the attempt. They told him to go and see for himself. Brockie did so but didn't return. So Winston followed him anxiously, after asking Haldane to wait a few minutes before following suit. He found Brockie coming out of the latrine, but they couldn't talk in view of the sentries. Winston went into the latrine to consider his options and decided on immediate action. While the sentry turned away to light his pipe, Winston jumped up to a ledge of the wall and dropped over it.

Then he crouched down and waited for the others. Nothing happened for half an hour, and he grew anxious as he watched the owner of the house come out into the garden several times while Winston concealed himself in the shadow of the wall. When all was quiet, he managed to communicate to a prisoner on the other side to give Haldane and Brockie a message in the dining room. A quarter of an hour passed before Haldane and Brockie came out to the latrine and Haldane attempted to climb the wall. But he was barely half way over when a sentry spotted him and levelled his rifle, then ordered him back inside. Winston continue to wait restlessly on his own. He had relied on Brockie being able to talk to the locals in their own language when they crossed the Transvaal. Finally, Haldane tapped on the wall to tell him that the sentry was too alert for him to make any attempt.[2] Winston was now on his own.

He digested the change of plan and decided to carry on, although it was far too dangerous to tramp on foot without any knowledge of Afrikaans. He would have to dart out and reach the railway as quickly as possible, then head for the seaport at Lourenço Marques. He walked out of the garden and past another guard, straight into the middle of the road. He was fortunate to be wearing an ordinary civilian suit. He had no difficulty reaching the railway, and carefully chose a place a couple of hundred yards from the station, to hop on to a train at a steep gradient before it speeded up. He reached for the coupling between two wagons and climbed in one of them. There were only empty coal sacks for company.

Escape to Danger

The goods train rattled its way slowly towards Moçambique in the night. Just before dawn, he decided it might be wise to leave the train in case he was discovered. He was near Witbank, east of Pretoria, when daylight came, and he jumped off. Then he waited cautiously by the track, intending to hop on to another train the next night, and carry on to the Portuguese port.

Meanwhile, in the prisoner-of-war camp, the guards began searching for him. In view of what they felt was an emergency, and in the hope of a quick capture, they distributed leaflets with a picture of him across the Transvaal. His description read: "Englishman 25 years old, about 5 ft 8 inches tall, average build, walks with a slight stoop, pale appearance, red brown hair, almost invisible small moustache, speaks through the nose, cannot pronounce the letter 's,' cannot speak Dutch, has last been seen in a brown suit of clothes."

Having not eaten or found anything to drink, Winston headed for some lights, which he believed emerged from an African kraal. Moving closer, he found it was a coalmine with a private house near the entrance. He hesitated, not knowing if the occupant might be English or a Boer enemy. The man who cautiously opened the door in the night held a gun pointed directly at him. Winston introduced himself as Dr. Bentinck and claimed he'd lost his way after falling off a train. How else could he explain arriving alone in such a desolate place on the Highveld?

But evidently it didn't sound right to the stranger, who told him to go inside the dining room, while he kept his pistol aimed at Winston. Gradually, the man pressed him to say who he really was and what he was doing at the mine. Since the mine manager was obviously English, Winston admitted he had escaped from a Boer prisoner-of-war camp. They relaxed and the manager put away his gun and invited him to hide in the coalmine, where he remained.

Soon afterwards, on December 14, a terse message arrived for Jennie by telegraph from the Reuters news agency. It said simply, "Churchill escaped."

Winston continued to remain in the coalmine at Witbank while the Boers carried on searching for him. They posted a reward for him of £25 alive or dead, while he was concealed underground in a stable for the pit ponies, where white rats stole his only candle to eat and left him in pitch darkness. After three days alone in the dark he became disoriented and ill. The mine manager confided in an English doctor who advised them to bring Winston above ground to recover, since he was confused and edgy. They locked him up in a storeroom first, then took him to a railway wagon outside the colliery, which was about to head for the coast. They gave him plenty of food and a semi-automatic Mauser. Then the wagon was shunted into place by the engine at Witbank station, where it was linked to the Lourenço Marques train.

In the meantime, he remained hidden from sight beneath bales of wool in the wagon while the train made its way closer and closer towards the Portuguese border, where it was shunted onto a siding. It was eighteen hours before the train started up again and continued until it crossed the border into Portuguese East Africa.

When he jumped down into a goods yard at Laurenço Marques, it was four o'clock in the afternoon on December 21. He went immediately to the British Embassy and telegraphed Milner that he was safe. After a hot bath and clean clothes, he had dinner. Then he began telegraphing, first to Souza to exonerate the sentries at the camp, in case they were in trouble. And he read the latest newspapers.

Defeat

What he saw was that the British defeats by the Boers were even worse than defeat by the Russians had been in the Crimean War fifty years previously. It was not the kind of news he'd grown up with. He would have asked himself what was wrong with British politicians and the army. He may have instinctively been reminded of a popular stirring march he had often heard as a boy, because of its certainty and pride. Military marching songs were composed to rise easily to the surface of a soldier's mind after marching to them with the rhythmic stamp of army boots so many times before. They were a metaphor for initiative, courage, determination, and bravery on the battlefields.

We're the soldiers of the Queen, my lads
Who've been, my lads, who've seen, my lads

In the fight for England's glory, lads
When we've had to show them what we mean:
And when we say we've always won
And when they ask us how it's done
We'll proudly point to every one
Of England's soldiers of the Queen.

It was being played in the music halls and by military brass bands in Victorian public parks, and by recruiting officers who used it to entice young men from the villages and the farms to "take the queen's shilling," as a contractual agreement to join up and fight for the British Empire against the heathen all over the world—to knock them into shape as civilized and peace-loving members of the colonies. But something appeared to have changed in the spirit and valor of the British.

> Neither Haig, Edmonds, French or [Aylmer] Haldane are to be particularly criticized, for what was happening was the slow transition under twentieth-century pressures of a small, colonial-oriented, traditional, above all personalized army, into a much larger, professional and technically oriented army; and this transition caused the personalized senior level promotion system to become antiquated, as it were, in mid-stream.
>
> Nor was the system simply one of protectors and *proteges*. There were many countervailing currents, such as the "cavalry" thesis of Edmonds, who maintained that after Haig obtained the post of Commander-in-Chief, he continued French's policy of promoting cavalrymen—Gough, Allenby, Byng and Birdwood, for example— who all commanded armies.[3]

And there were all sorts of effects of other frictions and jealousies and insecurities. For example, "Hamilton's problem in South Africa, when appointed Chief of Staff for General Kitchener was that Kitchener saw him as a rival; he feared that he himself would be sent home, and replaced perhaps by Hamilton. So, reportedly, he would not let Hamilton do anything, and if Hamilton wrote a minute, Kitchener would allegedly blue pencil it out of recognition."[4]

England had prospered from its initiative in inventing the English Industrial Revolution. It had created employment at home and throughout the colonies as Britain had become "the workshop of the world," with factories across the industrial north and midlands, and the five towns of the potteries, which were linked to each other by canals and railroads and roads leading to England's coastal ports, from where British manufactured goods were shipped to British colonies and all over the world.

The United States had been quick to follow Britain's example by industrializing with its railroads and its inventors and manufactories in a Second Industrial Revolution. Inventors and innovators like Thomas Edison and his team of artisans electrified New York City and other American cities. Germany followed suit, and so did Japan, which soon modernized its fleet and army to attack Tsarist Russia, which was much slower to industrialize.

The Great Industrial Exhibition of British and Commonwealth and international goods had been organized by Prince Albert in 1851, and proudly displayed in the famous "Crystal Palace" in London. Many of Britain's notable achievers had attended the opening, including scientist Charles Darwin, novelist Charles Dickens, Lewis Carroll, Mary Ann Evans, the famous female author who wrote under the pen-name of George Eliot, and Alfred Lord Tennyson, who had celebrated the Charge of the Light Brigade in verse. It was the first World's Fair to show the achievements of industrialization and Victorian culture. But, only ten years later, the Prince Consort died suddenly at the young age of forty-two.

The bells that tolled in St. Paul's Cathedral did so not only for Albert's death, but sent out a message across London which signified a moment of national crisis. For everyone knew that Victoria had been entirely dependent on Albert, although they had been patronizing about him when he lived, because he was a foreigner. But now they realized that Britain had effectively lost its leader. The mood of the nation faltered, lost its balance, and slowed down, looking bewildered, like a horse that loses its rider. Britain's royal family almost never recovered from the calamity, as outpourings of grief matched the Queen's own deep suffering at her loss. She retreated from life to Balmoral and became the mourning image of death.

"There is no one to call me Victoria now," she cried—and imposed mourning on everyone else. Her happiness had ended. And so, by extension, had Britain's.

To complicate matters further, it happened at more or less the same time as the American Civil War, arguments about slavery in the South, and a diplomatic conflict with the Northern States. Not only did the virtues of family life crumble with the death of the head of the royal family, but domestic virtues and bourgeois values were left stranded without leadership. The extraordinarily long period of mourning was a metaphor that symbolized the weakening of the family of nations in the commonwealth.

Her favorite courtier, Benjamin Disraeli, attempted to charm and encourage her, and give her more self-confidence as a woman, when he was re-elected as Prime Minister in 1874. And she became resigned to being the grandmother of Europe. It was when Britons became "Victorians."

Attila and the Huns

Meanwhile, Germany's steel industry in the Ruhr Valley employed nearly three thousand staff and workers in fifty ironworks in 1850, when the German Empire was created. By 1870, the German nation aimed to compete with Britain in heavy industries. German firms, like Krupp, modernized and adapted to change, to become the biggest producer of steel in Europe, while Britain was still mired in mourning for Prince Albert and grief for the Queen. When America and Germany began to compete for trade with Britain, the United States showed itself to be better at commercialization, and German industry worked hard with government contracts to modernize the German Navy. They also began to specialize in chemicals and dyes.

The so-called "Boxer Rebellion" in China against the West was put down in 1900 by a combined force from Britain, France, Russia, Germany, America, and Japan. The German troops lost face by arriving after the other forces had already battled and taken Peking, where the heaviest fighting took place. They were made to look even worse by a speech given by the Kaiser to his troops. He told them to be merciless in battle in the spirit of the Huns.

"Should you encounter the enemy," he told them loftily, "he will be defeated! No quarter will be given! Prisoners will not be taken! Whoever falls into your hands is forfeited. Just as a thousand years ago the Huns under their King Attila made a name for themselves, one that even today makes them seem mighty in history and legend. May the name German be affirmed by you in such a way in China that no Chinese will ever again dare to look cross-eyed at a German."

His speech was the reason why old soldiers in Britain began to refer to the Germans mockingly as "Huns." And the old saying, "Scratch a Russian and you find a barbarian," began to be transferred to Germans instead. (Russia, being neither European nor Asian, had been viewed as exotic, with its Orthodox Church chanting, and equated more with Byzantium and the Middle East.) Now it was the Kaiser's Germany which was equated with the barbarian Huns.

Spioenkop

Britain had reached its economic peak in the middle of the century, but then began a decline that continued up to the time of the Boer War. Some claimed its loss of confidence began when Prince Albert died and the queen withdrew from the world to live with Albert's spirit for the rest of her life. British aspiration dwindled, except for a handful of exceptional men. Winston was one of them.

When he read that General Buller's forces had been pushed back from Colenso while attempting to relieve the siege of Ladysmith, Winston was shocked. He was determined to leave for Durban by steamer. He was escorted to the docks by a group of armed Englishmen who feared that Winston might otherwise be seized and kidnapped by the Boers and returned to a prisoner-of-war camp. Once in his cabin, he wrote to the *Morning Post*.

He arrived at the docks in Durban in the afternoon on December 23, to find an eager and cheering crowd waiting for him at the quay. They escorted him to the Town Hall, where he regaled them with the story of his escape from the Boers. He left by train an hour later, anxious to return to the battlefront. He arrived in Pietermaritzburg one month after he'd left on the same railway line. General Buller had set up his headquarters close to the spot where the armored train had been ambushed. He spent Christmas in the platelayers' hut, near where he had been captured by the Boers.

"He really is a fine fellow," Buller wrote to a friend the next day, "and I must say I admire him greatly. I wish he was leading irregular troops instead of writing for a rotten paper. We are very short of good men, as he appears to be, out here."

With all the gloom and despondency of the British defeats, the press made much of Winston to encourage the others, and announced that he had accepted a commission in the South African Light Horse. Winston was a soldier again. He wrote to Jennie in the New Year that he was now a lieutenant, without having to give up his position as a war correspondent. At the same time, he also wrote to his lady-friend, Pamela Plauden, that "Buller himself is worth very little." It seemed that, regardless of his undoubted patriotism, Winston knew that something was very wrong with the army culture. But he had to take care in his articles not to aggravate too many people at the top, or risk being accused erroneously of disloyalty.

Although he gave her a firm opinion that "the Boer Republics are wearing thin," the difficulty of any such affair was to separate wishful thinking from reality—it might go either way. The Boers were absolutely determined to hold on to what they considered to be their land, after all their pioneering hardships and hazards for generations, and after successfully tearing down forests to till the land, then create and establish a culture, from being farmers to building towns and cities—just as the Americans had done when they had trekked west and built their own homesteads. The Boers had trekked to the Transvaal in their own ox-wagons, circled them under attack, and fired with their rifles to protect themselves and their families from the peoples who surrounded them and outnumbered them. The attacking enemies were well-organized and brave warriors, the Zulu and the Xhosa. They and the Voortrekkers suffered heavy losses of life. The Matabele had moved south at more or less the same time that the Dutch settlers had travelled up north from the Cape Province, and met somewhere in the middle. Both parties had managed to survive. Their problems now came from the British.

The Voortrekkers

There was no doubting that the Boers were determined to resist the incursions onto their land. Winston wrote in the *Morning Post* of one man he had seen who had touched his heart. "I have often seen men killed in war," he wrote, "thousands at Omdurman, scores elsewhere, black and white, but the Boer dead aroused the most painful emotions."

These Afrikaans, Dutch, French, and German Protestants had fled from violent religious and military upheavals, and from wars of persecution by the

Roman Catholic Church and its armies in the Spanish-ruled Netherlands in the 1830s and 1840s—at the same time as other emigrants escaped slaughter in the revolutionary turmoil in the Spring of Nations in Europe, some finding a safe haven in the Cape Colony of South Africa. It had been founded by the Dutch and taken over by the British when Holland's economy foundered and collapsed. They surged into the interior in their covered ox-wagons to found their own homeland in the Great Trek.

It was little different from the pioneering days in the "Wild West" of America, with comparatively small groups of families with their horses, cattle herds, sheep, and hens. They moved together for protection like nomads against the well-regimented forces of native warriors, all riding and surging towards the Promised Land of the Book. Most were poor farmers from the East Cape, but some, like Piet Retief, came from the West Cape, leaving the insecurity of frontier life in the Cape Province. The land and weather had been too harsh for farming, and they were squeezed for survival between an inflow of thousands of British immigrants and British administration that favored the others, including the indigenous Xhosa tribes.

News reached them of a "Promised Land" which was more fertile, in what would become the Orange Free State and the Transvaal. There was also serious conflict between the hardworking farmers who needed labor and the British Empire's insistence on freeing all slaves, as was also being done in North America. Those families were hard-bitten and accustomed to shortages and mere subsistence farming. But they were also shrewd hunters who shared a religious fervor for the land and the Old Testament, with their ancestors' names of each generation painfully written into the flyleaves of the family Bible. It was the only book they knew—usually read to them by the father of the household, if he could read—otherwise in the Dutch Reformed Church.

When the Voortrekkers migrated to Natal in 1837—which was Zululand— they sent a delegation of a hundred representatives to King Dingane the following year, to negotiate a treaty. After the king signed it with their leader Piet Retief, Dingane changed his mind and had the entire hundred guests murdered in their huts when they slept at night. The treaty had given the Voortrekkers land by the Tugela River. Dingane then sent a regiment of well-trained and disciplined warriors against the rest of the families, and slaughtered 500 of the Voortrekkers, then stole all their cattle.

Andries Pretorius took leadership of the remaining families and was determined to retrieve their cattle and sheep and take revenge on Dingane. In response, Dingane sent some 15,000 to 20,000 Zulu warriors to wipe out the Voortrekkers. The families defended themselves courageously in the customary way of frontier pioneers, by encircling their ox-wagons into a protective *laager* and firing at the enemy from in between and underneath them. Although overwhelmingly outnumbered, the Voortrekkers made a vow to God that they would honor the date of December 16, 1838 by commemorating it, if they were delivered from the Zulus. Their victory over the Zulu attack became known as the "Battle of Blood River," because the waters of the Ncome River turned red from the slaughter. It was their turning point.

They established the Republic of Natal in 1839 between the Tugela River and Port St. Johns, in accordance with their original treaty with King Dingane. Britain annexed it in 1843. And many of the Boers packed up their belongings and their families and livestock and trekked even further north to get away from them, joining up with other pioneering families there and establishing homesteads, ranches, and farms. These illiterate and semi-literate poor farmers who only read one book, the Bible, believed they had entered the Nile Valley in Egypt and were "God's Chosen People."

But there were other people there before them, and inevitable conflicts also with the Ndebele tribe, ruled by Chief Mzilikazi in the Transvaal. The Boers overcame all the odds against them by their hardiness and persistence, their shrewd hunting tactics, their sharpshooting skills with their muzzle-loaders, and their horsemanship. Their small pioneering settlements merged into several small Boer Republics, and then the Orange Free State and the Republic of South Africa. But when valuable mineral resources were discovered in Bloemfontein and on the Reef, the British annexed the land in the Boer War in 1900.

"If I were a Boer"

The particular man Winston referred to as having touched his heart was in his sixties, "with firm aquiline features, and a short beard." He had refused to surrender to the British. "Even when his left leg was smashed by a bullet, [he] continued to load his rifle until he bled to death." Next to him he saw the body of a teenage boy, shot through the heart. Further away were two British riflemen with their heads smashed in. Winston was so deeply moved at what he saw in battle at Spioenkop that he turned down an invitation from the Conservatives to stand at the next General Election in Southport, in order to continue under fire at the battlefront.

In the meantime, the indomitable Jennie had helped to organize and equip a hospital ship named *Maine*, and arrived, in charge of it, in Durban on January 28. Winston met her and his brother Jack there, and took Jack back with him to the front at the Tugela River. Jack was now an officer in the Territorials. Addressing the despondency in England in one of his newspaper articles, Winston wrote that some British citizens have a duty to shoot straight, "but all of us remain cheerfully determined."

Jack was wounded and sent back to Jennie's hospital ship. As for Winston, he wrote to Pamela on February 25, "I was very nearly killed two hours ago by shrapnel." His attitude was quite simply that they must be more determined than the enemy. But few could be as determined as the Boers, who felt their land and their identity slipping away from them. Three days later, two cavalry squadrons commanded by Lord Dundonald were about to enter Ladysmith. With him was Winston's friend Ronald Brooke. He invited Winston to join them.

It was a cool evening and Winston's horse was fresh. They passed first over stony ground. The British cavalry pushed on with the sound of artillery. An armed picket approached before they could put their horses into a gallop. They paused to identify themselves as the Ladysmith relief column. Then, Winston wrote, "from out of trenches and rifle pits artfully concealed in the scrub a score of tattered men came running, cheering feebly, and some crying. In the half-light they looked ghastly pale and thin. A poor white-faced officer waved his helmet to and fro, and laughed foolishly, and the tall, strong colonial horsemen, standing up in their stirrups, raised a loud resounding cheer. Then we knew the siege of Ladysmith was over."

After dining with the town's defenders, he never lost sight of the predicament of the Boers. "I would treat the Boers with all generosity, and tolerance, even providing for those crippled in the war, and for the destitute women and children . . . To last, a peace must be honorable." He wrote later that the British should "devote themselves to stimulating and sustaining the spirit of the people by measures of social improvement and reform."

Joseph Chamberlain praised his reports from South Africa. He was Secretary of State for the Colonies, and although he never became Prime Minister, he was viewed as the most important politician at this time. Meanwhile, Winston's novel, which he called *Savrola*, had finally been published, and he read the reviews. He was relieved to see it highly praised, particularly for its deep insights. And some phrases had made their impression on the book critics' minds, such as his description of "a degenerate imperialism."

Winston laid out a rule for the final phase of the action in South Africa in his newspaper articles, which he hoped would stand as a model for the government and the military to follow: "Beware of driving men to desperation—even a cornered rat is dangerous. . . . Those who demand *an eye for an eye and a tooth for a tooth*, should ask themselves whether such barren spoils are worth five years of bloody partisan warfare and the consequent impoverishment of South Africa."

But as it would turn out, not everyone was as wise or compassionate as he was. He became disillusioned with the Conservative Party and turned away from it, partly because of its attitudes to the Boer War. "If I were a Boer," he said later on, "I should be fighting in the field."

His sympathies wavered, because he did not distinguish one group of people from another by its color or race, nationality or religion. And he knew from Darwin's hundreds—even thousands of scientific studies—that all human beings were related to each other from the same stock. He was in revolt against "jingoism" that resulted in mindless and brutal attitudes towards different people, like the Kaiser with his Hunnish mindset.

He was horrified at the poverty of the Boers. It was an insight of the other half of the world with its completely different societies that no one in England ever saw. Even so, he knew that if he pushed the points he wanted to make in his newspaper articles too far, there would be a backlash from the generals and politicians alike and they would close ranks against him to prevent him from telling the truth. He was aware from his reading of the classics that the result of bad news is that the messenger gets killed to prevent it from leaking out.

From Winston Churchill's vantage point and his philosophical way of seeing events unroll, he would have seen the war in South Africa as the beginning of the fall of the British Empire, partly as a result of favoritism and cover-ups and personal squabbles in the army culture, that would affect not only events in the South African war but also in the First World War, with Sir Ian Hamilton, Haldane (who didn't like him), and Kitchener, who felt insecure against him.

"Inquiries after the war showed that British commanders had been incompetent, that forces had been sent into combat without clear orders, proper maps or sufficient intelligence, and that equipment had been completely inadequate. Leo Amory, who was a reporter in the field for *The Times,* wrote, for example, of the disaster of Spion Kop: no effort was made beforehand to ascertain the shape of the position to be occupied, or to furnish the officers entrusted with its capture with such information."[5]

CHAPTER ELEVEN

BELOW THE POVERTY LINE

WINSTON'S SHIP BROUGHT HIM BACK TO England from South Africa before the Boer War was over. It was not an honorable end that he had repeatedly called for in his newspaper articles, and he felt well out of it. He could do no more, although it was in the hands of casual and scheming administrators and an incompetent British army with a bespattered reputation. But even Winston could never have imagined what would besmirch it next. Meanwhile, Kitchener achieved fame and was ennobled as "Lord Kitchener of Khartoum" for winning the Battle of Omdurman, which secured British control of the Sudan.

Winston found a copy of *Vanity Fair* magazine on the ship, with a cartoon of him by the popular artist who called himself "Spy." There was an article with it that said, "He is a clever fellow who has the courage of his convictions. He can write and he can fight. . . . And it is probable that his every effort, military or literary, has been made with political bent." Winston must have grinned at the writer's prescience. He landed at Southampton on July 20 and went to Oldham five days later, where he was adopted as their prospective candidate for the General Election.

Over ten thousand people turned out in the streets with flags and drums beating and shouted themselves hoarse for two hours, he told his brother afterwards. Next day, in Oldham's Theatre Royal, he described to a mesmerized audience how he had escaped from the Boers and holed up at the Witbank colliery. As soon as he mentioned the name of one of the men who had helped him, Mr. Dewsnap, the Oldham engineer, someone in the audience shouted, "His wife's in the gallery." It was followed by cheers.

Concentration Camps

Back in South Africa, there was nothing for either side in the battle to cheer about. Winston had been right about the Boers refusing to put down their guns. The guerrilla battles of their commandos continued, despite the overwhelming size of the trained British forces. Regimented British soldiers would advance in the open with not a single enemy in sight, and suddenly be confronted by a squadron of Boers rising from trenches concealed at their feet and shooting them down in an instant. On other occasions—as Kitchener complained plaintively—"The Boers are not like the Dervishes who stood up to a fair fight. They are always running away on their little ponies." The Boer hit-and-run tactics continued to be effective against an outmoded British Army.

It was a war of attrition to see which side would be worn down first. The sturdy Dutch farmers were hardier than the British soldiers and accustomed to privations. But each side was determined to win. The popular opinion in Britain was that none of the British generals was any good. And since the war had drifted off course and lacked deliberate focus, General Buller was replaced by Lord Roberts. The British government now sent its biggest military force ever overseas, hoping to crush the Boers with overwhelming force. But the guerilla commandos were led by excellent generals and a last-ditch dedication to fighting on. It was mass against minimalism, and the minimal guerilla forces continued to win for a while; then not so much.

Roberts took back several cities in the traditional manner of previous wars and annexed the Republic of South Africa, declaring the war was over. But it continued with small commando raids, as Winston had warned it would if there was no compromise. There was considerable sympathy for the Boers in Europe. Queen Wilhelmina of the Netherlands sent a Dutch warship for President Kruger and his family and the Boer government, ignoring a British naval blockade. Meanwhile the Boer Republics were incorporated in the Union of South Africa in 1910.

Boer prisoners of war were shipped out of the country. But although Roberts had assumed the commandos would down arms when their leaders did, the Boer forces stubbornly continued their guerilla tactics—they simply could not be stopped. The British government was forced to think again and change its traditional tactics that didn't work. Now, blockhouses that contained small groups of half a dozen soldiers were built across the two republics—eight thousand of them to restrict the movement of Boer commandos. And there was a scorched earth policy to destroy any homes that gave, or might give, concealment or support to the guerilla forces, in order to cut off their supplies. British troops made constant sweeps of the countryside and destroyed crops to starve them out. They even poisoned the wells—a move unheard of in civilized western societies. Then they rounded up Boer women and children into tented camps, even with their African women servants. Some Boer auxiliaries were persuaded to change sides, but not many.

Concentration camps to confine dissidents had already been used by the Spanish, and the Americans in the Philippine-American war. Now Roberts began to set them up to house refugees whose homes were burnt down. When Lord Kitchener replaced Lord Roberts, he extended the camps for women and children, locating them close to train stations so that they could be supplied. 25,630 men were sent overseas when captured, leaving about 2,000 women and children in the camps. Food was sparse and the conditions were poor. Bad personal hygiene led to the spread of measles, typhoid and dysentery. Insufficient medical care resulted in deaths whose numbers increased sharply. 4,177 women, 22,074 children under the age of sixteen, and 1,676 men died from starvation, exposure and disease.[1]

The British public were shocked when they found out. A report caused a government inquiry.[2]

Emily Hobhouse, the Leader of the Liberal Opposition in Parliament, visited the camp with £200 worth of groceries and bales of clothing. Sir Alfred Milner contributed a truck. She sent her report to a committee with recommendations for reforming the camps. She described that part of the country as silent and lifeless and prone to dust storms. She saw a few burnt farms.

The Bloemfontein camp was a good two miles from the town, "dumped down on the southern slope of a *kopje*, right out on the bare brown *veld*, not a vestige of a tree in any direction, nor shade of any description. There are nearly 2,000 people in this one camp, of which some few are men—they call them 'hands-up' men—and over 900 children":

Imagine the heat outside the tents and the suffocation inside! We sat on their khaki blankets, rolled up, inside Mrs. B.'s tent; and the sun blazed through the single canvas, and the flies lay thick and black on everything; no chair, no table, nor any room for such; only a deal box, standing on its end, served as a wee pantry. In this tiny tent live Mrs. B.'s five children (three quite grown up) and a little Kaffir servant girl. Many tents have more occupants. Mrs. P. came in, and Mrs. R, and others. And they told me their stories, and we cried together, and even laughed together, and chatted bad Dutch and bad English all afternoon. On wet nights the water streams down the canvas and comes flowing in, as it knows how to do in this country, under the flap of the tent, and wets their blankets as they lie on the ground.

While we sat there a snake came in. They said it was a puff adder, very poisonous, so they all ran out, and I attacked the creature with my parasol. I could not bear to think the thing should be at large in a community mostly sleeping on the ground.

The death-rate among staff was also high, indicating that the dire effects were not deliberate but due largely to the incompetence of the army and Milner, who was responsible for the camps. Apparently no one in charge knew enough about hygiene and the spread of germs, particularly among crowds of refugees confined together in camps in the sub-Saharan heat.

Separated from their families, who were dying in British camps, and their homes destroyed, the spirit of the Boers was broken. When the war was finally over, "Families left the camps with a tent, bedding, and food for a month. Where possible, tools, seeds, livestock and vehicles were handed out by the British."[3]

Winston Under Fire

Jennie had not met Winston at Southampton, because she was marrying army Captain Cornwallis-West. He was twenty years younger than her. Ten days after his return, Churchill was being entertained on the terrace of the House of Commons where he met "all sorts of members," and felt his political future was assured. Newspapers gave him a paragraph whenever he opened his mouth. As well as Oldham, he made speeches in several other towns in the coming months, although he admitted he found it tiring. The *Times* filled an entire column when he spoke about the evident weakness of the British Army in the event of a war in Europe. He warned that few were preparing against it, despite the suspicion that the European powers, "armed to the teeth, viewed us with no friendly eye." He contemplated the situation with anxiety.

He told his Plymouth audience that he had been trained in the theory and practice of war for seven years, and knew enough to say there was little in military administration that a sensible businessman could not understand. Although British soldiers possessed courage, it was no reason why their weapons should be out of date. The government should act wisely. His speech appeared in the weekend *Times*.

He was happy with his speechmaking, which he considered he had mastered, and managed to flatten out all the interrupters in the end, to the delight of the audience. He also spoke at the annual dinner of the Institute of Journalists, who represented almost the whole of the press who, hopefully, would continue to quote his speeches and applaud him.

Nevertheless, he was urged to practice repeating, "The Spanish ships I cannot see, for they are not in sight," to pronounce his "s" properly, but said he would never learn to do so.

He rented a bachelor flat in Mayfair, where he lived and kept his office for the next six years. Neither pleasure nor relaxation would keep him away from his future in the industrial city of Oldham with its working-class voters, where he set up his campaign headquarters. Polling took place on October 1, and was spread over a period of three weeks.

He became a Member of Parliament at the age of twenty-five, going on twenty-six. And his new book was published soon afterwards, making him the author of five books, with money coming in from most of them. Now he would be paid also as a lecturer, to tour all over England with speeches about the Boer War. He spoke in Scotland and Ireland. In London alone— where Lord Wolseley, the Commander in Chief of the British Army, was in the chair—he earned £265 (a year's salary for a young professional man). Wolseley said that Winston held everyone's attention for an hour and a half.

The Conservative candidate at Oldham invested the capital for him in a quick money-making scheme, although Winston confessed he couldn't understand the prospectus.

He began the America tour in New York on December 8. Mark Twain introduced him to the audience by telling them that his mother was an American.

He met President McKinley in Washington. In Albany, he met newly elected Vice-President Theodore Roosevelt, who would become President several months later when McKinley was assassinated by an anarchist. He followed by lecturing in major cities in Canada. While there, he met up with Pamela. They were still friends although they had ended their romance by mutual agreement.

He learned of Queen Victoria's death when in Winnipeg, and left for England ten days later, taking his seat in Parliament on February 14. He had become aware by now that he would be in the public eye for the rest of his life.

When, in his maiden speech, he said, "If I were a Boer I hope I should be fighting in the field," Chamberlain remarked lugubriously to his neighbor, "That's the way to throw away a seat." But Churchill went quickly on to add, "We have no cause to be ashamed of anything that has passed during the war . . ."

Maiden speeches are not often reported in the Press, but the *Daily Express* described it as "spell-binding." He was evidently perfectly at home, made the appropriate gestures to his words, and was in tune with the audience in the crowded House. Inevitably, he would be compared with his father, Lord Randolph, and *Punch* magazine did so. Despite Winston's different voice and manner, they claimed he possessed "the same command of pointed phrase; the same self-possession, verging, perhaps, on self-assurance; the same gift of viewing familiar objects from a new standpoint; the same shrewd, confident judgment."

Two other useful attributes were noted by the *Daily Chronicle*. They were candor and independence.

But his remark "If I were a Boer" offended many of the Conservatives. Letters of protest were written to the newspapers. In reply, he wrote in the *Westminster Gazette* that "While the Boer cause is certainly wrong, the Boer who fights for it is certainly right." And "neither side has a monopoly of right or reason."

Only two weeks after his maiden speech, he had the confidence and courage to raise a matter long on his mind about the military and political custom of the "cover-up," by stating, "Perhaps it will not be entirely agreeable to many of my friends on this side of the House if I say that I have noticed in the last three wars in which we have been engaged a tendency—arising partly from good nature towards their comrades, partly from dislike of public scrutiny—to hush everything up, to make everything look as fair as possible, to tell what is called the official truth, to present a version of the truth which contains about seventy-five percent of the actual article."

Not satisfied only with that, he went even further. "So long as a force gets a victory somehow, all the ugly facts are smoothed and varnished over, rotten reputations are propped up, and officers known as incapable are allowed to hang on and linger in their commands in the hope that at the end of the war they may be shunted into private life without a scandal."

In spite of his provocation, his audience must have recognized the truth of what he said, since it turned votes in favor of the government. And the Secretary of State for War (St. John Broderick) wrote to him to say "you filled the house and held it." Churchill's correspondence was now so great that he was obliged to hire a secretary to cope with it.

Not long afterwards, he criticized St. John Broderick, the Conservative leader, when he opposed a 15 percent increase in military expenditure, by arguing that it was too small to make the army stronger. And, in any case, it was unnecessary, since any attack on Britain would come from the sea. "A better army does not necessarily mean a bigger army."

Opposing his own party made him enemies. Nevertheless, he was always alert and ready to pounce. And if he did not succeed the first time, he returned to the kill. His stooping shoulders that leaned keenly forward gave him the stance of a predatory eagle, ready to pounce on its prey.

In this case it was in the cause of efficiency and effectiveness, with economy. Too much money was being wasted instead of improving the technology or increasing skills. It was the very point over which his father, Lord Randolph, had resigned fourteen years earlier. Churchill stood up to read out the letter of resignation his father had written in 1886. He had kept it and knew it by heart. And he'd had long enough to think about the issue and also observe it at the front for himself. "This is a cause I have inherited," he said. Then he listed the points of his argument against having three army corps. One, he said, is quite enough to fight savages, and three are not enough to fight Europeans. He reminded them of how glibly Ministers talked of a European war, without noticing the changes that had taken place in war. A modern war, he said, can only end in the ruin of the vanquished and the exhaustion and economic dislocation of the victor.

"We do not know what war is," he insisted. "We have had a glimpse of it in South Africa. Even in miniature it is hideous and appalling." It was on a strong economy and a strong Navy that Britain's power and prosperity depended.

His own party was shocked that he attacked their policy. But the opposition parties praised his sentiments and courage. Churchill now found himself at the head of a group of dissatisfied Conservatives. The Liberal Lord Rosebery invited him to his home at Durdans, near Epsom, for Sunday. Another leading Liberal, Sir Edward Grey, invited him to dine with him at Asquith. The Liberals shared many of Churchill's views and wanted a strong Britain with a social policy which would benefit the mass of the population and reduce extremes of poverty and deprivation.[4]

Churchill drifted steadily to the left, mainly because of the attitude of the Conservatives to the Boer War. In the autumn, he protested against the execution of a Boer commander, and worked quietly to prevent the execution of another one. "I was in revolt against jingoism," he would declare many years later. Balfour and Chamberlain had handed the war over to the military in order to relieve themselves of responsibilities.

His Mission

Churchill's sense of mission was stimulated when he read Seebohm Rowntree's book on poverty in Britain.[5] Sociologist and social reformer Rowntree and his team studied 46,000 people, representing two-thirds of the population of the city of York. He excluded only people who could afford a domestic servant. He discovered that nearly half lived in poverty, around 20,000. Twenty-eight percent were living in "most serious" poverty or "absolute poverty"—meaning that they were unable to acquire food, fuel, or clothing. In about a quarter of cases, the chief wage-earner was either dead or disabled, or otherwise unable to work. In over half the cases he was employed but was paid a pittance. The study revealed that poverty was widespread in Britain and not only in the metropolis of London.

Rowntree's lectures were a major influence on Liberalism in England—certainly on future Prime Minister Lloyd George. Winston Churchill considered abandoning the Conservative Party for the Liberals. When speaking at Blackpool in 1902, he said he was deeply shocked and expressed sympathy with people who had only the workhouse or prison as options to escape their present situation. American labor was better fed and healthier—there was no reason why the same should not apply to England.

Winston Churchill was twenty-seven when his eyes were opened to the precarious life of most people in Britain. "Imagination recoils," he remarked. But people did not wish to contemplate "the slum, the garret and the gutter." He made a summary of the disasters that befall the working man, in particular the results of unemployment, sickness, or death. Then there were the evil housing conditions that Rowntree had studied. It occurred to him that they would be better off living as subjects of the islands of the Southern seas. He wrote to a leading Birmingham Conservative, "I see little glory in an Empire which can rule the waves and is unable to flush its sewers."

His disappointment with the Conservative party continued to grow. He considered whether to reply to the growing invitations from the Liberal Party. He finally decided to attack the Government failure to use taxpayers' money in the most economical and beneficial way. He was congratulated on his budget speech on April 14 by Sir Edward Hamilton, who was the Permanent Financial Secretary to the Treasury. Churchill approached Balfour to serve on a committee over controlling government expenditure. He accepted, but Churchill still found differences of opinion with his party leaders. Every month there were further breaches. He found his enthusiasm for the Government's positions waning. He stayed with Lord Rosebery at Dalmeny and raised his intention of pressing for a joint action against Brodrick's Army scheme by an aggressive group containing both Conservative and Liberal members willing to vote against unnecessary military spending.

After talking to a leading local Conservative who had expressed similar opinions, he came away with an idea of a coalition to inject vitality into the Conservative Party. He confessed to broad, tolerant, moderate views, for compromise and agreement, a central party, freer and more efficient. Now he hinted to Rosebery his plan for a middle party to control government spending, since it was impossible for a private member acting alone to have any effect. At the same time, Chamberlain wrote to him of his belief that Churchill would never settle down as a loyal supporter and that he recognized the possibility that sooner or later he would drift across the floor to the Liberal cause.

Arguments about tariffs and Protectionist legislation split the Conservatives and Liberals further apart. Churchill supported free trade and his views were considered too extreme for the Conservatives. Churchill decided there was no future for free-traders in the Conservative Party. At a free trade meeting in Birmingham he made a spirited defense for it, but had still not decided to join the Liberal party. But then he was asked by Lord Tweedmouth if he would stand as a Liberal in Sunderland. Meanwhile, his views did not please his Oldham constituents. And the General Purposes Committee informed him that he had forfeited their support in the event of an election. The choices that lay open to him were whether to seek election as an independent Unionist free-trader or join the Liberals. Meanwhile, he had begun to vote against the Conservatives. And he was cheered loudly by the Liberals.

Churchill finally accepted an invitation by the Liberals of North-West Manchester to stand as a free-trade candidate with their support, stating that Britain should have a higher regard for people's rights and rely on liberty and justice. On April 22 he spoke at length on upholding the rights of trade unions. His speech was followed by one presenting a plan for more Irish control over Ireland's affairs. He then attacked the Government's Aliens Bill. It had been introduced to curb Jewish emigration from Russia to Britain. He was concerned to protect the "simple immigrant, the political refugee, the helpless and the poor." His speech was reported in the *Manchester Guardian*.

He was twenty-nine when he entered the Chamber of the House, bowed to the Speaker, and, after a brief glance at the Conservative benches, strode this time to the ranks of the Liberals, and sat down beside the Opposition leader, Lloyd George.

Ever since he crossed the floor, Conservatives have characterized his move as disloyal or undependable. But to understand why he did so we must recognize his coming of age with his discovery of how the poor and jobless struggled to survive in England, and the realization that only the Liberal Party possessed the understanding and compassion to serve the greater majority of Britain's population, not just the upper classes.

Chapter Twelve

WINSTON'S REBELLION

Winston's goal was now not only to persuade the British public of the advantages of Liberalism, but also to discredit the Conservatives. He appears to have been rather like some of the clergy at discovering from the scientific evidence of evolution that they had been fooled; and he resented his naïveté, even his stupidity at having been associated with the Conservative Party. His eyes had been opened at the plight of most of Britain's population, despite his having been brought up in the Conservative social class. On June 4 he attacked Balfour's protectionist policies, since he believed in the full benefits and economies of free trade, and he denounced the government's Aliens Bill, since he believed in liberty. The Bill was withdrawn three days later.

Jennie invited him to a ball given by Lady Crewe, who was married to a leading Liberal. Winston was introduced there to an attractive girl of nineteen named Clementine Hozier. Her mother had been Jennie's friend for years. Clementine said later, "He never uttered one word and was very gauche—he never asked me for a dance, he never asked me to have supper with him . . . I had been told he was stuck-up, objectionable etcetera. And on this occasion he just stood and stared."

She had already planned to be rescued from him if necessary, and her escort stood by to ask her to dance at an appropriate signal. "What was she doing," he asked her, talking to "that frightful fellow Winston Churchill?" Her dancing partner was one of many people who felt that Winston had let down his class.

To explain why the ruling classes considered Winston such a turncoat when he should have been one of them, they were the land-owning classes of aristocrats and minor landed gentry who expected their class to stick together.

They had been educated together at leading British public schools and universities, and appointed each other to senior positions in the civil service, the armed forces, Parliament, and the Church. They owned estates of a thousand and up to thirty thousand acres that may have included mines, residential real estate, or value-added industrial properties. It required considerable courage for Winston Churchill to stand up against their united opposition, which was bitter and hateful. Some even went so far as to call him the "Blenheim Rat."

Winston was spending his time completing his biography of his father at Sir Ernest Cassel's villa in the Swiss Alps. He was still writing to Jennie on every possible occasion and whenever he was away for a few weeks. "Never felt better," he told her in the clear Swiss air.

Back again in England, he spoke to Chamberlain in order to obtain more information about his father and the controversies and personalities of twenty years earlier. Chamberlain warned him he must expect abuse to be hurled at him for changing sides.

He began to move closer to the so-called "Welsh Wizard," Lloyd George, as they found more and more in common. He shared a platform with him on October 18 at Carnarvon. He remarked to a Scottish audience in Edinburgh that, "No one seems to care anything but about money today." Thirty-one of the current fifty-five Conservative Ministers were company directors, whereas the last Liberal Government had ruled against it as introducing conflicts of interest. His audience stood up and applauded at the end of his speech. But former Conservative friends had serious reservations about his attacks on his former party. And he continued to attack them for their economic laxness and the expenditures of the Army General Staff, who served simply as decorative functionaries at pageants in their gilded uniforms.

Churchill's speeches and his attacks were very effective, but the more he hit home the more resentful they were at his criticisms. It reached a point where he decided to leave his club because of the hostility of its members. Soon after, he was refused membership of the Hurlingham Club, where polo players had always been welcomed.

Politicians disliked the way he belittled Conservative Prime Minister Balfour. And at a country house party, he was told by a friend that everyone—men and women—admitted to wanting to tear him apart. But he was too focused on completing the biography of his father to be upset. As he told Jennie, he was attempting to receive a great deal of money for his book. And he was successful in obtaining the highest advance yet in Britain for a political biography.

As he was completing it, a Liberal was writing a biography of Winston.[1] Although the Conservatives castigated him, the biographer was full of praise for him, particularly as he expressed the virtue that Churchill wanted capital to be made the servant of the State instead of the master. Here was a change in politics at last, since Churchill claimed that "the true happiness of a nation is to be secured by industrial development and social reform at home, rather than by territorial expansion and military adventures abroad." It was a giant step from the vainglorious past of theft through power and glory to a more modern age, "animated by respect for right and justice."

It was a heavy burden to know better than anyone else, but Winston changed people's minds towards his own views in the course of time. "Already in the House of Commons," the biographer wrote, "he leads by a natural right which no man can dispute. He does what no one has thought of before and thinks the original thought that then comes to everybody's lips to express what all men have longed to say." Nevertheless, the author remarked, Churchill was "probably the best-hated man in English politics," after Joseph Chamberlain.

It appears that his first biographer had been struck by something particularly significant about Churchill's life and times that no one else had. It was that Winston had been born at a time when it was still customary for great powers to invade other nations' territories for vital resources they lacked. Stronger nations had always overpowered weaker ones in war. Now Churchill was proclaiming an obvious truth that it was not necessary to go to war if nations traded freely with each other for what each needed to advance their economies, instead of imposing tariffs. It was so obvious, and yet thirty-five years later, in the second half of his life, he would see Germany invade Norway and Russia for vital resources it needed for its economy, and Japan invade China for the same purpose.

Female Emancipation

Free trade was not the only subject that raised people's blood pressure; the other was an increasing number of annoying interruptions in the House by suffragettes like Christabel Pankhurst and Annie Kenny. They caused disturbances, were escorted from halls, fined, and refused to pay. What they were desperately seeking was martyrdom in prison in protest for women's rights. What angered Winston was the contempt they had for the value of free speech for others, and democratic principles, which they chose to ignore. But he deplored the use of the police force to silence them.

There are always extremists who do not understand the consequences of their actions. Nevertheless, the position of women in the Victorian and even the Edwardian Era in Britain was nebulous. It was the same in France, Germany, and Russia. They had no identity except as appendages of men— either fathers or husbands. They had little life of their own and rarely any money unless they inherited it. With the exception of domestic service— ranging from the lowliest servant to parlor maid, cook, or housekeeper—the only other, more genteel employment for women was that of a governess or nanny, or a lady's companion. The world outside of domestic service provided eleven- to eighteen-hour days of drudgery at machines in cotton or linen mills in the industrial north of England or the Midlands.

Women typists had to wait for the invention of the typewriter in 1877, but there were not enough of them to create a new class of clerical worker. Employers only began hiring women typists in greater numbers by 1920, when there were 286,000 female typists in the United States.

Meanwhile, few male-dominated institutions had any idea of the frustration that seethed inside women and caused them to rebel. Apart from the limit to jobs or professions, or vocations, their education was limited too. Although their frustrations did not create the psychiatric professions in Austria and America, it increased them considerably.

Churchill Rebuked

At the end of October, King Edward the Seventh invited Winston to dinner with the intention "to bring home to me the error of my ways." The King spoke angrily to Winston against his attacks on the Prime Minister. And Winston accepted the King's rebuke meekly.

On his birthday, he wrote to Jennie, "Thirty-one is very old."

He received a letter from Hugh Arnold-Forster at the War Office—whose Army expenditure he had criticized—wishing him recovery from a debilitating illness. He wrote to Winston that although he didn't agree with his politics, he thought he was the only person in his party who understood the problems of the army, and that he shared his views.[2]

When Balfour resigned as Prime Minister, and the King sent for Campbell-Bannerman to form a new Government, Churchill was offered a Ministerial position in it as Financial Secretary to the Treasury under Asquith. He requested rather to be Under-Secretary of State at the Colonial Office, and it was accepted. Winston became a Junior Minister only a few days after his birthday. He was now a member of the British Government.

On his first day in office Churchill appointed Edward Marsh—a Colonial Office clerk two years older than him—to be his Private Secretary. Marsh agreed, and they would work together for the next quarter of a century. "The first time you meet Winston," Pamela Plowden cautioned him, "you see all his faults, and the rest of your life you spend in discovering his virtues."[3]

In 1906, the Liberal Government called for a General Election. Churchill issued a manifesto against any form of tariffs and for a reduction on armament expenditure. He also claimed he would like to see the Irish allowed the power to manage their own affairs according to Irish ideas, but opposed separation from the United Kingdom.

His book on Lord Randolph was published, and described by the *Times Literary Supplement* as among the two or three most exciting political biographies. Lord Rosebery praised it by letter. In it, Churchill referred to his desire for an England "of wise men who gaze without self-deception at the failings and follies of both political parties."

Winston's Triumphs

Winston and Edward Marsh took the train to Manchester on January 4 to launch his first election campaign as a Liberal. They took a walk through the slum areas of the constituency before campaigning for eight days. When a heckler quoted back at him something Winston had said previously as a Conservative, he replied that he'd said a lot of stupid things when he was in the Conservative Party, but that he'd left it because he had no wish to continue saying stupid things.[4]

Churchill was elected with a majority of 1,241. Six other Conservative seats were overturned and replaced by Liberals. It seemed that Churchill had energized the party, and the Liberals rode to victory on a landslide. His success was compared to his father's and to Benjamin Disraeli's.

Working at the Colonial office with the help of experienced older civil servants and his Secretary Edward Marsh, Churchill's first task was to draw up a constitution for the Transvaal. Ever since the Boers had been devastated by the burning down of their homes and the losses of their wives and children from malnutrition and diseases in the camps of tents, he had advised conciliation instead of punishment, and now it had become his responsibility. He advocated responsible self-government for the Transvaal to replace strict controls. The cabinet accepted his proposals to establish equal rights for Boers and Britons alike.

Equalizing racial issues in a multicultural country like South Africa in 1906 was not easy. For one thing there was the problem of indentured Chinese labor in the mines where working conditions were appalling. The Liberals were committed to allowing them to return home to prevent them from being used as slave labor. Churchill described the situation as an immoral contract. The cabinet agreed to repatriation, even though conditions in China for laborers were little better. That was why they had left to come to South Africa in the first place. The government also disallowed any further recruitment, aiming at eliminating any Chinese labor in future. In Winston's words, it was an "evil inheritance" and a "sordid experiment."

Another controversial issue was the part that Lord Milner had played in the infringements and frictions which had led to the Boer War. The tendency was almost inevitably to find scapegoats and pile on the blame or cover up the causes and culprits. Lord Milner was supposed to be in charge but had overlooked the ill-treatment of labor in the mines to benefit the mine owners, and neglected conditions in the concentration camps where Boer families had been sent after their homes were destroyed. Churchill knew that there would only be injustice without reconciliation, but he could not forget the camps, even though he had left South Africa before they had been set up. Instead, he introduced a general motion in the House condemning the flogging of Chinese coolies.

The Conservatives were out for somebody's blood, preferably Churchill's, whereas he felt they should be satisfied that Milner had no more authority or responsibility. Having supported men who made fortunes out of the mines for years, Milner was now poor and discredited.

Churchill's gift with language seldom went unnoticed. And some members of the Opposition chose to scrutinize what he said and pick on the words he used to discredit Milner while pretending to be conciliatory towards him. It was a Parliamentary gift he had inherited from his father. But they said it was evidence of Winston's mischievousness. One Conservative MP called it "pompous and impertinent," but Winston knew who he was dealing with. Nevertheless, Balfour requested that both of Churchill's amendments be rejected with contempt.

In fact, Winston had deliberately chosen his tactics to suit the situation and avoid what he saw as a possible class cover-up of Milner's misdeeds. He discredited Milner's reputation before he could be whitewashed by the Conservatives. His language was described by one Conservative member as "bitter and empoisoned." But, as Churchill explained to Milner's successor, no other course would have prevented Lord Milner from being censured formally by the Conservatives and then left to continue in his position with his authority intact. Now he was finished. Even so, the conditions of labor in the mines continued to be appalling.

The German Kaiser

Winston took a well-earned holiday at the end of the year. He was invited to live on Baron de Forest's yacht off the coast of Deauville, where he gambled at the casino and won. He took a train from Paris to Cassel's villa in Switzerland. Sir Ernest Cassel was a firm friend of the King. Winston and Sir Ernest climbed the Eggishorn mountain in the Bernese Alps together. He told Jennie that he'd needed a mule to get back home. He went on to Berlin, then visited the Kaiser as his guest in Silesia. Kaiser Wilhelm was King Edward's nephew. And Prime Minister Campbell-Bannerman sent him a message from the King, "to warn you against being too communicative and frank with his nephew." Winston wrote to Jennie that he'd been warned to mind his Ps and Qs—to be candid but say nothing.

The Kaiser had invited Winston to observe the German Army maneuvers. Winston spoke to the German Kaiser for about twenty minutes, during which the Kaiser praised the fighting qualities of the Herero tribe in the German colony of South-West Africa, where the German army was ruthlessly suppressing their revolt. Churchill remarked later to Lord Elgin at the Colonial Office on the impressiveness of the massive force of the German military machine and its terrible firepower. But he added that he thought they had a lot to learn from the British army. Even so numbers, quality, discipline, and organization are four good roads for victory.[5]

He was in Venice for a week before taking a trip through Italy, driving with Lionel Rothschild in his motor car. "At forty miles an hour!" he exclaimed to Jennie. Except for the German Kaiser, three of his hosts for the two-month vacation—Cassel, Rothschild, and de Forest—were Jewish. It revived a remark previously made about his father, that Lord Randolph only had Jewish friends.

Aristocratic English Guest: "What, Lord Randolph, you've not brought your Jewish Friends?"

Lord Randolph: "No, I did not think they would be very amused by the company."[6]

Perhaps it was because both Lord Randolph and his son were such great admirers of Benjamin Disraeli (although Disraeli had been an Anglican).

After returning to London, Churchill sent a polite letter of thanks to the Kaiser for "Your Majesty's kindness."

He was thanked by the Prime Minister, on his return, for his successful work on the South African settlement, which left government in the hands of the Boers. Nevertheless, it was questioned by the Opposition on the grounds that the British Government could not abandon responsibility for the black population. "Our duty," Churchill, wrote to Elgin, "is to insist that the principles of justice and the safeguards of judicial procedure are rigidly, punctiliously and pedantically followed." So clear and insistent was Churchill with every single word, to ensure he could never be misunderstood or doubted, or overruled, that "Elgin asked him to paste them over so that junior officials would not see them," since they sounded like reprimands.[7] Justice was always his central theme.

When a Zulu revolt in Natal was put down, Winston protested to Elgin about the "disgusting butchery of the natives." But there was no doubt who was in charge in the Colonial Office.

As far as rule was concerned, he maintained that there was always a just compromise between capitalism and socialism. As he told a Glasgow audience, he did not aim to restrict energetic competition, but he wished to draw a line below which people would not be allowed to live and labor. He wanted free competition upwards but it must not run downwards.

His Restless Energy

Churchill was now thirty-two, and his experience, his skills, and his interests were wide. He was being considered for a cabinet position. So he must have seemed abstracted when he met the daughter of the Chancellor of the Exchequer at a dinner party. In those days, in a man's world, it was customary for young ladies to be excellent listeners and flatter important men. Having no career or vocation themselves and being inexperienced in the world, they had little of their own conversation except for polite trivialities. Churchill had so far been entirely self-absorbed, but finally caught Violet Asquith's eye and asked her how old she was. She was nineteen. He sighed despairingly at his own advanced age and the passing of time. After chatting with her politely for a while, he said disparagingly of himself, "We are all worms, but I do believe I am a glow-worm."

He was in France by mid-September, where he attended French Army maneuvers. He was far more impressed by them than by the "crude absurdities" of the German "theatrical display" he'd watched with the Kaiser in the previous year. He travelled to Moravia, Italy, Syracuse, and Malta. From there, he went on an Admiralty cruiser to Cyprus, where he encountered demonstrators demanding union with Greece. He telegraphed Elgin to brief him about local conditions, then embarked by cruiser to the Eastern Mediterranean and through the Suez Canal, the Red Sea, and Aden.

He praised the accommodation to Jennie and claimed he was becoming a seasoned mariner. Then he was on to Berbera to study the Somaliland Protectorate at first hand. While at sea, he prepared six long memoranda about things he wanted done, which he sent to the Colonial Office. As the Senior Civil Servant wrote to Elgin, "He is most tiresome to deal with & will I fear give trouble—as his father did—in any position to which he may be called." Churchill loved to stir up individuals and departments to keep them constantly on their toes, instead of being vapid, self-satisfied, and inert.

He wrote again to Jennie when he reached Mombasa, then took a train with his Secretary and entourage through the Kenya Protectorate. "Wherever I wished to stop," he wrote her, "it stopped." From the carriages, he wrote, he could see every animal in the zoo—zebras, lions, rhinos, antelopes, ostriches, giraffes . . . As he told Jennie, "On turning round the corner of a hill & coming into a great wide plain of dry grasses we saw, almost five hundred yards away, a rhinoceros quietly grazing. I cannot describe to you the impression produced on the mind of the grim black silhouette of this mighty beast—a survival of pre-historic times—roaming about the plain as he & his forerunners had done since the dawn of the world. It was like being transported back into the stone age."

Inevitably he couldn't resist writing to the press about what he saw, and sent several accounts from Nairobi to the *Strand Magazine.* He would rewrite them as part of a new book later on, called *My African Journey.* At Jinja, the Nile departs from Lake Victoria to begin its journey to the sea. He could see the potential for a dam at the Ripon Falls to produce electric power. From Jinja, he and Edward Marsh travelled through the Uganda Protectorate on foot and by canoe for three weeks. He celebrated his thirty-third birthday on their journey north, continuing by steamer down the Nile. At the same time, he was writing dissertations and instructions about the standards and wages of the working classes, and how to provide comfort and insurance against unem-ployment and sickness, and old age.

They were at Khartoum on December 23, where his old servant Scrivings fell ill with cholera and died on Christmas Eve. They had all eaten the same food, and worried who would be next. Amid the general gloom, he made all the arrangements for the funeral. Scrivings was given a ceremonial send-off at the cemetery by the band of the Dublin Fusiliers, who played an appropriate funeral march, while Churchill and his party waited uncomfortably for the danger period to pass. But no one else was struck down with cholera. He made arrangements to ensure that Mrs. Scrivings—who had been the Churchills' cook for ten years—would be looked after, and her children.

They boarded a special steamer from Khartoum to Cairo. He worked on the boat at Aswan on the need for a new railway through Uganda, to join the two lakes—Lake Victoria and Lake Albert—the "Victoria and Albert Railway." He discussed the scheme and its cost with the Financial Secretary to the Treasury, to catch the Congo trade.

He continued working on trying to provide security for the working classes, and proposed social reforms, including insurance against accidents and sick-ness at work, and provisions for old age. He knew the German system, which already covered those eventualities. British people too required aid from the State. It was a recurring theme—"competition upwards but not downwards."

He had been out of England on a five-month tour of parts of the British Empire that impressed him so much that he wanted to protect the magnificence and beauty of all he had seen and felt. He had also observed the chaos and squalor and poverty, and cruel violence, in which so many of its inhabitants lived. And it was obvious to him that they needed the help and leadership that Britain could provide in order to develop the best conditions for their wellbeing.

Now back in Britain, he spoke in Manchester on January 22, and was in Birmingham the next day to organize training and apprenticeship programs. They were the "Untrodden Fields in Politics" which he wrote about in *The Nation* on March 7 on social and economic independence for the working man.

In the same month, he met Clementine Hozier again at a dinner party in London. She had been engaged twice since they had last met in 1904. This time he devoted all his attention to her. Jennie's influence was evident in the choice, since his mother knew exactly the type of young woman he needed. Winston was genuine and sincere and had little or no patience with shallow or artificial women. Nor was he looking for an heiress, as many young men did at a time when family fortunes invested in agricultural property were evaporating with industrialization. He didn't need to—he was a high earner.

Everyone who met Clementine remarked on her gorgeous red hair and bright blue eyes. She was intellectually self-possessed, with her own original ideas and opinions, and enjoyed her own company. Her family had no money, so that she was obliged to make her own clothes in a fashionable era, when her frocks sometimes looked crushed for lack of alternatives and domestic servants to iron them.

The type of people whom Winston enjoyed were all originals, like Asquith, Lloyd George, and Admiral Fisher—as had been the great Victorian adventurers and explorers. There was still great originality in the Edwardian and post-Edwardian Eras, but stereotypes had begun to appear with a greater number of young people going to universities, and there was now greater confidence in eating out since Lyons opened its first "Corner House" in Coventry Street, and the Trocadero.[8] It contributed to a new "Café Society," and more people began to imitate each other. Even the idiosyncratic Slade School of Fine

Art was beginning to produce painters who tended to copy each other in a typical Slade School style. The fashion industry also began producing replicas that would eventually lead to popular mass production of clothing.

Not long afterwards, Winston invited Clementine to Blenheim. She hesitated to accept his invitation at first, since she guessed he would propose to her. "She was down to one last cotton frock and the struggle to dress in the manner expected of a lady in Edwardian society daunted her."[9] But she went in the end. Winston invited her to walk in the garden with him. It began to rain, and they sheltered in the ornamental Temple of Diana. He plucked up enough courage to ask her to marry him, and she accepted.

"Everyone felt curiously pleased at this wedding, but it was Jennie, earthy Jennie, who knew by instinct that her son had found the right woman. No money—she brushed that aside—Winston was an earner. No, it was something else which made her rejoice, the sure sense that behind this gentle loveliness lay qualities of steel—absolute integrity and fortitude that would not snap if things went ill for Winston."[10]

Their honeymoon began at Blenheim, where Winston wrote first to Jennie, to express his gratitude for her contributions to his life and wellbeing. "Best of love my dearest Mama. You were a great comfort and support for me at a critical period in my emotional development. We have never been so near together so often in a short time. God bless you. What a relief to have got that ceremony over! And so happily. Your loving son, W."[11]

CHAPTER THIRTEEN

PUBLIC AND PRIVATE LIVES

————

DESPITE THE CONSIDERABLE RANGE OF INTERESTS and activities in Winston's private life—which might have created an impression that he loved showing off—he was more of an introvert than an extravert; shy or seriously self-absorbed at the dinner table, resisting making a spectacle of his clumsy dancing at balls, and confiding in only very few friends. His skills with the written word and his panache with his speeches in Parliament had serious purposes in mind. And he could be obsessively single-minded in order to achieve those purposes. Why should he not feel pleased with himself when he did? Nevertheless, when news of his engagement leaked out to the public on August 15, Clementine began to have nervous, even anxious, second thoughts, because he was such a public celebrity.

Forty-eight hours later, he made a major speech at Swansea on Anglo-German relations, in which he sought to enlighten individuals and news media, "who try to spread the belief in this country that war between Great Britain and Germany is inevitable." There was no collision of primary interests—although some people may have been nervous at the perceived buildup of the German Navy or Britain's Fleet. The Naval policy of any nation would naturally be based on reasonable measures for its defense, including modernization of its technologies. "Why," he exclaimed, Germany is among our very best customers!"

As for people who argued that Britain and Germany were rivals and a danger to each other, he speculated that it was probably only about 15,000 mischief-makers, "snappers and snarlers" in both countries who raised the danger of war, and who wanted it. Are we all sheep? Working-class people all over the world have a common interest in peace.

Meanwhile, he and his fiancée had arranged to marry in mid-September. But Clementine hesitated. She quailed at the competition of public life with their private life. It "laid constant claim to both his time and interest."[1] She considered herself "stupid and clumsy in that relation," even "naturally self-reliant and self-contained." It required the warmth of his reassurance and his own confidence to sweep away her doubts. And her family had also reminded her of her two previous broken engagements—a third would create an impression that she was undependable.

Just before their wedding, he was asked to arbitrate for the electrical workers' trade union, and agreed to do so. They were married three days later at St. Margaret's, Westminster, in the same parish as the House of Commons. She was now twenty-three. Lloyd George was one of the witnesses who signed the register. He was Chancellor of the Exchequer.

"Clemmie very happy and beautiful," he wrote to Jennie from Blenheim on the first day of their honeymoon. He had rented a house on Bolton Street, and went with his bride from there to Lake Maggiore and then on to Venice." We only loitered and loved," he remarked to Jennie—"a good and serious occupation for which the histories furnish respectable precedents."

Before returning to Britain, he introduced his new wife to Baron de Forest in Moravia, and then to his constituents in Dundee, to whom he spoke of government-financed pensions for the over-seventies, in his fight against the humiliations and deprivations of the poor. His next step would be to plan an unemployment insurance scheme to which the State would contribute.

It was at this point, in 1909, that the First Lord of the Admiralty, Reginald McKenna, pressed the cabinet to increase the size of the British Fleet by building six new dreadnought-class battleships, when Winston and Lloyd George wanted the money for social reforms instead. And the Conservative opposition upped the number of battleships to eight, making them even more hard-pressed to reconsider the expenditure. The controversy over one or the other brought derisive laughter from the Conservatives: What were Churchill's reasons for preferring social reform? "Of course," they jeered, "it cannot be from conviction or principle. The very idea of his having either is enough to make one laugh."

Winston was anxious to retain naval supremacy, but felt certain that it could be achieved just as well with only four extra battleships in that financial year. On the other hand, construction prospects would be considerable for as many as three million workers in Britain's ship-building and engineering industries. "Big Navy" was in conflict for funds with Churchill's unemployment insurance scheme. Prime Minister Asquith came out in support of a compromise with six new battleships but, after four months to think about it again, agreed to only four, on condition of another four being built in 1910.

Even so, the conflict between protecting the British Isles from possible attack and providing unemployment insurance for the working-classes gave the opposition an opportunity to undermine him and cast doubts on his character. Then his insurance scheme was set back by Asquith. It caused Churchill to complain at the Birmingham Liberal Club that, while the vanguard of the British people enjoyed all the privileges of the age, our rearguard struggles in conditions which are barbaric. He called for humanity and justice. And, in a single new Bill, he managed to establish a principle of minimum wages for low-paid employees, and a "right" for tea-breaks and breaks for meals. Then, on May 19, he introduced a Labor Exchange Bill, which was something entirely new.

Private Lives

While explaining the new Bills to the public, he supervised preparations to move in to their new London home at Eccleston Square. Clementine was expecting their first child. Letters he had formerly sent to Jennie went instead to her at Blenheim; "The marble basin has arrived . . . The window is up . . . All the bookcases are in position . . . The big room is papered . . . the bathroom well advanced."

As well as waging war on poverty, Winston held the rank of Major in the Queen's Own Oxfordshire Hussars and took part in annual military camps of the Oxfordshire Yeomanry. But he waved it aside when Clementine gave birth to a daughter whom they named Diana, on July 11. And he found peace and quiet for his wife while involved again in industrial arbitration when a strike threatened to paralyze the coal industry. Sir Edward Grey wrote to thank him for his firmness in averting a strike. Congratulations from Asquith and the King followed.

But with opposition by the House of Lords to Lloyd George's budget, he had no time for any accolades to enlarge his ego; he was on to another

matter of even greater importance: that August he had a lengthy talk with
Count Metternich, the German ambassador in London, about the substantial
increase in Germany's naval construction program.

The following month, Clementine was still recovering from the birth in
Southwater, while he was warning of the dangers of class warfare if the House
of Lords voted against the budget, which had already passed with a majority in
the House of Commons. It was, he cautioned, a clear case of the rich getting
richer and the poor getting poorer.

Some of the words he used angered the King, causing his private secretary
to write a protest to *The Times*—a situation without precedent. They must
both have gone mad, Winston remarked, before attending Army maneuvers
in Leicester. To encourage Clementine in her misery, he wrote to her on the
train, "Dear Clemmie, do try to gather your strength." She would have to
play her part if there was an election in the autumn. But he understood the
strain that his continual activities were placing on her. And he imagined his
private conversations must be awfully dull for her, since she wasn't also in the
political trade.

Travelling in his cousin's motor car with Edward Marsh, they went to observe
German army maneuvers. He visited the Franco-Prussian War battlefield at
Metz. It seemed to him not so long ago that the French had been defeated in
1870. There were the bodies of each individual soldier buried exactly where he
fell, dotted in hundreds instead of being lined up like regiments. They drove
across the Vosges Mountains to Strasbourg in Alsace, where the German army
had annexed territory from France at Alsace-Lorraine. He wrote to Clementine
on their first anniversary. The bells of the old city, he said, had reminded him
of the chimes which had saluted their wedding at St Margaret's.

"A year has gone by," he wrote. He expressed the thought that she had
brought him the light of happiness. His thoughts dwelt on their baby daughter, and he wondered what she would grow into. He wished a bright star to
shine for her.

After more driving through Germany, they reached Würtzburg, where the
German army maneuvers were to take place the following day—five Army
Corps and three cavalry divisions in action. He wrote to Clementine afterwards that he had been loaned a very good horse from the Emperor's stable
to ride around on. He and the Kaiser chatted with good humor about the

Socialists. "As to the German Army," he remarked, "it is a terrible engine. It marches sometimes thirty-five miles in a day." The difference between the imperialists and the Socialists in Germany represented two entirely different populations—nothing unites them. He had only another two minute talk with the Kaiser on the final day of maneuvers. "He was very friendly—"My dear Winston" & so on." He made friends with the Turkish representative—a man named Enver Pasha.

While Winston was abroad, Asquith took Clementine to a political meeting in Birmingham. "There's Mrs. Churchill!" And they all cheered.

Winston drove to the battlefield at Blenheim, where his ancestor had beaten the French in 1704. Only a few days later he was speaking to his constituents in Dundee. Then he was focused on compiling a book of some of his speeches, called *Liberalism and Social Problems,* which was published a month later—to be followed by another one called *The Public's Rights.* On November 3, he made some notes for the cabinet on German naval intentions, which pointed out that the only limit on its expansion was money, and predicted a severe financial crisis in Germany as a consequence. He expected internal tensions to arise out of it.

Soon afterwards he was severely shaken by an unexpected incident at Bristol station, where he'd arrived with Clementine. He was attacked by a suffragette named Theresa Garnett who tried to strike him in the face with a whip. When he attempted to protect himself by grabbing both her wrists, she almost pushed him off the platform, while Clementine prevented him from toppling onto the line by hanging on to his coat.

Nevertheless, he made a strong speech against the motion of the House of Lords, who rejected the Liberal budget. His adversary was Lord Milner, who claimed it was the duty of the Lords to vote against it. They did so by 350 votes to 75. And a general election was called. The Liberal war-cry was "The peers versus the people."

The General Election

Winston led the Liberal Campaign against the House of Lords in the General Election. He described them as a played-out feudal arrangement, anachronistic and obsolete, which now required a smashing blow from the electors to finish it off. Asquith was most complimentary about his choice of words and phrases and his rhetorical skills. By the end of all the noise and fury, the Liberals had retained their political power, and Churchill kept his seat in Dundee with the same majority he had before. When the election results were announced, he was appointed Home Secretary. His new position gave him the responsibilities for the police, the prisons, and their prisoners. Only Sir Robert Peel, the founder of Britain's police force, had held the office when as young as Winston.

What always challenged him was breaking new ground, giving the responsibilities deeper thought than hitherto, and becoming master of its territory, before moving on to bigger and more interesting challenges. Right from the beginning he developed a program of prison reform. First off, he separated criminals from political prisoners, which improved conditions for any suffragettes who had been arrested for disturbing the peace. He decriminalized a number of lesser offenses and separated juvenile delinquents from hardened repeat criminals, reducing the number of prisoners.

He advocated regular books from the libraries for prisoners, lectures, and entertainment. In each situation he viewed prison from the perspective of the inmate rather than that of a vengeful society. Revenge was the way of the leading criminologist Hans Gross in Austria. Gross stereotyped anyone who was different as a potential criminal who had to be crushed *before* he set out to destroy the State. Winston made special concessions for the aged and feebleminded prisoners, whereas all had been treated the same way before. He had the evidence for his reforms in past statistics, which showed that out of every four discharged convicts in 1903 and 1905, three were back in penal servitude.

He had hoped, on taking his new position, that he could recommend reprieves for some about to be hanged for committing murder. But after studying existing cases who had been sentenced to the death penalty, he found he was unable to recommend reprieving any of them. Forty years later, he told friends that having power over life and death had been very distressing.

Winston was the main speaker when proposals to curb the power of the House of Lords were introduced in the Commons. The point he made was that they had enjoyed all the privileges of a well-ordered society but, when it came to voting responsibly, they allowed themselves to be dictated to and told what to vote for and against.

When he left England for a two-month vacation with Clementine on Baron de Forest's yacht, he found several pouches of work from the home office waiting for his attention at Athens. They had been sent by his personal secretary, Edward Marsh. He plunged into the work in his usual obsessive and compulsive manner.

He was provided with security against brigands at the port of Smyrna in Turkey. Viewing the countryside from the front of the engine, he saw the landscape as a world of rising and ruined civilizations in which the individual was almost irrelevant. It was that, and his studies of the worthless lives that so many poor people lived, which influenced his objective and philosophical worldview of history.

Public Life

That thought may still have been at the forefront of his mind after he returned to Britain to face the eruption of a coal strike in the mines of the Rhondda Valley. There seemed to be only minor incidents of window-breaking in two of the pits, but the chief constable had appealed to the army for four hundred soldiers, despite already having 1,400 county police at his disposal. When Churchill was informed they were on their way, he phoned the chief constable for information before deciding to halt the infantry. He also stopped the cavalry at Cardiff. Instead, Winston ordered only two hundred constables and seventy mounted police to be sent to South Wales. As he informed the King afterwards, the local police had dealt with the problem before the reserves even arrived. But what was potentially incendiary was the ever-present fear of the upper classes of a possible revolution, inspired by Marxist propaganda.

Strikers moved to a nearby village named Tonypandy and deliberately wrecked several shops, provoking another appeal from the chief constable for troops. Winston allowed him only a squadron of cavalry in reserve, to be kept out of the way if not needed and avoid provoking the miners to more vandalism. Then on November 8, he sent the strikers a conciliatory message. He was violently attacked for it in *The Times* and other Conservative newspapers, according to which he should have sent in troops to protect private property.

Private property was still considered more important to protect than the public, since it was owned by the middle and upper classes. It was something that Charles Dickens had continually depicted in his novels. And, although this was no longer Victorian England, the working classes still had no vote. It made them almost invisible to politicians, whereas Winston was attempting to establish the value of the individual above the value of property. Only the more intelligent and thoughtful *Manchester Guardian* defended Churchill's actions. The strikers accepted his offer of a parley. But riots broke out again in Tonypandy ten days afterwards. "The police were quite strong enough," Winston reported to the King. But "the owners are very unreasonable as well as the men."

He may have felt embattled between strikes in the Welsh coal mines and suffragettes demonstrating at 10 Downing Street in London, who battled for women's rights to vote. Prime Minister Asquith had to be hurriedly bundled into a taxi for his protection, and another minister was badly hurt in their attacks. Churchill watched the police trying to cope as they attempted to remove Mrs. Cobden-Sanderson. Four days later, he was repeatedly interrupted by a male supporter of the suffragettes, Hugh Franklin, who followed him to his train afterwards and attacked Winston with a riding whip.

Winston was in favor of women having the vote, but the suffragettes were wrongly convinced he was their opponent. And whatever he might try to do for them, he knew their movement was so unpopular with the public that no Bill would be passed in their favor. Their cause had gone beyond the boundaries of reason into such bizarre extremism that they had already burnt down over a hundred private houses, and the Prime Minister's wife admitted she was sick with fear of them. Like the Irish, their cause had become so inflamed that now they would stop at nothing until they destroyed their own case out of lack of proportion. Most people were afraid to take sides—except for extremists.

Meanwhile, the Liberal Party was still in power and Winston Churchill was thirty-six. All he could see before him as priorities now were discussions with the Conservatives about Ireland, the Poor Law, boy labor, insurance, and modernizing the navy.

It was the last item he was working on at home when a messenger arrived from the Home Office in haste with an urgent message. There had been a burglary in the East End by three armed men. That fact alone was unusual, since guns were rarely seen or even spoken of in London or any of Britain's industrial cities. Consequently, police constables were not issued regular firearms. All they had to protect citizens and themselves was a wooden truncheon. The Metropolitan Police preferred to keep it that way rather than imitate New York or Chicago where shootouts between gangsters and police had become almost commonplace.

Six policemen had attempted to arrest the thieves and another individual known as "Peter the Painter," who was a Russian anarchist. The burglars had shot and killed three of the policemen. They had been followed to a house in Sidney Street. The men were armed with Mausers, which had a greater range than revolvers issued to the Metropolitan Police for emergencies. As a consequence, a senior police officer had summoned twenty Scots Guards armed with rifles from the Tower of London. The criminals were now shooting from the house and had killed another policeman.

Churchill left for the Home Office to seek more information and advice at 11:15 a.m. He considered it his duty to see for himself what was going on. He found an unusual scene for London, with gunshots from every window and bullets striking brick walls. Police and soldiers were armed with rifles.

He went round the back of the premises to make sure that none of the criminals was managing to escape from the rear of the building. And when the fire brigade arrived, he prevented any firemen going in, in case they were shot. As a result, the house was burnt down by a fire started by the anarchists, and some died in the blaze—one shot, the other suffocated by smoke. Peter the Painter was never found. And the fire burnt itself out.

Once again he was attacked by the Conservatives in the house and by the Conservative press for being too prominent: gentlemen were supposed to avoid being featured in the newspapers. But Churchill knew from Britain's Intelligence Service that it was more likely a terrorist attack connected with the imperial Russian secret police, the Okhrana, that kept a watchful eye on Russian émigré circles in London.

The Agadir Crisis

Clementine was pregnant again. And the King offered her a ticket to his own box for the coronation in Westminster Abbey, so that she could sit privately and in comfort. The coronation of King George the Fifth took place on June 22. Winston and Clementine rode together in the procession. When their son was born they named him Randolph, after Winston's father.

Four days later, he was met by renewed hostility from the House of Commons. He continued to keep up a brave and positive front in public, but Winston was prey to dark moods of depression, which he named his "black dog." It was partly because he was a high achiever and partly because of the continued hostility against him from the upper classes. He had heard only recently of a doctor in Vienna who was developing a reputation of sorts for getting rid of that kind of thing. Fortunately, although his work had been incessant, his recent moodiness seemed to have vanished at the thought of his darling Clementine.

It was during the summer of 1911 that a crisis erupted in North Africa that threatened to develop into war. A German gunboat called the *Panther* was sent to a port in Morocco called Agadir. Although it was part of France's sphere of influence, under an Anglo-French agreement of 1904, France asked Britain to send a gunboat as a challenge to the unacceptable German action.

"This would be a serious step," Winston wrote to Clementine from the Home Office. According to tradition, Britain would have to be prepared to go to any lengths necessary.

He wrote to Lloyd George that Germany had a minor claim that could be dealt with if amicably stated, subject to Britain being safeguarded. He advised that the subject should be kept in the open. Lloyd George warned Germany openly. But Germany chose to denounce his words as "a warning bordering on menace."

Churchill now issued a warrant to Britain's Secret Service for the inspection of correspondence. It meant that anyone suspected of receiving instructions from Germany had their letters opened. After which Churchill was able to inform Grey that "we are the subject of a minute and scientific study by the German naval and military authorities, and that no other nation in the world pays us such attention."

Two days later he informed the King that he had been impressed in the commons by the widespread agreement among MPs that Germany must be prevented from having her way by the threat of force.

"It seems," he wrote later to Clementine, that, "the bully is climbing down, & it looks as if all will come out smooth and triumphant." Four days later, he told her that the Germans were going to settle with the French on a friendly basis. Nevertheless, he addressed a meeting of the Committee of Imperial Defense on August 23, by outlining the dangers facing France if Germany were to launch a military attack on French Morocco, and the part Britain would have to play.

The German army, he predicted, would break through the line of the River Meuse on the twentieth day of war, and the French army would fall back towards Paris. The odds seemed high against anything other. The momentum of the German advance would weaken the more it was extended. The Russian army would begin to exert pressure on the Eastern Front from the thirtieth day. The British army would be in place in Flanders by then. By the fiftieth day, German forces in the West "should be extended at full strain both internally and on her war fronts." It would become more severe each day and ultimately overwhelming without victory. Then, "opportunities for the decisive trial of strength may occur."

As the Agadir negotiations continued on August 30, Winston suggested to Grey that if they failed, they should propose a triple alliance of Britain, France, and Russia in order to safeguard the independence of Belgium, Holland, and Denmark. And Belgium should be told that, if her neutrality was violated, we were prepared to come to her aid. Then we must take whatever military steps were required, including taking our main fleet to its war station in to the north of Scotland. He emphasized, "Our interests are European, not Moroccan."

Churchill received a letter marked "Secret: destroy" on September 2. It was from the Secretary of the Committee of Imperial Defense, Sir Charles Ottley. It provided details of the immediate concentration of the German High Sea Fleet at Kiel. He sent the letter to Lloyd George with his comments. After studying the Admiralty's North Sea dispositions again, Winston found himself to be deeply concerned. On September 13, he asked Asquith, "Are you sure that the ships we have at Cromarty are strong enough to defeat the whole German High Sea Fleet? If not, they should be reinforced without delay."

Churchill was particularly annoyed at the Admiralty's complacency. He asked Asquith, "Are you sure that the Admiralty realise the serious situation of Europe? I am told they are nearly all on leave at the present time." One lapse, he knew, as stupid as that revealed at their previous meeting, "& it will be the defense of England rather than that of France which will engage us."

He was now determined to replace Admiral McKenna at the Admiralty and eager to create a naval war staff to plan for a possible war. The matter of who should become First Sea Lord was already being discussed when Asquith wrote to the leader of the House of Lords, Lord Crewe, that he was satisfied Churchill was the right person. Five weeks prior to Churchill's thirty-seventh birthday, Parliament reassembled on October 24, 1911, when it was announced that Winston Churchill would be First Lord of the Admiralty.

Chapter Fourteen

THE COMING WAR

———

Only after it was officially announced that he was First Lord of the Admiralty did Winston realize the full impact of the huge responsibility he had agreed to undertake. It was the challenge of defending the British Isles from attack by enemies and preventing any possibility of blockades that might result in starvation for its population. And to undertake either of them meant ensuring that Britain had enough of the types of battleships needed for the tasks, the armor, the ammunition, and personnel with all the necessary skills. Then there was the task of acquiring enough money to keep the Navy modernized, managed, and maintained.

Britain had effectively ruled the waves ever since it great hero Horatio Nelson's victories against Napoleon's forces at the Battle of the Nile in Egypt and the Battle of Trafalgar. What gave Winston confidence was that funding for the Fleet had so far been generous, since Britain was proud of its Royal Navy, and it had sufficient battleships to protect the British Empire, in spite of the fact that it was spread all over the world.

Now he had to draw up an analysis of the situation for the cabinet, to recommend establishing a naval war staff to prepare for war, since the Royal Navy was the sole guarantee of preserving the territory and economy of the State. His first principle was to recognize what dangers he anticipated. His second was the best means to meet those challenges, based on past events in history when Britain had been in danger from attacks. His third principle was how to use the war material he possessed in the most effective ways.

Churchill would spend the next two and a half years developing the navy and preparing it to prevent war if possible, and to win the war if not. He visited all major naval installations and the dockyards, learning important aspects of gunnery at sea, and naval strategies and battle tactics. He carefully studied new developments in Germany's naval construction. And he particularly focused on improving morale in the British Navy.

Former British Prime Minister Balfour wrote to congratulate him on his new position, for which he saw the benefits of a new look and attitude and new skills to energize the British Navy. Within only two weeks of taking office, Winston wrote to Prime Minister Asquith on November 5, "I have come across one disconcerting fact: there is a shortage of 120 twenty-one-inch torpedoes, meaning that thirty of our best destroyers would have to go to sea without reserves of any kind other than the two they carry." It would take until April or May at the very earliest to fill the gap, so that all reserves of ammunitions and torpedoes would be available.[1]

His office and home for the next two and a half years would be on board the Admiralty yacht, the *Enchantress,* with its staff of nearly two hundred officers and ratings. He left Cowes to inspect the dockyards and the submarine depot at Portsmouth on his first tour of inspection. Three days later he joined other naval vessels escorting King George and Queen Mary on their visit to India for the Durbar in Delhi. It was a reminder that the long sunny relaxed Edwardian era was over, and formality and public rituals had returned.

Winston's third voyage began on November 17 when he launched the new battleship, the *Centurion,* at Devonport. His fourth voyage was to inspect the torpedo boat destroyer, the *Falcon.* He made a tour of inspection of Portsmouth Royal Naval Barracks on December 9. It was his fifth such trip in less than six weeks, and it included the Royal Navy submarine school.

He was conscious also of a need for air superiority, and always drawn to the possible uses of new technologies, as well as the continued need for naval dominance. War in the air was the most recent branch of the science of war. He had to establish principles and conditions for a naval air service, which he considered to be the most dangerous profession for a young Englishman. He wanted young and capable airmen. Whereas the army used its pilots in defensive ways, like reconnaissance, while avoiding air battles whenever possible, he envisaged naval aircraft would be used more to attack the enemy with machine-guns and drop bombs on their installations. It became part of the training of the Royal Naval Air Service.

Preparations for war also presented opportunities to develop friendships across party lines, in the hope that purely political party interests would no longer take precedence over honesty and common sense, nor create irrational biases. One friendship he attempted to make across political lines was by writing to the newly elected leader of the Conservative Party, Andrew Bonar Law. It required tact, since politics were still as lethal as conflicting religions in which faith in the group was all that mattered in siding with them.

Sir John Fisher, a former Admiral of the Fleet, visited him and wrote him letters of encouragement. Winston replied eagerly and established a friendly relationship with him, too. Fisher planted in his mind the concept of a Fast Division of warships and using oil fuel instead of coal. He encouraged him to develop fifteen-inch guns for battleships. Fisher had always been an outspoken and controversial figure. He was now seventy, while Winston was little more than half his age. Some people were shocked at Winston's instant friendship with him, but he found Fisher's enthusiasm and zeal for naval science and technology refreshing and rewarding. He was, after all, a naval officer of considerable experience. Churchill outfitted the Royal Navy with new guns, as Fisher suggested.

The Arms Race

One "sinister and disquieting fact" that concerned him as the German navy grew rapidly by the end of 1911 was their simultaneous funding which further enlarged the already powerful German army. As Winston pointed out, it was a bureaucratic military machine supported by a "powerful Junker landlord class." He put the idea about that, if Germany ceased its arms buildup, Britain would follow suit, "not only by words and sentiments, but by action."

He hoped that Asquith's firm response to the Agadir Crisis, and Lloyd George's strong speech about it in the Mansion House, had succeeded in stalling an outbreak of war. He viewed postponement as important, since he did not believe in the inevitability of war. And he still hoped for a more democratic approach from Germany in the meantime. But that country was still firmly divided between the Junker landlords and the people. Meanwhile, he thought that Russia's swift recovery after its defeat in Manchuria by Japan was "a great corrective" to German aggression. He shared those thoughts with his friend, Sir Ernest Cassel, who was on his way to meet the Kaiser in Germany. If Germany would slacken its arms buildup, he said, it would be met with goodwill from England.

He wrote to Fisher three days later to inform him that flights of airplanes would shortly be attached to naval battle squadrons on a regular basis, and that the number of British submarines under construction had already begun to increase. Nevertheless, some Conservatives attacked him for not doing enough. They wanted to "show the flag." He warned them not to encourage a further arms race, and reminded them of Napoleon's principle of concentrating superior force in decisive war zones, rather than weakening the Navy by dispersing its strength all over the place just to make a show.

When Sir Ernest returned from his visit to the Kaiser in Berlin, he arranged a breakfast meeting with Winston and Lloyd George, and informed them that "a major German naval expansion was imminent."[2] The Kaiser had speeded up a six-year construction program, instead of the twelve new battleships which had been previously planned. Churchill advised Grey on the same day that Britain should make a firm response and invite Germany to slow down their Naval schedule to twelve years instead of six, so that "friendly relations would ensue," and allow Britain to slow down, too.

Cassel had obtained a copy of the new German Naval Law from the Kaiser before it was published. It revealed that the Kiel Canal between the Baltic and the North Sea was to be deepened to allow bigger battleships through by 1915. It would allow twenty-five German battleships to be sent swiftly to the North Sea and endanger Britain whenever Germany chose to commence hostilities. That innovation alone would require the Royal Navy to have at least forty battleships available for protection within twenty-four hours which, of course, they did not possess.

He circulated the new German Navy Law to the cabinet on February 14, from which it was clearly evident that Britain's naval construction now needed a substantial boost, since Germany's new plan was to build twenty-five new battleships, twelve battle cruisers, eighteen extra small cruisers, and more than fifty submarines. Fifteen thousand more officers and men would be added to their present 86,500. By April 1914, Germany would be in possession of the biggest navy with the most modern battleships and cruisers in the world. And, as Churchill pointed out, they would be maintained on a permanent war footing.

When asked for his opinion, he informed the house on March 18 that Britain would have to build two battleships for every German one.

He continued to propose slowing down German production by mutual agreement, in order to postpone war for another year, in the hope that if money were circulated to German consumers instead, a war might be postponed still further. There seemed to be a fatalism about the buildup of German war potential which he did not share—as if they were prepared to take one huge risk for the sake of demonstrating that they could dominate Europe.

To Clementine, he wrote, "We shall be much stronger in a year." And he waited for the Kaiser to agree to his offer of a "Naval Holiday" from construction. In the meantime, he continued his inspections of the naval dockyards at Portland, and wrote to Clementine that he had discovered more waste of money in refitting and repairing ships unnecessarily, just to provide work. "I wish I had nine lives like a cat," he told her. Then he would have more time to be even more thorough. But he praised the Admiralty men under his command and considered himself fortunate to have them.

Winston noted that the Kaiser had still not published Germany's new naval program. He wrote Cassel a letter intended for the Kaiser to see. It emphasized all the problems of a land war that Germany would have to face in Europe, instead of focusing on its naval buildup. Meanwhile, the king formally inspected the Fleet at Weymouth on May 9 and 10, where a demonstration showed airplanes detecting submarines below the water and other planes dropping bombs on targets. Newspaper reports now revealed that the press had come to think of Winston as a naval man rather than as a politician.

But his hopes of postponing war were shattered when the Kaiser dismissed his idea of a "Naval Holiday" out of hand and had the new German Naval Law passed in the Reichstag on May 21. Now Churchill directed all his time and energy to preparing the Royal Navy for the hazards of war with Germany. According to the *Daily Express*, "He is here, there, and everywhere."

Now that the German navy laws were known to the public, Churchill felt able to seek additional Navy Estimates from Parliament by explaining the need for more warships to secure the British Isles at sea.

On August 1, he was able to inform Clementine—who had been consistently unwell—that he would see her on Sunday, when perhaps they might find a nice sandy beach where he could build fortresses in the sand. "You might explore and report," he added.

During the remainder of the month and throughout September, he sailed around naval stations in Britain and watched firing practice and tactical exercises, inspected dockyards, observed new launchings, armaments workshops, shore installations, and studied all the latest technical improvements, including torpedo technology. He also did his best to encourage the French Ministry of Marine to strengthen France's naval power, in order to focus Britain's naval activities on the North Sea. And he chose not to get involved in an alliance with the French, or anyone else, that might limit Britain's freedom to stand alone against German aggression.

He now spent his time and imagination on making naval personnel more comfortable and contented in their jobs and leisure time, by increasing the pay of lower ranks and improving recreation facilities on shore. He allocated funding for a football field in Harwich, a canteen and a reading room, billiard tables and bowling alleys, and ensured that sailors had places to stay overnight when ashore. But he had continual battles for funds with the Chancellor of the Exchequer over increasing sailors' pay, since Lloyd George protested at squandering money. Then, soon afterwards, the need for even more money arose.

While preparing the Navy Estimates for 1913–14, Winston's analysis of improvements in the German navy showed that a new German battle cruiser had superior armor which had to be matched in the constant struggle to compete with and overcome enhanced specifications; where new enemy armor required better shells to penetrate it, and better enemy shells or bullets required better armor to resist them. He also noticed that Austria-Hungary planned to build three extra battleships. Since they would certainly ally themselves with Germany, it would mean having to take further measures to compete for naval superiority.[3]

Pressures of work soon affected Winston's private life, when he was obliged to cancel some of his plans to be with Clementine. He had to keep offering apologies and providing explanations for his absences. One situation that kept them apart was his flying lessons at Eastchurch naval station and aerodrome on the Isle of Sheppey in the Thames Estuary. Flying was a young man's game, full of thrills and prone to fatal accidents in the fragile aircraft with simple instruments that didn't always work as they should. He would soon be forty in

1913. But the pilots were excited that the First Lord would want to be trained by them on how to fly dangerous airplanes. And his enthusiasm was as keen as theirs.

His cousin wrote anxiously to him, "Really, I consider that you owe it to your wife, family and friends to desist." But Winston continued, although he knew it was a dangerous pastime. Sometimes he went up ten times a day, and spent weekends at Sheerness to do so.[4]

Clementine was in London, doing what was necessary to move from their Eccleston Square home to the official residence at Admiralty House in Whitehall, where the rooms were more spacious and looked out over the Horse Guards Parade or St. james Park. And she joined him whenever possible on HMS *Enchantress*. He would always write to her soon after she left, to say how much he already missed her. Despite her anxiety at his flying, he continued it at Eastchurch and also at Hendon Aerodrome.

But they did manage to escape for a long holiday that summer. They were joined by Asquith and his wife and daughter. They took a train to Venice, then joined the *Enchantress* to sail on her through the Adriatic to the Mediterranean, where they visited Malta, Sicily, and Corsica. He discussed the defense of the Mediterranean with General Kitchener in Malta, but the two of them were still wary of each other.

Back in Britain, Winston tried again to make sense out of the Irish problem and Home Rule, which never satisfied anyone. He did his best to persuade the Ulstermen to sweep their problems away and out of their lives and into history. He discussed the situations afterwards at Balmoral with the King and Bonar Law. He had always respected British common sense, but this was one case where it would not prevail against so many emotional issues that were alternately bottled up or flaunted, and argued about from both directions; north and south, Protestant and Catholic, and the previous humiliation from one side set against a new one from the other. But he continued his efforts for a more peaceful Ireland, which was now even more important than before because of the looming dangers of war in which Britain could so easily be stabbed in the back by enemies in Ireland.

The Irish problem seemed insoluble, and he was convinced that, left to their own devices, there would be civil war with the north and south tearing each other apart to the last man, woman, and child. Each side would stop at nothing just to have its own way. Moreover, its abrasiveness was causing divisions in England, where some families refused to talk to each other.

In order to reduce naval costs for the traditional Grand Manoeuvres of 1914, and also to test Royal Navy strength, he organized a less costly but fully mobilized maneuver of the Third Fleet in the North Sea. As he explained to Prince Louis of Battenberg—a Lord of the Admiralty—it was an opportunity to rehearse naval actions there, instead of leaving things to chance in the event of hostilities with the German Navy.

Meanwhile, he continued his flying lessons in the autumn, in order to run up the necessary hours required for a flying license. He talked as much as possible with the airmen about the possibilities of aerial combat and bombing, and the training needed for it. He flew in an airship from Sheerness over the Medway and Chatham in October. "They let me steer for a whole hour myself," he wrote to Clementine. He also flew in a seaplane. Despite the relatively primitive aircraft, he believed absolutely in the future of aviation, and considered possibilities for air supremacy over any enemies.

Jennie

Although Jennie had been largely instrumental in arranging Winston's marriage, she had hoped to see more of him after their wedding, not less—it seemed to be a natural mark of possessiveness in mothers. But now she had a different problem to contend with: it was George, whom she had now finally lost to the celebrated actress Mrs. Patrick Campbell, ever since Jennie's own play had been tried out for a fortnight at the Haymarket Theatre and Mrs. Pat had been her leading lady.

> My dear George, Mr. Wheeler brought me your message. The d.n. will be made absolute on Monday and I understand that you are going to be married on Tues. You need not fear what I may say for I shall not willingly speak of you. And we are not likely ever to meet. This is the *real* parting of the ways. But for the sake of some of the happy days we had together—should you ever be in trouble and wanted to knock at my door it would not be shut to you. I am returning you my engagement and wedding rings—I say goodbye—a long, long goodbye. Jennie.

American Jennie Jerome from Brooklyn, New York in 1889, now Lady Randolph Churchill, with her two boys, Jack on the left, and Winston Churchill on the right.

War Correspondent for the *Morning Post* and Second-Lieutenant in the regular British Army in 1899, Winston Churchill arrives in Durban to cheering crowds after escaping from a Boer prison camp in the capital city of Pretoria, South Africa, in the Anglo-Boer War, at the age of twenty-five. Published in The Black and White Budget.

The Liberal-minded, red-headed Clementine Hozier in 1915 after she married Winston Churchill. Library of Congress.

Lord Randolph Churchill, British politician and Winston Churchill's father, has been described variously as brilliant, lovable, eccentric, nasty, and insane.

The young Winston Churchill in office as First Lord of the Admiralty in 1911. UK Government.

Blenheim Palace near Woodstock, Oxfordshire, the family home of the Dukes of Marlborough, where Winston Churchill was born and where he proposed to Clementine Hozier and she agreed to become his wife.

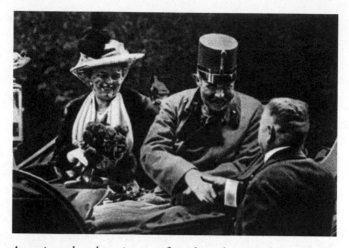

Assassinated only minutes after this photograph was taken on June 28, 1914. The official visit to Sarajevo of Austrian Archduke Franz Ferdinand (heir to the throne of the Austro-Hungarian Empire) and his wife Sophie. Their murders triggered the First World War.

Nineteen-year-old assassin Gavrilo Princip, who murdered the Austrian Archduke and his wife and caused two world wars and the deaths of millions.

The old Emperor Franz Joseph of the Austro-Hungarian Empire—a Habsburg family descendent of the Frankish Emperor Charlemagne. The victim of the assassination in Bosnia in 1914 was his heir to the dual throne. (This portrait taken about 1905.) Library of Congress.

German Kaiser Wilhelm II in one of his favorite postures for a picture postcard in 1905.

Tsar Nicholas II of Russia, on left, with his cousin, England's King George V, in Berlin, 1913. Photographer: Ernst Sandau.

Winston—still a reserve army officer in 1906—was invited by the German Kaiser to watch the annual autumn maneuvers of his Prussian army near Breslau, Silesia (Wroclaw, Poland). Photo by Imperial Court Photographer: S. Riegel.

General Herbert Lord Kitchener, national hero of the Battle of Omdurman in 1898, and commander in chief of the British Army during the South African War, was Chief of Staff in 1914.

Iconic 1914 recruitment poster for the British Army shows Kitchener's popularity. Library of Congress.

Field Marshal Sir John French, Commander in Chief of the British Expeditionary Forces on the Western Front. Library of Congress.

Field Marshal Sir Douglas Haig. Commander in Chief of British troops on the Western Front, who replaced French. (Taken after the First World War in Newfoundland in 1924.) Photo: S. H. Carsons and Sons.

British Prime Minister, the Right Honorable Sir Herbert Asquith, who was in admiring awe of Churchill and appointed him President of the Board of Trade, Home Secretary, and First Lord of the Admiralty. Library of Congress.

Prime Minister Asquith's twenty-one-year-old daughter Violet was fascinated with politics and obsessively in love with Winston Churchill. (Shown here much later on in 1915 when she was Helen Violet Bonham Carter, Baroness Asquith of Yarnbury.) Michael and Eleanor Brock: H.H. Asquith. *Letters to Venetia Stanley*.

Pragmatic Liberal Prime Minister David Lloyd George rose to power during the First World War and led a Coalition Government. Nicknamed the "Welsh Wizard," he appointed Churchill as Minister of Munitions, then Secretary of State for War and Air, and Secretary of State for the Colonies. Library of Congress.

French Premier Georges Clemenceau, known as "The Tiger." A formidable political journalist and newspaper owner, as keenly working for justice as his wartime friend Winston Churchill was. Library of Congress.

American General "Black Jack" (John) Pershing—the former Indian and Mexican fighter—was in command of all United States troops on the Western Front in 1917. Photo: George Grantham Bain.

Marshal Joseph "Papa" Joffre was Commander-in-Chief of French forces on the Western Front at the beginning of the First World War. 1915. *The New York Times.*

Young Colonel George S. Patton Jr. was fascinated by the new French invention of the Renault Ft Light tank on the Western Front in the summer of 1918. (World War I Signal Corps) Photograph Collection.

US Brigadier General Douglas MacArthur relaxing in a French chateau on September 19, 1918, all cleaned up for a photograph after German troops were driven out. National Archives.

Churchill's friend, General Sir Ian Hamilton—a decorated hero of several wars—was in charge of landing the Allied Armies in the Dardanelles Campaign, and was as determined as Churchill to discover why it failed. (Seen here in 1904 with Britain's Japanese allies during the battle of Shaho in the Russo-Japanese War.) Photo: P. F. Collier.

Field Marshall Sir Henry Wilson, Director of Military Operations and Intelligence at the War Office, passed information to Churchill of the German army buildup as early as 1911. He was assassinated by an IRA gunman on his doorstep in London in 1922. Library of Congress.

Canadian air ace Billy Bishop in a popular Nieuport of the Royal Flying Corps (RFC) in 1917. Fighter aircraft like this appeared only towards the end of the war, but by 1918 they swarmed the skies, providing support for infantry on frontline battlefields. Library and Archives, Canada.

American air ace First Lieutenant Eddie Rickenbacker with his SPAD S.XIII fighter-plane. 94th Aero Squadron, near Rembercourt, France.

From left to right, Field Marshal Paul von Hindenburg with the German Kaiser and General Erich Ludendorff, all apparently self-confident and in calm control of the war against the Allies. At German General headquarters in the Belgian town of Spa on January 8, 1917. Photo: Robert Sennecke.

British Nurse Edith Cavell, who was shot to death in 1915 by a German firing squad for helping allied soldiers escape from German-occupied Belgium in the First World War. Photographed here before the war in a garden in Brussels with her two dogs. Imperial War Museum.

Field Marshal and Chief of Staff of the Prussian army, Helmuth von Moltke the Younger in 1914, who blindly followed the Schlieffen Plan on the battlefields of the Western Front and lost his way. Private Collection: Wartenberg Trust, E. Bieber Atelier, Berlin.

Some years later, her sister Leonie spoke of accidentally encountering George Cornwallis-West when she was undertaking volunteer work in the war. She knew that he was anything but happy in his marriage with the outrageous Mrs. Patrick Campbell, who had remarked on marrying George, "Ah, the peace of the double bed after the hurly-burly of the chaise longue!"

George remarked to Leonie, "The day of my divorce was the saddest of my life."

To which she snapped back, "But the happiest of my sister's!"

Jennie would live alone for some years until her next marriage, but her life was continually busy with friends and social affairs. And, of course, with Winston, who was the most interesting man in her life.

Winston had spent the entire day at Eastchurch, toward the end of November, flying generally from shortly after noon to 3:30 p.m., and showing great promise according to his instructor. But he was concerned about the steering control, and had some difficulty getting the rudder to react smoothly and instantly. So they went up again with the instructor in the passenger seat. Shortly after their flight, the instructor went up again in the same plane and was killed when it crashed.[5] The tragedy induced the news media to persuade Churchill to give up flying. But he disliked the idea of abandoning a skill he had just begun to master.

Germany still refused to agree to a moratorium on naval construction. While preparing the Navy Estimates for the following year (1914–15), Winston decided to arm merchant ships that brought food to Britain, so that they could fight back if attacked by enemy cruisers or submarines, as well as ships converted as auxiliary cruisers. And now that the Fleet had converted to oil fuel, there was a need for oil storage depots. Naval air stations and facilities were required too. Then there was the cost of innovations like wireless telegraphy for sending secret communications at sea and in the air. But there were those who demanded substantial cutbacks in the Navy Estimates. Construction of at least one of the four proposed battleships had to be postponed as a consequence. Churchill could see disaster if there were any more reductions, and threatened to resign if the Navy did not acquire the four battleships it needed. Lloyd George finally agreed to accept the current Estimates if a definite reduction would be made in those for the following year. But Churchill stood firmly against it. He wanted Britain to be ever-ready for war.

Asquith argued with him to compromise. And Churchill agreed to small cutbacks in order to get the Estimates accepted by the cabinet for the coming year. He had three days to go before presenting the Navy Estimates to Parliament, when the Protestant leader in Ireland, Sir Edward Carson, rejected the Government's compromise over Home Rule.

On March 12, the cabinet learned from a series of police reports that Irish volunteers were likely to strike at police and military barracks and depots for arms and ammunition. The cabinet agreed it might be necessary to send more troops to Ireland to prevent it. Churchill issued a warning before taking action. He spoke at Bradford on March 14, then returned to London to finish preparing his speech on the Navy Estimates, which was scheduled to take place in three days.

At night on April 24, the Ulster Volunteers landed 30,000 rifles and three million cartridges at Larne in Ireland, and hurriedly distributed them. Churchill involved himself personally by appealing for conciliation. But many Liberals were furious that he had offered an amendment, although it was to enable negotiations to continue. But it was typical that any offer to one side in a heated argument would infuriate the other, and Churchill was caught in the middle.

The Kiel Canal

After his failure to conciliate the two sides in the Irish dispute, Winston turned once again to conciliating Germany when an opportunity arose—the Kaiser invited him to the naval regatta at the end of June in Kiel. Grand Admiral Tirpitz let it be known that he would like to see Churchill there. Winston was happy to go, hoping to discuss placing a limit on the number of battleships, and also on size. He would even be willing to allow inspections of each other's dockyards if it would allay suspicions and also reduce the extent of espionage between the two nations.

Foreign Secretary Sir Edward Grey hesitated to sanction Churchill's visit, anxious at what the news media and the public might make of it, and advised that the Kaiser be informed that Churchill was unavailable to visit Kiel.

Winston had continued his flying lessons and spent two weeks at the Central Flying School, although Clementine still did not approve: "so I did not write you from there as I know you would be vexed."

His instructor now was a young Royal Marine. Only six days after flying a seaplane with Winston, he and his co-pilot were both killed when it fell apart in the air and crashed into the sea. Clementine was expecting her third baby, and entreated him to give up flying. He wrote a long letter to her from the yacht on June 6, agreeing to abandon lessons temporarily while she was pregnant, but was reluctant because he had almost achieved the required amount of flying time to earn his pilot's certificate.

One of his more important innovations at the Admiralty had been to appoint Fisher to study the oil needs of the Royal Navy and locate an oil field that would make it independent if Britain could acquire controlling interest in it. Now Fisher recommended Anglo-Persian Oil Company, and Churchill obtained approval from the House of Commons to acquire a 51 percent share in it.[6]

Eleven days later, the Habsburg heir to the Austro-Hungarian Empire, Archduke Ferdinand, was assassinated at Sarajevo in Bosnia.

CHAPTER FIFTEEN

"KAISER BILL"

———

KAISER WILHELM HAD NOW BEEN EMPEROR of Germany for twenty-six years, which should have been enough time to brush aside the memory of Germany's greatest Chancellor, Otto von Bismarck, under whose considerable shadow the Kaiser had been hidden in his youth. He had learned a great deal from the "Iron Chancellor," as he was known, before he grew up and emerged into the harsh light of reality from out of Bismarck's shadow. First and foremost was the former Chancellor's guiding principle, which he had expressed clearly in 1808: "The weak were made to be devoured by the strong."

"Kaiser Bill"—as British Tommies would choose to call him with their customary irreverence for authority—became Kaiser Wilhelm II of Germany when he was twenty-nine years old. He was the oldest of Queen Victoria's grandchildren. Consequently, he visited England from time to time, where he admired and envied the British Navy. It had literally ruled the waves ever since Admiral Lord Nelson had defeated Napoleon and the French Navy at Trafalgar in 1805. But Cousin Willie was not always welcome, since his British cousins looked down on him and dismissed him as an upstart. For one thing, he was always boasting—which was frowned upon in British society, since people who felt they had to boast were evidently trying hard to conceal their mediocrity.

Although he was undeniably bumptious and inclined to vulgarity, what his British relatives failed to take into consideration was the physical deformity that most likely caused his pushy behavior: he was probably over-compensating for the withered arm he had been born with. Psychiatrist Alfred Adler would, very likely, have attributed his offensive behavior to an inferiority complex.

Whatever his British cousins possessed—whether admiration, respect, or battleships—Willy boasted he had it too. What he didn't possess, that they did,
was dominant naval sea power. Nor did he have their British sense of humor.

The "Great Man" Theory

The Great Man Theory of history is a nineteenth-century concept which
focused on the influence of heroes, or highly influential individuals, who initiate the direction history will take. It might be due to their charisma, their
wisdom, their intelligence, their audacity, or their political skills. For example,
most history books extol the virtues of Charlemagne, Napoleon, Alexander the
Great, Queen Elizabeth I of England, Eleanor of Aquitaine, Joan of Arc, the
Prophet Mohammed, and other influential leaders.

Historian and philosopher Carlyle most probably initiated the concept
when he stated that "The history of the world is but the biography of great
men." Economists like Karl Marx would point to economic conditions
instead, while sociologists like Max Weber would choose social influences.
There are plenty of alternative theories, like social discontent, evolution, fam-
ine, religion, or the clash of two great cultures in Hegel's theory. But it is clear
that the German Kaiser considered himself to be a great man—a mover and
shaker who could influence world events in his favor. Although the young
Winston Churchill was, so far, limited in experience and too modest to claim
the role of hero or knight in shining armor for himself, his energy and impatience, his personal magnetism, his aspirations, and determination to succeed
tend to demonstrate that, by his instincts, or his will, he was reserving a place
for himself as a leader of men. Without either of them realizing it, the two of
them were matched against each other like two fifteenth-century knights at
a jousting tournament.

"The goal of humanity lies in its highest specimens," wrote philosopher
and psychologist Nietzsche.[1] Whether the Kaiser fitted that category or not,
he evidently thought he did. There was a great deal of fatalism involved in the
beginning and outcome of the First World War. The dynamic of "the hero"
in society is difficult to dislodge because of the power of mythology, which
was still strong at this time, because of the ancient regimes in Tsarist Russia,
Prussia, the Habsburg Empire of Austria-Hungary, and Britain.[2]

When the young Kaiser had pushed Chancellor Bismarck out of office by forcing him to resign in 1890, Kaiser Wilhelm took over domestic and foreign policy. Had he not done so, the burly and bullying Bismarck would have prevented him from doing anything. Bismarck was a somewhat coarse and threatening Junker who had been Chancellor of Germany for longer than anyone else. It was partly because he was held in awe for increasing the size of the German Empire with a well-drilled and powerful Prussian Army, and partly because everyone was afraid of him. Only the German Kaiser was able to pull rank on him as a descendent of the Hohenzollern dynasty which had ruled Prussia for centuries. The young man knew he had to step out from under Bismarck's huge and threatening presence in order to be recognized and respected by his ministers and the German people. Until then, Bismarck had treated him disdainfully as an inexperienced little upstart. Bismarck had to go.

By that time, although Prussia was the most important state in the German Empire, the leading and influential Junker families who owned huge estates, and other elites, identified themselves more as Germans than Prussians. But despite Germany's huge size and its powerful army, the Kaiser suffered from constant anxiety that it could be encircled on the continent of Europe by France and Russia together. He couldn't fail to recognize the dangers of having to fight two huge enemies on two different fronts.

It hadn't seemed to worry Bismarck, because his shadow also fell over France, and kept the French in check. But it did worry the German Chiefs of Staff, including von Schlieffen, who had made a strategic plan against it, and his successor von Moltke who cherished the "Schlieffen Plan."

Despite that fear, Willie would often taunt his British cousins, as if daring them to strike him in retaliation, perhaps hoping they would make the first move. For example, while Britain was in conflict with President Paul Kruger of the Boers in South Africa, Willie couldn't resist stirring up trouble by sending Kruger a congratulatory telegram for defeating a British raid in the Transvaal. Willie could not help himself from being bombastic, unpredictable, impetuous, and tactless. And he must have been asking himself how the British Army was continually being beaten by a bunch of illiterate farmers.

He frequently made impulsive political decisions without consulting his ministers. In 1908, he was interviewed by the *Daily Telegraph* with disastrous results, when his loose mouth got ahead of his senses. Although he had intended to use the opportunity to encourage Anglo-German friendship, he became furious when baited by a British reporter. Irritated beyond his patience, and not gifted with a sense of humor, with which he might otherwise have brushed off some of the questions with a witty remark, he ended up alienating the British, the French, the Russians, and the Japanese, all at once. His best remembered remark was "You English are mad, mad, mad as March hares."[3]

His resignation was called for in Germany, at which he forced Chancellor Prince Bülow to resign. Even so, the crisis of confidence shattered his former ebullience, and he fell into a severe depression, from which it is said he never recovered. The British press had made him a laughingstock all over the world. Someone would have to pay for it, since vanity and pride featured importantly among national leaders, even in times as modern as the Edwardian Era.

Another cause for the war could be divined as his energetic pursuit of the reconstruction of the German Navy. Having admired and envied the superiority of the British fleet, it became his most important project, the fulfilment of his dreams to rival the British so that they would no longer disparage him. He appointed a new imperial Admiral of the German fleet, the very capable, indeed brilliant naval officer, Alfred von Tirpitz. Admiral Tirpitz developed a "risk theory," known as the "Tirpitz Plan." Its strategy was to force the British to accept German demands by threatening them with the might of a modern German Navy in the North Sea. He was given the go-ahead to build up the German Navy accordingly in 1897 and 1900. The cost led to strains on the German economy by 1914, as a consequence of constructing the highly costly dreadnought-class battleships, and opening up the Kiel Canal in 1895 to enable speedier shipping between the North Sea and the Baltic.

Now, said the Kaiser to Prince von Bülow, "I have got the British, despite their twisting and wriggling, where I want them."

Meanwhile, the Kaiser watched the affair in South Africa play itself out, and must have continued to wonder at the ineptitude of the British army in not being able to hold back a bunch of poor farmers with shotguns on little ponies. No doubt he calculated that if those dirt-poor peasants could beat the British again and again, he could do even better with his well-drilled and mechanized army of Prussian soldiers with their machine-guns and howitzers.

The dramas of current affairs had their effects even on Jennie, whose life generally ran along its own firm lines, regardless. "Darling Sniffy," she wrote to her sister Leonie, "Only a line to tell you that Winston tells us Poincaré has written an impassioned letter to the King imploring his aid. The fleet will be mobilized today probably . . . Money is getting fearfully tight here and one cannot get a cheque cashed and the banks will give no gold. But Winston says the financial situation will be easier as they are going to issue at once paper pound notes . . ."

The French President Poincaré was as shocked as the German Kaiser to hear of the assassination of the Austrian Archduke at Sarajevo in 1914. The aged and ailing Austrian Emperor Franz Joseph declared war on Serbia on July 28.

The Ottoman Empire

As for the Turks of the Ottoman Empire, it had originally come about by filling a power vacuum caused by the collapse of the Roman Empire and Persia. The Ottomans reached their greatest size by 1680, but failed to take Vienna in 1683 and declined—so that, by 1914, Turkey was known as "the sick man of Europe." It, too, was a family dynasty. It had benefited hugely from kidnapping Christian boys, converting them to Islam, and recruiting them as elite troops known as *janissaries*. Although slaves, they achieved an identity from being owned by the Sultan.

Serfdom was commonplace, and merely another word for slavery of the peasant majorities. They lived the most oppressive lives in Russia, where a landowner's wealth was counted in the number of slaves he owned.[4] As in Prussia and Austria, landowners had a legal right to punish their serfs, sometimes murdering them in the process. (To place it in the perspective of the times, most roads in France were built by "forced labor" from French peasants. Forced labor was abolished in the French Revolution in 1789). Landed wealth took dominance over commercial wealth in agricultural societies in which most people lived in the countryside.

Little was known of Islam in the West, because the Ottoman Empire was too far away from Europe, and a closed society. Most information came from books and rumors and myths that were hostile to it. Distorted legends based on historic nobles, like Count Dracula, were obsessed with tortures and death, and dreaded superstitions. Perhaps the first reasoned description came from Voltaire in 1742: "We must suppose that Muhammed, like all enthusiasts, violently impressed by his own ideas, retailed them in good faith, fortified them with fancies, deceived himself in deceiving others, and finally sustained with deceit a doctrine he believed to be good."[5] For some, Islam was just another form of Christianity. Historian Gibbon admired it for its speedy military conquests—since the highest aspiration for rulers everywhere, at the time, was territorial expansion. But to Montesquieu, it was just another form of despotism.

War causes vast changes and creates unintended consequences. The Crimean War was an expression by Russia to control parts of the Ottoman Empire. Until then (1853), Russia claimed to protect Orthodox Christians in the Muslim Empire, and France to protect Roman Catholics. Russia invaded Turkey on that pretext, provoking war from the Ottoman Turks. France and Britain allied themselves with Turkey and declared war on Russia in 1854. Since the Crimean War was the first war to be recorded by war correspondents and photographers working for newspapers, the general incompetence of both forces became clearly apparent. "The ill-equipped and poorly commanded armies became bogged down along the Crimean coast of the Black Sea. In September 1855, after a long siege, the Russian fortress of Sevastopol fell to the French and British." After which both sides hastened to make peace. "The abilities of the aristocratic officers leading the British Army had been discredited."[6]

Europe in 1914

Now that Austria-Hungary had declared war, the chess pieces for the First World War were about to be taken out of the little box where they had apparently been kept for such an occasion, to be set in place on the field of battle once again. The German Kaiser was bound to support Austria, his German-speaking neighbor. But this war would be different from previous ones, which had generally been fought for fear, hunger, or pride; whereas no one is entirely sure to this day why this one was fought.[7] Chancellor Bismarck would have considered it a folly.

After the Kaiser delivered an ultimatum to Belgium demanding a free passage for his troops, in accordance with his long-prepared war plan, he also sent an ultimatum to Russia and to France, It caused the Russians to prepare to defend Serbia by mobilizing its forces to strike at Austria.

Now, "Two million Germans were on the march, the greater part against France, and there were another three million trained men to back them up. France had nearly four million trained men at call, although she relied only on a million of the active troops in the first clash. Russia had more millions to call on than any, but her mobilization process was slower, a large part of her forces were in Asia, and even her eventual strength was hampered by lack of munitions."[8]

The only major European power not joining in the fight, so far, was Italy.

The training and outfitting and arming of these immense forces was due to the military theory of mass, which had been developed by the Prussian military strategist von Clausewitz, who had been an officer in the Napoleonic Wars—in 1866 against Austria and 1870 against France—which ended in victory. One of Napoleon's best known sayings was that "wars are won by the big battalions." Although not necessarily always true, in fact the concept of overwhelming force had stuck with the military in the West ever since. Colonel Foch also pointed to advances in firearm technology to strengthen an offensive. But that too was not necessarily the case, and actually contrary to the experience of the American Civil War, the South African War, and the Russo-Japanese War—all three of which were the most modern wars.[9] In fact, they brought movement to a standstill. But that did not concern the Army Chiefs of Staff, who operated in "monastic seclusion," preferring academic theories on paper to the realities of war.

But the Germans did pay attention to the introduction of the machine-gun and also heavy artillery to overcome modern defences.[10] As military strategist Captain Liddell Hart pointed out, using only two machine-guns for defense could paralyze attacks from a thousand men.[11] Another factor that could slow war to an endless crawl with heavy casualties was that "multitudes serve only to perplex and embarrass."[12] Even with the swifter form of transport of railways, armies comprising millions could clog up the arteries of movement and communications.

Inability to control the forces mobilized began to be revealed before the war had even started. But reason had already become drowned by the state of nervous excitement that "wrecked the delicate process of negotiation." In other words, the First World War opened with the type of wild impetuosity more often associated with the New York Stock Exchange, where emotions and greed run riot over reason and logic.

The Schlieffen Plan

The German Foreign Office received the telegram from the German Ambassador with the news on July 30, 1914, that Russian mobilization had commenced and would not be halted after the Tsar's decision. Now, according to Germany's Schlieffen Plan, immediate mobilization of the German Army was required to launch a swift attack on France before the huge Russian armies could be organized in the east for their slow but relentless sweep to strike at Austria, in order to protect France from its forces. France and Russia had signed a secret military agreement to defend each other if either was ever attacked.

Tsar Nicolas's relationship with France was an important one since—although Russia had recovered remarkably quickly after its defeat in the Russo-Japanese War only nine years previously—they were behind other leading European nations in industrialization, and required enormous loans for that purpose. France's President Poincaré provided the loans because France needed friends in Europe, since the Napoleonic wars had caused so much havoc and hatred toward the French.

Now the telegram from St. Petersburg meant that war had arrived. But was there any way that mobilization could be halted? Kaiser Wilhelm did what he always did when he received an official document that required thought and consideration—he made copious notes of his thoughts in the margins: in this case of the letter from the German Ambassador in St. Petersburg.

If mobilization can no longer be retracted—WHICH IS NOT TRUE—why then did the Tsar appeal for my mediation three days afterwards without mention of the issuance of the mobilization order? That shows plainly that the mobilization appeared to him to have been precipitate . . . Frivolity and weakness are to plunge the world into the most frightful war, which eventually aims at the destruction of Germany. For I have no doubt left about it: England, Russia and France have AGREED among themselves . . . to take the Austro-Serbian conflict for an EXCUSE for waging a WAR OF EXTERMINATION AGAINST US. Hence Grey's cynical observation to Lichnowsky as long as the war is CONFINED to Russia and Austria, England would sit quiet, only when we and France MIXED INTO IT would he be compelled to make an active move against us.

As was so often the case, the Kaiser's rambling thoughts centered on himself and Germany with its perennial fears that the German Empire would be encircled by its enemies in Europe. That had been the purpose of von Schlieffen's plan in the first place—to strike a blow at its old enemy, France, before the French could mobilize against Germany.

That is the real naked situation . . . which, slowly and cleverly set going, certainly by Edward VII, has been carried on, and systematically built up . . . and finally brought to a conclusion by George V and set to work. . . . The net has been suddenly thrown over our head, and England sneeringly reaps the most brilliant success of her persistently prosecuted purely ANTI-GERMAN WORLD-POLICY, against which we have proved ourselves helpless, while she twists the noose of our political and economic destruction out of our fidelity to Austria, as we squirm ISOLATED in the net. A great achievement, which arouses the admiration even of him who is to be destroyed at its result!

A Third-Rate Power

Despite the Kaiser's usual self-absorbed paranoia, in fact British Foreign Secretary Edward Grey had no such intentions and would have preferred to sit back isolated from Europe's dangerous hatreds and conflicts. He knew what few others did: that Britain's Empire was overextended and costly to maintain. Thirteen years previously, the then Prime Minister Balfour had remarked that "the conviction was forced on him that we were for all practical purposes at the present moment only a third-rate power." Unfortunately, Britain possessed interests in conflict with and crossing those of the great powers of Europe.

In other words, it would be better to be as far removed as possible from the Continent of Europe.[13] At that time, as the First Lord of the Admiralty, Lord Selborne, had remarked bitterly to his colleagues, Britain possessed only four battleships in the Far East to France and Russia which would soon have nine.

Winston Churchill, with his considerably dry wit, would write of that period just before the First World War, "We have engrossed to ourselves, in a time when other powerful nations were paralysed by barbarity or internal war, an altogether disproportionate share of the wealth and the traffic of the world. We have got all we want in territory, and our claim to be left in the unmolested enjoyment of vast and splendid possessions, mainly acquired by violence, largely maintained by force, often seems less reasonable to others than to us."[14]

Meanwhile, Germany was on the rise and sensitive to criticism, while Britain was arrogant and complacent, as each eyed the other warily. The Kaiser was eager to bring England down, and England was contemptuous of the new-rich upstart. It was not a recipe for friendly relations.

But was there a last chance to avoid the fate that the Kaiser feared? He wrote on in the margins of the letter, apparently attempting to whitewash his legacy for the sake of posterity:

> And we walked into the net and even went into the one-ship program in construction with the ardent hope of thus pacifying England!!! All my warnings, all my pleas were voiced for nothing. Now comes England's so-called gratitude for it! From the dilemma raised by our fidelity to the venerable old Emperor of Austria we are brought into a situation which offers England the desired pretext for annihilating us under the hypocritical cloak of justice, namely, of helping France on account of the reputed "balance of power" in Europe, i.e., playing the card of all the European nations in England's favor against us! [He meandered on to the end:] And our consuls in Turkey and India, agents, etc., must fire the whole Mohammedan world to fierce rebellion against this hated, lying, conscienceless nation of shopkeepers, for if we are to be bled to death, England shall at least lose India.[15]

When the Kaiser read a report that the French might agree to give up their alliance with Russia, he said eagerly to his Chief of Staff, von Moltke, "Now we can march, with all our forces, towards the east alone." They would take on Russia, instead. But Moltke stiffly replied that it was impossible. "The advance of armies formed of millions of men . . . was the result of years of painstaking work. Once planned, it could not possibly be changed."

To which the Kaiser answered petulantly, "Your uncle" [who had been the victor of 1870] "would have given me a different reply."

Despite his "Willy-Nicky" notes of affection to his cousin and their being photographed for posterity in each other's uniforms to embark on putting down the Boxer Rebellion in China, one of Willy's paranoid anxieties was the immense size of the Russian population—twice that of Germany's—so that it always posed a threat. Better to have a go at them now, while they were still unprepared, and before they were fully industrialized and might swamp the German Empire. It must have been a compelling thought.

To understand a little more of how the Kaiser's mind worked, he had a conversation with the financier Max Warburg in 1914, which Warburg made a note of: "Russia's armaments, the great Russian railway constructions were in his opinion preparations for war which could break out in the year 1916 . . . Beset by his anxieties, the Kaiser even considered whether it would not be better to attack first instead of waiting."[16, 17]

At the same time, Willy managed to undertake more reasonable discussions with cousin Nicky about how they both might share the pieces of Turkey together as it continued to fall apart—although Turkey's own modernization program continued to thwart them.

In any event, Moltke had his wish, and nothing could stop his alarm clock from ticking away once he had wound it up. So the German armies continued to march on France, through Belgium. However, the dialogue between him and the Emperor had indicated hesitation, and at least one double agenda on the Kaiser's part. It also revealed the "rigid limitations of the military machine as well as the military mind."[18] The Schlieffen Plan, on which Germany's war strategy and tactics were based, was what controlled the German war from the very beginning, and it was inflexible—hence the atrocities to anyone who got in its way. It crushed them like a heavy tank.

Russia with its peasant population, its geography, its vast territory, and its limited industries, armaments, and technology was bound to be slower to act than the other nations. Germany had the central position and the easiest terrain to cross. It could and would strike directly and heavily at France, while holding off the Russians until France was crushed, and then turn on Russia. The only factor that might prevent it was France's fortification system, which was why Germany intended to sidestep it and go through Belgium, as von Schlieffen had planned. The question of violating Belgian neutrality, and calling into play their treaty with Britain for its protection, was a risk they decided to take. Von Schlieffen had warned his staff before dying that it would come to a fight and they must keep the right wing of the force stronger than the left.

The French plan was based on the tradition of the offensive—only attack with enough ardor and they would be bound to win. But that too was not necessarily the case. What won wars? Was it audacity, overwhelming numbers, superior technology, war craft, or deception? Nobody knew with certainty, so fashions changed. Meanwhile, all complacently carried on with self-assurance; otherwise none would have mobilized in the first place. Evidently each nation imagined it would win in its own traditional way.

The French Chief of Staff, General Michel, was convinced the Germans would come through Belgium and was keen to prepare the necessary defenses to stop them. But since his move did not fit in with French tradition, he was replaced by General Joffre, who planned a headlong offensive instead. According to Winston Churchill, Joffre was another taciturn general, like Redvers Buller in the Boer War, utterly devoid of imagination or even common sense, who could not explain himself. And so "a million Frenchmen advanced to meet a million and a half Germans."[19]

CHAPTER SIXTEEN

THE FIRST WORLD WAR

IN VIEW OF CLEMENTINE'S PREGNANCY, WINSTON took care to say nothing about the tense mood in the House of Commons and in diplomatic circles in Europe as a result of the assassination of the heir to the Habsburg Empire. In fact, it was the Irish conflict that was overheating the minds of Londoners, not Austria, since a conference was planned at Buckingham Palace on July 21. And there had been several assassinations of heads of state before—generally by anarchists or vagrants, or by other mentally unstable individuals. What was unusual about this one was that Austria blamed the entire nation of Serbia for the wilful action of one half-educated and rebellious teenager.

Winston wrote to Clementine of the conference, "We are preparing a partition of Tyrone with reluctant Nationalist acquiescence. Carson absolutely refuses." Sir Edward Carson was the leader of the Ulster Volunteer Paramilitary Force and, some would claim, the creator of Northern Ireland. But two days later it was agreed that Ulster could establish independence from Dublin's rule, and Carson was happy. The cabinet was about to conclude its meeting, when Grey received a communication and read out the Austrian ultimatum to Serbia. It was harsh and threatening. From the previous discussion of the squabbles between snarling parishioners in Ireland, attention switched to the more serious affairs of aggressors who might change the map of Europe forever unless they could be stopped.

"Europe is trembling on the verge of a general war," Winston wrote to Clementine.

He dined that night with a German industrialist who was in touch with the Kaiser and predicted a series of situations that could result in war between

Britain and Germany. If Russia attacked Austria then Germany must enter the conflict. Then France must march. What would England do?

The question caught Winston's attention. That, he said, would be up to the cabinet to decide—but that Germany would be wrong to assume we wouldn't be involved. Unfortunately, the Kaiser had apparently been told by his brother, who had visited the King, that Britain would definitely *not* be involved. And the Kaiser had chosen to believe the King of England—despite his brother's habit of getting meanings and emphasis wrong when talking in a foreign language. Winston begged his friend not to let the Kaiser wage war on France.

Despite the unyielding wording of the ultimatum from Austria, Serbia replied in a conciliatory manner, and agreed to suppress all anti-Austrian activities in the country. They also promised to bring anyone connected with the murders to justice, adding that they were willing to submit the case to the International Tribunal at the Hague, or even to the Great Powers.

The German Kaiser was impressed. "It was a moral victory for Vienna," he wrote, "and with it every reason for war disappears." But he thought the Austrian Army should occupy Belgrade as a warning.

So Asquith told the King on July 25, "There seems to be no reason why we should be anything more than spectators." Consequently Winston traveled to Norfolk by train to join Clementine and their children at the seaside.

He phoned Prince Louis from the Post Office in Cromer and obtained the latest news that Austria was not satisfied with Serbia's reply. He returned to the beach and built sandcastles on the seashore for his little son and daughter, then returned again to the post office later in the day, when Prince Louis informed him that Austria had rejected Serbia's answer.

The likely sequence of events began to look clearer: if Austria decided to invade Serbia, it would motivate Germany, Russia, and France to involve themselves in the affair. Germany might even strike swiftly at France and defeat it at the outset, to get it off the chess board, in order to attack Russia. And Germany would not hesitate to attack Belgium in order to go through France. Britain would be obliged to honour its treaty to protect Belgium's neutrality, and be embroiled in a war against Austria and Germany.

It was at that moment that Winston remembered the position of the fleet and believed he had asked Prince Louis not to let it disperse from the North Sea. But Prince Louis thought differently; that he had been left to decide for himself.

Back in London at the Foreign Office, Grey told Winston that Austria was determined to impose war on Serbia. They decided to issue a statement that the dispersal of the British fleet had been halted. The news appeared in *The Times,* looking innocent enough; but Winston hoped that the Kaiser would understand his message. Even so, at that morning's cabinet meeting, most ministers opposed any British action against Germany in response to its invasion of France. Their point was that Britain did not have a formal alliance with France. The Liberal Ministers were completely against war.

Attacks by Air

Nevertheless, Winston's first duty was to make sure that, if war came, Britain would be prepared against naval or air attacks. He sent armed guards to all ammunition depots and oil tanks, and also to man all coastal lights and guns. And he took other measures and precautions in the Mediterranean and along the North Sea coast. Oil tanks and ammunition stores were protected by anti-aircraft guns, while aircraft were gathered around the Thames Estuary to prevent possible attacks by airships.

He lunched with Kitchener, who was in London to receive an earldom. Winston was impressed by Kitchener's understanding of the likely effects of Germany attacking France, so he asked Asquith not to let Kitchener be sent back to Egypt in case he was needed in Europe. Asquith had Kitchener's train stopped, made him Secretary of State for War, and brought him back to London.

On July 28, the German High Command suggested that Austria-Hungary should immediately march on Serbia in case someone should change their mind, while Grey pressed Austria to turn away from war. But the British Ambassador in Vienna told Grey that the Austrian public were eager for it, that they had "gone wild with joy" at the prospect of war.[1]

The British First Fleet had not dispersed and looked formidable in the Channel, off of the Isle of Wight. Winston sent it back to the North Sea in the hope of discouraging the Germans from attacking Britain's East Coast. By that time Austria-Hungary had declared war on Serbia.

"My darling one & beautiful," Winston wrote to Clementine, "The preparations have a hideous fascination for me . . . I cannot feel that we in this island are in any serious way responsible for the wave of madness which has swept the mind of Christendom. No one can measure the consequences . . . The sailors are thrilled . . . But war is the unknown & the unexpected!"

The following day, the cabinet agreed to his request for precautionary defensive measures, like civilian craft to be removed from naval harbors, armed guards positioned at bridges and viaducts, and observers placed on the coast to report on any hostile ships.

Next day he received a message that the First Fleet was now back in the North Sea. But on July 31 there was strong opposition by Liberals to any involvement in war on behalf of France. Churchill told them he agreed that Britain should remain neutral, since there was no treaty. Nevertheless, he also authorized his naval advisers to meet with the French Naval Attaché in London and discuss what should be done if they ever became allies in war. And he asked the cabinet to authorize full mobilization of the Fleet. Ministers were divided. Lloyd George was undecided. Churchill was as impatient as usual, but reluctant to commit to going to war for France if Belgium was invaded. It would depend on British public opinion in the end.

Then there appeared to be a possibility that Austria and Russia might negotiate a formula that Germany had suggested. Soon after 9:00 p.m., F. E. Smith visited him with Max Aitken (later Lord Beaverbrook). He told them of the possibility of war being prevented. So they sat down at a card table to play away the time while they waited for fresh news. The cards were dealt, when a messenger delivered a red dispatch box. Churchill opened it with his skeleton key. He found "it contained a single sheet of paper." He read aloud the message on it: "War declared by Germany on Russia."[2]

Edith Cavell

Although the German armies had crossed into Luxemburg, they did not cross the Belgian frontier immediately. Instead, they sent an ultimatum on the morning of August 3, which demanded the right of their troops to cross Belgium. Impatient to attack the border, their vanguard was already sweeping through Luxemburg. They crossed the Belgian frontier that afternoon. A British ultimatum to Germany to maintain Belgian neutrality was due to expire at midnight on August 4. Germany made no reply and their troops continued to advance deeper into Belgian territory.

The following day, the British Expeditionary Force reached the town of Mons in Belgium. The First German Army, under von Kluck, drove south through Mons to the French border. It consisted of 580,000 troops. The Allied troops numbered only 336,000, of whom about 36,000 were British. The majority were French. They took up positions along the Mons-Condé Canal.

Edith Cavell was a trained nurse working in Belgium. She first came to the notice of a British publication when she wrote to the *Nursing Mirror* on August 21, 1914, to tell them that some Belgians who spoke to German troops in German found them vague about where they were, imagining themselves to be already in Paris, which was their destination. They were evidently bewildered and could not understand what quarrel they were supposed to have with the Belgians, or why they were there.

Nurse Cavell's father was a vicar who had brought her up to help people less fortunate than herself. Her Anglican beliefs persuaded her to help anyone who needed it, because she could not let anyone die. She worked in several hospitals as the Victorian century turned into an Edwardian one, and became the matron of a nursing school in Belgium in 1907. Professional nursing developed so much in the next three years that she published a professional nursing journal called *L'infirmière*. She began training nurses in three hospitals and twenty-four schools, as well as thirteen kindergartens in Belgium a year later. She moved to Brussels when the German Army occupied it. From then on, she sheltered British soldiers and helped them to escape to neutral Holland. She saved the lives of any soldiers, whether from Britain, France, or Germany. But her equal treatment of the Germans did not save her from their firing squad.

At first, Edith Cavell was offered safe conduct to Holland with other British nurses, but most refused. At the same time, a British soldier who had reconnoitered the village of St. Symphorien with his bicycle failed to return. He was the first British soldier to be killed by the enemy in the First World War.[3] He was buried in the village with others who got in the way of the German war machine.

Fourteen months later, the forty-nine-year-old British nurse, Edith Cavell, was about to be executed by the Germans for helping British and French prisoners-of-war to escape to neutral Holland in order to join the Allies. After being lined up for execution, she was struck by four bullets, one of which killed her instantly by piercing her heart.

Considerable anti-German feeling was expressed by the British when her murder became known. But that was only the beginning of the German atrocities in Belgium.

Naval War

Churchill was convinced that Germany's next step would shortly be to attack Russia's ally, France. He left his friends playing cards and walked across the Horse Guards Parade to the Prime Minister's office at Number 10. Once there, he told Asquith that, despite the cabinet's earlier refusal, he wished to order immediate mobilization of the fleet. Then he walked back to the Admiralty and gave them the order.

"Cat dear," he wrote to Clementine at one o'clock in the morning, "It's all up. Germany has quenched the last hopes of peace by declaring war on Russia, & the declaration against France is momentarily expected." She had written to him on the previous day to declare that war would be lunacy. Now he had a chance to agree with her. "But the world is gone mad—& we must look after ourselves—& our friends." He told her he hoped she would come to London for a day or two.

At the same moment that Germany aimed to defeat France, to get her out of the war, the Russian government now requested that France should honor the Franco-Russian Treaty of 1894 by coming to her aid. So far, the expected progress through the alliances and treaties was going like clockwork. Germany's initial drive would be through Belgium. Soon after midday on August 2, Britain informed Germany that it would not allow German ships through the English Channel or the North Sea to attack the French coastline or French shipping. A copy of the warning was sent to British naval commanders in those areas with orders to "Be prepared to meet surprise attacks."

No German armies had yet crossed the Belgian frontier at that point, although their forces had occupied Luxemburg. On the morning of August 3, the cabinet learned that Germany had sent an ultimatum to Belgium. It meant that Britain was now committed to insisting on maintaining Belgium's neutrality. Nevertheless, German forces crossed the Belgian border that afternoon. Grey warned the House that their act was a violation of Britain's Treaty of 1839, which now obliged Britain to go to war on Belgium's behalf. "Now,"

Grey said privately to Winston, "we shall send them an ultimatum to stop their invasion of Belgium within twenty-four hours."

Back at the Admiralty, Churchill requested that Asquith and Grey give him immediate authorization to undertake the combined Anglo-French dispositions to defend the Channel. Unless expressly forbidden, he would now act accordingly. On August 4, *The Times* complimented him as the one Minister "whose grasp of the situation and whose efforts to meet it have been above all praise." The British ultimatum was to expire at midnight.

While the cabinet waited impatiently and anxiously for an answer all day, the German cruiser, the *Goeben,* bombarded a French North African port, while a German light cruiser, the *Breslau,* bombarded Bône. British warships followed both of them, but could take no action unless fired upon, since Britain was not at war. Anticipating another favorable reaction from Asquith, Churchill telegraphed the Admiralty, "If *Goeben* attacks French transports you should at once engage her."

At noon on the same day, Asquith wrote, "Winston, who has got on all his war paint, is longing for a sea fight in the early hours of the morning to result in the sinking of the *Goeben.*" Churchill was told by the cabinet to wait until the ultimatum had expired one hour after midnight. He telegraphed all ships accordingly.

German troops penetrated deep into Belgian territory that afternoon. As soon as the ultimatum expired, Winston authorized a signal to be sent from the Admiralty to all ships and naval establishments: "Commence hostilities against Germany."[4]

In the meantime, Bonar Law had already started to plot Winston's downfall. But when it came, Kitchener would be able to say to that brash young man of whom he had once disapproved, "There is one thing they cannot take away from you—the fleet was ready."[5]

The Fall of Antwerp

The British Expeditionary Force would have to be shipped across the Channel, and Churchill had sealed off the English Channel against any German intervention. The BEF began to be transported to the Continent within two weeks. One hundred twenty thousand men arrived without any loss of vessels or lives.

Meanwhile, Churchill was anxious about Clementine and their children, in case of a mischance of war, since they were still on vacation by the North Sea. She was seven months pregnant. He wrote to tell her there was little chance of a raid, but that Cromer provided a landing place for the enemy. "I wish you would get the motor repaired and keep it so that you can whisk away at the first sign of trouble."

Meanwhile, the German attack on Belgium had been planned to run seamlessly, with nothing and nobody allowed to stand in the way of its timing. The plan, as revised by Moltke, was heavier than necessary and deadly effective. It established a detachment of troops under General von Emmich, to open out a corridor into the Belgian plain north of the Ardennes, ready for the advance of the main troops when, after a temporary check on August 5, a staff officer named Ludendorff became famous for occupying the fortress of Liége. The fort was held stubbornly, but fell because of the invention of heavy Howitzers with enormous destructive power that took everyone by surprise. The Belgian Army fell back on Antwerp.

On August 6, the British light cruiser, the *Amphion*, destroyed a German minelayer and captured its crew. But it was sunk almost immediately by one of the mines. A hundred and fifty British sailors drowned, and so did their captives. Churchill immediately related the tragedy to the House of Commons and the news media, and was complimented for his frankness by the *Manchester Guardian*.

Unable by temperament and common sense to be limited to a passive role in war, Winston recommended an assault on one of the Dutch islands, which might be fortified and used as a base from which to attack German shipping and an air base to bomb the Kiel Canal. The Naval war staff he had set up to advise him considered such an operation impractical, so he continued searching around for other opportunities to attack Germany. He obtained cabinet approval for a naval blockade of Germany's North Sea ports, to prevent food coming out or going in. Volunteers were applying to fight with him; among them the rising patriotic poet Rupert Brooke. Churchill persuaded Kitchener to send Britain's last military division to France, after convincing him that the Admiralty was ready and able to protect Britain against invasion on its own.

Two days later, Kitchener appeared in his doorway at the Admiralty looking like the ghost of Hamlet's father. He brought tragic news that the Belgian forces at Namur were in German hands. It meant that the road from Belgium to the Channel ports was open. Churchill spoke to Lloyd George at the

Treasury. It was their first confidential meeting since the war had erupted, and he needed a reaction and some advice from someone he trusted and respected. Their talk gave him confidence. He immediately signaled to the new naval Commander-in-Chief, Admiral Jellicoe, to instill confidence in him too, in order to prepare him for the seriousness of the situation as French and British armies fell back from the German onslaught on August 26. He had obtained cabinet approval to send the marine brigade to Ostend in order to pressure the enemy to divert their forces from the main German thrust.

Far on the other flank of the Belgian plain, the French offensive had opened on August 7, but was soon halted. The main thrust into Lorraine by the French First and Second Armies began on August 14, but was stopped in a battle at Morrhange-Sarrebourg on August 20 when the French armies were appalled and demoralized by the extent of the war material bombarding them. Although led by offensive tactics, they were stopped in their tracks by the deadly defensive killing power of machine-guns and Howitzers.

It was the German attack on Liége that opened General Joffre's eyes to the reality of the German advance, since French Intelligence had greatly underestimated the number of German troops that the French forces now faced. The French armies everywhere were taken by surprise. As for the British troops, after resisting six German divisions, they fell back on August 24 with their French Allies. Then they began to retreat in earnest, largely because of Sir John French's "sudden revulsion of mind and emotion," as military strategist Liddell Hart phrased it.[6]

Clementine was with Winston in London when news arrived of Britain's first naval victory. The British fleet had sunk three German cruisers in the Heligoland Bight without losses. As a show of united confidence, Asquith and Opposition Leader Bonar Law spoke at the Guildhall. When Churchill was asked to speak, to rousing cheers, he told the public that he was absolutely sure that they had only to endure to conquer, and victory would be found at the end of the road.

But the British and French forces were in retreat after only thirty days of war, and a cloud of depression hovered over England. Winston attempted to raise morale by using encouraging words, and managed to do so with his colleagues. One wrote to him that "You inspire us all by your courage and resolution."[7] Kitchener asked him to take over the entire responsibility for the aerial defenses of Britain from the War Office. He agreed, and set up communications between Hendon Aerodrome and the coast, to attack any enemy aircraft that might attempt to strike London. A historic event took place on the same day, when a Royal Naval Air Service pilot dropped a bomb on a German army unit close to the frontline. Twenty-four airplanes were sent to newly established bases fifty miles inland. They were commanded by some of the airmen who had taught Churchill to fly.[8]

Now the newspapers headlined all sorts of stories about a continuing retreat. *The Times* wrote describing a bitter retreat from Mons, "of the broken bits of many regiments," of British soldiers being battered by marching. Asquith asked Winston to respond with a more uplifting report of successes, and he did so. His article was published on September 5, after which the Prime Minister requested more of "his best journalistic condiment." His articles benefited by his not knowing all the unexpected complications that had emerged in the fog of war in every army in the front lines. Had he known at the time, he would have been stunned. Even a century later it is difficult to make sense of what still looks like total chaos everywhere.

Churchill travelled to France on September 10. Only Asquith knew of his trip. He investigated the Dunkirk fortifications and studied the air bases and the first armored cars, which were armor-plated Rolls Royce motor cars. He discussed the defense of the port with the French Governor and encouraged him. On his return, he sent the Marine Brigade over at Kitchener's request, to distract German forces which were moving cavalry units towards the Channel. Then he electrified an audience at the Guildhall with his public speech. According to the *Manchester Guardian* it was full of determination and belligerent phrases that stuck in the minds of the audience and hardened their own determination—about how the bulldog breed hangs on to its enemy and never lets go until it finishes them off. He didn't deny the dangers, and caught the imagination of the public, who liked to think of their own stubbornness being compared with the British bulldog breed.

The Lust for Battle

There was no doubt that Winston possessed a lust for battle and longed to be in the thick of it again. It was the attraction of all the challenges and the willingness to take on an army that had been preparing for war for years and was fully equipped for it. It even seemed to be an added stimulus to his over-developed sense of responsibility that Britain was losing to the Germans: it got his adrenaline flowing. On September 14, Asquith wrote, "When I hear Winston say that the last thing he would pray for is peace, I'm inclined almost to shiver." Winston returned to France at Kitchener's request to explain to Sir John French, the Commander-in-Chief, why the British Expeditionary Force should be in position along the coast to protect the Channel ports together with the Navy.

He observed French artillery in action while there, with German shells bursting over a nearby village. Most of their technology was new or modernized. It was a first view of a war that would soon become a normal way of life. A week later, the enemy sank three British cruisers with 1,459 officers and men losing their lives. He was blamed for the catastrophe, although he had warned them to take precautions against the risks. He made a third visit to France to encourage the marines and airmen to attack the German lines. Five days later he was back there again and as dissatisfied as ever.

"You should be swelling with pride," Clementine told him, instead of depressed. "The PM relies on you and listens to you more and more. You are the only young vital person in the Cabinet."

But German troops advancing to the Channel had reached Ypres by October 2 and were ready to cut off the port of Antwerp. Asquith viewed the possibility as being worse than the fall of Namur. Winston's fifth visit to the Continent was halted for an immediate meeting at Kitchener's house, where Grey and Prince Louis were waiting to inform him that the Belgian Government had decided they could no longer hold Antwerp. The Belgians were ready to abandon the port with its huge fortifications. He and Kitchener decided how to send British troops to hold on to the city. All resistance would collapse if the military left—the Germans would race to the coast and Dunkirk and Calais would be gone. The British Isles would be in danger if those ports were overrun.

Churchill offered to go to Antwerp himself, to report the situation back to Kitchener and persuade the Belgian king to hold on to the city. He departed on a destroyer for Ostend, and drove to Antwerp. The Belgian Prime Minister agreed to hold out for ten days, but only if he received reinforcements by the fourth day. Churchill agreed to provide them, and that the first two thousand marines would arrive the next morning. He stayed in Antwerp to wait for them.

Then, to the astonishment of Prime Minister Asquith, Winston telegraphed to offer his resignation as First Lord of the Admiralty, in order to take military command of Antwerp and resist the German onslaught. The offer was conditional on his being awarded the rank of commander of its forces. He felt it was his duty to achieve victory in a battle in which he was already deeply involved.

Asquith was amazed and impressed, but declined the offer. When questioned by the cabinet, he read out Winston's telegram. It was received with incredulous laughter since, if accepted, he would be in command of two major-generals and several experienced brigadiers and colonels, who would hardly be flattered to be commanded by a former second lieutenant. Nevertheless, Kitchener had faith in him and told Asquith he would have no hesitation in commissioning Winston as a lieutenant-colonel. Asquith shook his head—he wanted Churchill back in London immediately. But Antwerp was under German bombardment and Winston was stuck there.

An Italian war correspondent observed Winston smoking a huge cigar and watching the battle thoughtfully but with unconcern under hails of fearful shrapnel. He was in his element. He informed Kitchener that night that the Belgian ministers were determined to fight where they stood, whatever happened.

By midday there were 8,000 British troops in Antwerp and a further 40,000 on the way. Winston remained, leaving the Admiralty in London without a head. But the Belgians changed their minds and decided to abandon the city before heavy German howitzers were brought up. He returned to England on the morning of October 7, when Clementine gave birth to their daughter Sarah. He visited them on arrival and then reported to the cabinet on Antwerp.

Sir Edward Grey spoke to Clementine by phone from the cabinet room, to tell her he was sitting next to a hero. "I can't tell you how much I admire his courage & gallant spirit & genius for war."

When Winston spoke privately to Asquith he was still overcome by what he had experienced in Belgium, and was as keen as before to get back into the army. He asked Asquith not to view his career in a conventional way, but to place him in command of a military force instead of his present position. It was not that he was after glory, but he couldn't bear to think that the direction of the war was in the hands of dull-witted generals who were devoid of intelligence, imagination, or spirit. He referred to them as "dug-out trash" who had been bred on the obsolete tactics of twenty-five years earlier. Antwerp had been a revelation to him about how not to run a war.

As usual, he had analyzed the problems and quickly diagnosed their cause before everyone else—this would be a war led by generals whose sole experience had been set-piece battles against primitive and poorly armed tribesmen in the colonies. Few even realized the change or recognized the potential of the new technologies, and those who did had no idea how to handle trenches and barbed wire, machine-guns and Howitzers, airplanes and submarines. It required a different breed of leaders with imagination, initiative, and élan.[9]

The additional six days that Winston had persuaded the Belgians to hold on for allowed the British Expeditionary Forces to return safely and reform in Flanders. And the 40,000 reinforcements on the way were turned back. But despite what he had achieved, Winston was ridiculed by the Conservatives in the House. Bonar Law—who knew nothing about what had happened—called it "an utterly stupid business," and claimed that Churchill must be mentally unbalanced to go into "danger at a time like this." Both the *Morning Post* and the *Daily Mail* criticized him. The incident became known as the "Antwerp Blunder." It may even have been the origin of the dismissive expression "twerp!" Churchill's position had been weakened.

Resignation

Now he felt frustrated at the absence of opportunities for effective action. Since Prince Louis was dropped as a negative influence on the Admiralty, Churchill wanted to appoint the enthusiastic Fisher in his place, because he was full of eager ideas. Fisher was now seventy-five and the king was against the idea, arguing that Fisher was too divisive. But Churchill knew it was a typical reaction to new ideas, when others disliked change and were often too slow-witted to move with it before it was too late. He saw the same problem with dull and slow-witted army officers who simply did not understand when situations were no longer the same as they had been when they were originally trained. That was why he was always under fire from them. Churchill responded to the king's remark by hinting at resigning. He preferred to go to war as a soldier. The king consulted with Asquith before agreeing to accept Fisher as First Sea Lord. Now Winston felt he had a zealous partner to work with.

The *Goeben* and the *Breslau* bombarded the Russian Black Sea port of Odessa on the same day that Fisher took up his new post. Asquith immediately sent an ultimatum to the Turks to get the Germans out of Constantinople, but they refused. Churchill asked Fisher to investigate the possibility of bombarding the forts of the Dardanelles to give the Turks some encouragement. The bombardment was carried out at the beginning of November. It lasted for only ten minutes and obliterated all their heavy guns, which were not replaced.

It was out of this episode that an idea began to emerge and grow in Winston's mind for a campaign in Turkey that would end in his disgrace.

CHAPTER SEVENTEEN

WINSTON IN DISGRACE

THE ALLIED RETREAT TO THE MARNE took place after four British divisions moved up to Mons on August 22, preparing to advance even further into Belgium. Almost as soon as they arrived, General Sir John French learned that the German attack on the previous day had now taken his plan to cross the Sambre River out of the equation. He agreed to make a stand at Mons to cover the French left flank. But then he heard on the following day of the certain fall of Namur and the existence of the German Third Army on his exposed right flank. He gave orders to retreat that night. And the Allies fell back, "not a moment too soon."[1]

Although British forces retreated later than the Allies, they moved faster and further. Sir John French had been eager to begin with but, now faced with overwhelming force, he appeared to be struck numb, just as General Joffre had been struck blind. When told that the Germans had reached the Meuse, Sir John asked some French officers what the enemy were likely to do. Lanzevac contemptuously replied, what did he think—fish in the river? In view of the difficulty of language, the sarcastic barb failed to pierce Sir John's ego, but he resented the other officer's attitude. On the other hand, he was far too alarmed to make an issue of the insult when he discovered that his Allies had withdrawn and left him isolated, helpless and bewildered. Fortunately, Kitchener intervened to straighten him out.

Meanwhile, General Joffre had recovered his sense of location to formulate a new plan, since his original one was now in tatters. The German Command had lost touch with the situation through poor communications, so that all troop movements had begun to lose their meaning. The idea of

Sedan appealed to them because they had enjoyed victory over the French there before. Most significantly, German troop movements had been too fast and outran their schedule, so that their supplies could not catch up with them, leading to hunger as well as fatigue. They could find little to eat except for raw turnips and unripe fruit. Forced marches and hunger reduced them to wandering creatures who were half asleep. Then Moltke lost touch with his commanders as a result of lack of pre-planning some means of communication with them, since the cavalry had destroyed the telegraph system in France.[2]

"Thus, in sum, so much grit had worked into the German machine that a slight jar would suffice to cause its breakdown. It was delivered in the battle of the Marne."[3]

This was the friction of war that military strategist von Clausewitz wrote about after campaigning as an officer in Napoleon's wars. Once the world war had been unleashed, everything that could possibly break down on every side did so. It was typical of the obscurity of war and its unreliable information on the movements of generals, troops, and technologies, food supplies and ammunition. According to military strategist Liddell Hart, the battle of the Marne changed everything by placing the Germans on a different route than the Schlieffen Plan had intended. And there was a gap that the French Fifth Army failed to drive through while it was open. Now the fact that twenty-seven Allied divisions were confronted by thirteen German ones was evidence that Moltke had deviated from Schlieffen's original plan. Joffre had to reshuffle his cards under pressure. Now General Joffre formed a fresh army, led by General Castelnau, to maneuver around to the rear of the German flank. But the Germans had already recovered their senses. Even so, the fact remained that Moltke had not managed to seize the Channel ports—or not thought of it—and had left the British troops to evacuate through Calais, Boulogne, and the coast, up to Le Havre.

It was very likely the confusion that Churchill had been envisaging as he had sat thoughtfully puffing away at his huge cigar in Antwerp, oblivious to the shells falling all around him as he concentrated on analyzing the present situation, considering what he expected to happen, and deciding what needed to be done to turn it into an Allied victory. Strategic planning was one of his strengths. And, although not always right, he was not often wrong.

On August 24, the Belgians attacked the rear of the German right wing, which eased the pressure on their Anglo-French Allies. King Albert launched another sortie on September 9.

With all the sound and fury of the battle fronts, Sir John French had the illusion that his troops were attacking the Germans, whereas they barely held their ground. It appeared that he thought the war would be over in three months because of the strain on Germany that would surely result in its collapse. He seemed not to want to do anything more.[4] His confused state of mind may have resulted from a severe heart attack: he was sixty-two, and his doctor had warned him to go carefully.

This was when the battles slowed down to an abysmal halt and troops dug primitive trenches from which they were discouraged to leave by the murderous onslaughts of machine-gun fire and Howitzer shells, into which any courageous or foolhardy troops who showed themselves were instantly wiped out.

Revenge

Asquith told Winston it was time that "he bagged something and broke some crockery." With Fisher at his elbow, waiting to be unleashed, Churchill ordered a heavy force to concentrate all its attention on the victorious Admiral von Spee, who had just sunk two British cruisers. Admiral Sir Christopher Cradock had gone down in one of them—and, once again, Churchill had been blamed for the defeat. Now, six weeks after the disaster, von Spee was tracked to the Falkland Islands and six of his eight ships were destroyed by the British Navy.

By now, the tragedies of war began to affect Winston personally. His cousin Norman was killed at Armentières, his friend Downey was killed at Ypres. The British Army attempted to hold the line at Flanders, and kept the Germans from advancing. The Western Front was established with trenches, barbed wire fencing, and machine-gun posts, where more of Winston's friends were killed. He wrote to his brother Jack at Ypres, "It would take the edge off much if I could be with you."

He was forty when Asquith created a war council with Grey, Lloyd George, Kitchener, and Churchill. His thoughts that winter were on Turkey and Bulgaria. He was good at analyzing situations and seeing their weak points, and possessed what von Clausewitz called "a sense of location," because he had travelled to so many countries and could instantly bring places and their topography to mind. He was also aware of previous battles that had been fought there, and what had been the fatal flaws which had enabled one army to destroy another.

On December 5, Asquith wrote of Winston that he wanted "to organize a heroic adventure against Gallipoli and the Dardanelles, to which I am altogether opposed." Winston first considered a Greek Army allied to the Royal Navy in a combined attack on the Gallipoli Peninsula.

When the war council received a telegram which disclosed that the Russian Army was desperately short of ammunition and therefore wanted something to distract the German army, Churchill planned a Baltic campaign. He was intent on formulating a plan which would stop the war with one overwhelming stroke. He was aided by his Admiralty Secretary and Edward Marsh. He had succeeded in a minor way by organizing a bombing raid by seaplane on German warships, but that was more of a minor skirmish. He brought up his Baltic plan, which he felt was better than the defensive trenches on the Western Front. Could they not use the power of the Navy more directly on Germany?

He had considered another plan to land at a Greek port, and one to land 100,000 troops in Syria to relieve Russia from Turkish pressures. Maurice Hankey, a former Colonel of the Royal Marines, thought a blow could be struck through Turkey with a combined force of British, Greek, and Bulgarian troops who ought, he wrote, to capture Constantinople. Fisher was impressed and sent Winston a plan to defeat Turkey and Austria-Hungary. It involved landing 75,000 British troops south of the Dardanelles, landing a Greek force on the Gallipoli Peninsula, and a simultaneous naval attack to force the Dardanelles with old battleships. Admiral Fisher was eager for it, if it could be mounted immediately.

The idea of a diversionary campaign in Turkey to help their Russian Allies turned up again when Britain's Ambassador to Russia sent a telegram to Grey. It informed him that Russia was under severe attack by the Turks and wanted Britain to mount a diversion which would force the Turks to withdraw some of their forces. Grey asked Kitchener for his opinion, and Kitchener asked Winston. Before Winston could consider the request, Kitchener visited him at the Admiralty, eager for a direct answer. Winston thought that a naval attack on its own would not be enough, that it wouldn't be effective unless they could organize a combined military and naval assault. He insisted that at least 50,000 men should be within three days distance either to seize the Peninsula when it had been cleared, or to take Constantinople if a revolution occurred. All would be lost, he emphasized, if the naval operation succeeded but there was no follow-up by the Army. Kitchener promised to find the men.

Winston returned to his advisers at the war office, who told him there were no spare troops available. But Kitchener became more determined, convinced it was "the only place." So Winston sought advice at the Admiralty for a naval bombardment and landing on its own. They were skeptical about a purely naval attack. He telegraphed Admiral Carden, who was blockading the Dardanelles, with the same question, although Winston himself was still keen on the Baltic operation. In his opinion Germany was still the enemy, not Turkey. Fisher tried to get Balfour to support his scheme, on the grounds that possessing Constantinople would enable them to prevent wheat being distributed from the Black Sea.

Admiral Carden replied the next day, "I do not consider Dardanelles can be rushed. They might be forced by extended operations with large numbers of ships." At the War Council meeting that afternoon, Winston hoped to be told to go ahead with his Baltic operation instead. He had recommended seizing Borkum and landing near the Kiel Canal. Lloyd George was in favor of landing at Salonika. F. E. Smith had sent a plan to land on the Turkish coast. But Kitchener was all for Gallipoli and Constantinople, which would answer Russia's appeal for help.

They discussed Admiral Carden's suggestion for the Royal Navy alone to force the Dardanelles with ships. When Winston raised that plan with the Admiralty, he found that his advisers too thought that a naval bombardment could be enough, since the earlier ten-minute one had impressed them. So Churchill telegraphed Carden for details of a proposed plan.

The Western Front

At their War Council meeting on the following day, Churchill again pressed for his Baltic plan as the most potentially effective one, and put forward the details. Fisher supported him and claimed it would take him no longer than three months to seize Borkum. Asquith gave Winston the authority he required.

The situation on the Western Front had worsened in the winter months. Hankey proposed a trench-crossing machine, and Winston gave it some thought. He wrote to Asquith about fitting together a number of steam tractors with bullet-proofed armored shelters and machine-guns. The caterpillar system should enable it to cross trenches under fire, and their weight would crush any wire entanglements. Forty or fifty could be positioned under cover of darkness and destroy all obstructions while sweeping enemy trenches with machine-gun fire and tossing grenades out of the cabins. Asquith recommended the idea to Kitchener, who had a number of designs made at the War Office.

Their daily discussions were far too crucial for Winston to socialize in his spare time, which he did not enjoy anyway, and had no patience with small-talk, having none himself. He could only talk about the war nowadays: "My God!" he said when invited as a guest to Walmer Castle on the Kent coast. "This is living History. Everything we are doing and saying is thrilling—it will be read by a thousand generations, think of that!" The whole Asquith family were great admirers of his. "His eyes have the glow of a genius," Asquith said, as if mesmerized by him.

Carden sent the Admiralty War Group another telegram on January 12, which provided a detailed plan for the proposed Dardanelles naval campaign, and indicated it could be undertaken one month hence. Fisher was as enthusiastic as ever, and even suggested adding their most modern battleship, the *Queen Elizabeth*, which was about to be tested off Gibraltar. The idea transformed Winston's thinking away from his Baltic campaign to the Dardanelles. The QE could outgun the *Goeben* and the *Breslau*, placing Constantinople at the mercy of the British fleet. It might even persuade Enver Pasha—who was now the Turkish Minister of War—to abandon his German ally.

Asquith listened wordlessly to all the proposals before voicing his own conclusion. It was that the Admiralty should consider a possible naval action in the Adriatic immediately, and also prepare to bombard the Gallipoli Peninsula in February with the objective of taking Constantinople.

Gallipoli

Planning went ahead immediately with the ships that Carden asked to be fitted with mine-bumpers. An airfield was situated on a convenient Greek island. The

Adriatic plan was abandoned altogether at Fisher's request, since he advised that the Dardanelles campaign would require "our whole available margin." According to his enthusiastic assessment, their success there would 'influence every Mediterranean power.'

But Fisher seemed hesitant the following day, as if he'd had time to think it over and was now less sure of his claim not to require troops. He wrote to Admiral Jellicoe for 200,000 soldiers to act in conjunction with the fleet. Otherwise, he said in a complete turnabout, "I just abominate the Dardanelles."

Churchill, who had been swept away by Fisher's zeal for the plan, now found the old Admiral's behavior erratic, even bizarre. And some others viewed Fisher's disruptiveness as a portent of failure for the entire operation. "He is old & worn out & nervous," wrote the Assistant Director of Operations at the Admiralty.[5] He added that Fisher was a "failing old man, anxious for popularity," who did not want to be blamed for anything that might go wrong.

Fisher even offered to resign on February 25. Apparently he didn't want to see huge losses of life attributed to him. Then, the next day, Fisher wrote to Asquith to insist on military cooperation or he was against the plan. Nevertheless, the Prime Minister ordered the Dardanelles campaign forward—at which Fisher got up abruptly from his seat and hurriedly left the room. Kitchener followed him out to ask him what he intended to do. Fisher said he would resign as First Sea Lord.

All those remaining at the conference table enthusiastically expressed their own reasons for considering the operation important. Later on, Fisher changed his stance again by telling Winston he would support it.

The bombardment was planned for mid-February, but had to be postponed to wait for the necessary mine-sweepers. Then Winston's advisers at the admiralty argued that a military force *was* needed after all, to follow up the naval success on land. The Prime Minister agreed to troops, and the 29th Division was allocated for the Gallipoli Landing.

The war council met again on February 16, and agreed also to send redundant Australian and New Zealand troops from Egypt to Lemnos, as reserves for the Gallipoli landing. The Dardanelles campaign had now become a combined military and naval operation. Admiral Carden began bombarding the outer forts of the Dardanelles as a preliminary step to force the Straits. At that point, Kitchener informed them of news of a Russian setback that required the 29th Division. If taken away, it would leave only 30,000 Australian and New Zealand troops to achieve the landing at Gallipoli. This change of plan struck Lloyd George, Asquith, and Grey as unacceptable, and they all argued against Kitchener.

Admiral Carden reported that bad weather prevented any more firing during four days of poor visibility. Meanwhile, Winston requested that the 29th Division be sent to the Dardanelles. "We might be in Constantinople by the end of March," he told them hopefully. But Kitchener was now convinced that the Turks would withdraw from the Peninsula even if faced with the power only of naval gunnery on its own. So that, when Asquith asked to be reassured that the Australian and New Zealand troops were good enough, Kitchener intimated that they were all right, "if a cruise was all that was contemplated" for them. Asquith attempted to press him again to use the 29th Division. But Kitchener was evasive and refused to commit himself. Even so, the Prime Minister was so convinced of the positive effects resulting from the operation that he remarked philosophically, "One must take a lot of risks in war."

The decisive factor at the last moment was Kitchener's belief that the Turks were weak—although Churchill thought otherwise.

On February 28, Winston heard from the Grand Duke Nicholas that Russia would send 47,000 men to attack Constantinople from the Black Sea as soon as the British Fleet forced the Dardanelles, and his eagerness revived. He received a further boost of confidence on March 1 when the Greeks offered 60,000 troops to fight against Turkey. The 29th Division no longer seemed necessary. Now he waited anxiously for Carden's attack. Then the Russians wanted to annex Constantinople themselves, and rejected any Greek participation in the campaign.

Friction of War

So far, the Conservatives had not been invited to participate in any aspects of the war. Now Churchill felt that an all-party coalition might help to develop war policy, despite their continued quarrels. He persuaded the PM to invite Bonar Law and Lansdowne to the next war council meeting on March 10. But the meeting turned out to be a failure, as the Opposition leaders sat silent and unhelpful.

Fisher had heard intelligence that the Turkish forces had run out of ammunition. Since it would take weeks for more to arrive from Germany, he was convinced that the moment had now arrived for the landings on Gallipoli. So Churchill instructed Carden to feel free to "press the attack vigorously," which was what the Admiral had previously requested. But Kitchener suddenly changed his views on the Turks again. Instead of despising them as an easy walkover—as he'd constantly expressed before—he now decided they were a serious threat, and the attack must therefore wait for the 29th Division to arrive first.

The Decisive Moment

This was the decisive moment for Winston. But Fisher's and Kitchener's sudden turnabout made him uneasy. Then he received a signal from Carden which described the situation as an "unsatisfactory mine-sweeping operation," owing to heavy fire. It seemed to make no sense to Winston, because there had been no casualties. And if Kitchener was right about the Turks running out of ammunition, it didn't ring true. It left Winston feeling puzzled and anxious.

Then Carden decided not to wait for the Army, and planned his attack for March 18. But two days later, he became ill and passed his command to Rear-Admiral John de Roebeck. Churchill telegraphed the new commander to ask if he was satisfied with the plan, or wanted any changes to it. De Roebeck said he was satisfied and would attack in forty-eight hours.

At 10:45 a.m. on March 18 de Roebeck launched the naval attack on the Dardanelles. Six British and four French battleships entered the Straits and pounded the fortifications. By 1:45 p.m. there was no more return fire from the forts. It was time to withdraw the ships and introduce the minesweepers. Instead, the French battleship *Bouvet* hit a mine and sank with over 600 sailors. Soon after 4:00 p.m., the British battleship *Irresistible* began to list and was immovable. De Roebeck halted the operation immediately to rescue men from the *Irresistible*, when a third battleship, the *Ocean,* struck a mine.

As it turned out, British casualties were light—only fifty sailors dead and twenty-three wounded—despite the loss of three battleships. But the minefields had still not been swept. And Turkish guns continued firing from both shores. Fisher and Churchill assumed that de Roebeck would make a second attack soon. Fisher was so eager that he ordered two more battleships for de Roebeck, and told the War Council that a loss of twelve would have to be expected. They authorized de Roebeck to continue the attack if he thought fit.

De Roebeck telegraphed them next day to say he was ready for imminent action, but for the floating mines, and weather was bad. Then he had a change of mind, saying that the Army must go ashore first to demolish the forts before he could send his ship through the Narrows. He was now told that Kitchener had given orders to wait for the 29th Division from England, which would take three or four weeks before they could arrive.

As a result, de Roebeck telegraphed that he would suspend the naval operation. His message was received on the morning of March 23, advising of a decisive strike in mid-April, "rather than risk a great deal for what may possibly be only a partial solution." Churchill sent him a telegram to urge him to try once more, and reminded him that he also had aircraft at his disposal—and that the minefields must be swept. Before sending this telegram, he showed it to the cabinet in Downing Street. It included the words, "We do not think that the time has yet come to give up the plan of forcing Dardanelles by a purely naval operation." The cabinet agreed with the wording. Asquith made a personal record: "The Admiral seems to be in rather a funk."

But when Churchill returned to the Admiralty, he found that Fisher and the other two Admirals in the war group supported de Roebeck and wanted the telegram cancelled. Churchill returned again to Downing Street to obtain Asquith's signed authority to send the telegram. But now the Prime Minister was suddenly filled with doubts and would not overrule Churchill's most senior advisers at the Admiralty.

Churchill considered resigning immediately in the face of an impossible situation. Otherwise all he could do in the circumstances was to watch events unroll which he was powerless to prevent.[6] Instead, he was isolated. But he realized that resigning would not achieve anything. All he could do was telegraph de Roebeck to ask him to think again, and leave it in his hands.

When Churchill dined with Asquith that night, he found him disappointed. But there was no doubt that an attack by ships alone would not be repeated. The Army's opinion was that long-range Naval fire on forts was not enough unless infantry occupied the forts and held them afterwards.

De Roebeck simply waited for the Armies to assemble and were ready to attack, attempting merely to assist them with supporting fire. This was quite different from what Winston had been led to believe. The admiral left the fighting to the army, without even sweeping the minefield or sailing through the Narrows. Every decision was made either by Kitchener or by General Sir Ian Hamilton or his commanders. The entire operation had effectively been taken out of Winston's hands, and he could do no more than passively observe events that would ruin his reputation.

What he had considered his "Golden Age" in the admiralty was finished. Although he was still First Sea Lord, never again would he be a central player on war policy in Asquith's Government. No war council even met. And Kitchener did not even bother to send him any plans for his information or remarks. The Gallipoli Landings were a disaster; and despite securing the beachhead and cliff tops and fighting hard and long for five days, they had nothing to show for their efforts but a confusing shambles.[7]

The Opposition Conservative Party pointed accusing fingers at Churchill as the culprit for the waste of funds, shipping, and lives. Fisher disappeared after going home to bed. A search was made for him. "I have resigned," he told them when found. He said he was off to Scotland. Bonar Law received a great deal of information on the fiasco from him before he left, which the Conservatives would exploit to the full to destroy Churchill.[8]

The only mistake that Churchill had made was not taking his own advice. During the South African War against the Boers, he had cautioned the British Government not to push them into a corner but always leave them an avenue of escape. "Never corner a rat," he'd said, "or it will leap at your throat in desperation." But he had reviled some of the Conservative leaders, ridiculed others, and treated them generally with contempt, without understanding that they were frightened men. Values had changed since the Industrial Revolution, and the landed gentry were losing their wealth as a result of rising costs and falling revenues from their estates. They were also losing their way and their sense of purpose. Meanwhile, he had turned away from them to support the unprivileged and poor, the ill and the unemployed, the widows and orphans. He had been oblivious to the fact that the

Conservative upper classes hated him for it. Now Bonar Law was ready to leap at his throat and tear him down.

Jennie

"Poor Winston," said Jennie. "It never entered his head that a small-minded, gloomy man like Bonar Law could detest him. He detested nobody. He could only think about winning the war. Now he brooded in anguish . . ."[9]

The only war correspondent whom Kitchener allowed to report from Gallipoli returned to London in June and wrote in his diary: "June 10, 1915. This evening I dined at Lady Randolph Churchill to meet Winston . . . I am much surprised at the change in Winston Churchill. He looks years older, his face is pale, he seems very depressed and he feels keenly his retirement from the Admiralty. But even if he be the creator of the Dardanelles Expedition, he is in no wise responsible for the manner in which it is being carried out . . . It was only towards the very end [of the evening] that he suddenly burst forth into a tremendous discourse on the Expedition and what might have been, addressed directly across the table in the form of a lecture to his mother, who listened most attentively. Winston seemed unconscious of the limited number of his audience, and continued quite heedless of those around him. He insisted over and over again that the battle of March 18th had never been fought to a finish and, had it been, the Fleet must have got through the Narrows. This is the great obsession of his mind and will ever remain so."[10]

The war correspondent, Ashmead Bartlett, remembered after leaving the dinner, Winston at the open door, crying out into the night, "They never fought it out to the finish. They never gave my scheme a fair trial."

Jennie wrote to her sister Leonie on September 11, 1915: "It was too sad my missing seeing the zeps considering one passed over the house and all the maids saw it and the shrapnel bursting around it . . . Winston and Clemmie have gone to the farm. Lovely day, but I am feeling sad mostly about Winston."

A month later, Jennie was raging to her sister: "This slow and supine government are now beginning to realise what Winston has preached for the last six months. If they had made the Dardanelles a certainty, which they could have done in the beginning, Constantinople would have been in our hands ages ago . . . There is a minute of his, written the beginning of June, in which he warned the Government that Germany will not bring back troops from Russia to the West but will lose them to march through Serbia . . . But nothing will make them listen—Winston is on the war-path!"

But when Asquith formed his new War Committee it did not include Winston. Meanwhile, Winston suffered horribly with guilt of quite another sort. One after another of his friends was lost fighting the war at the Front. Jennie wrote to Leonie on November 12, 1915: "I want you to know before you see it in the Press that Winston has resigned and is going to join his regiment at the Front next week."

Beaverbrook visited the Churchills in Cromwell Road and found the whole household turned upside down as they prepared Winston for the trenches. According to him, Jennie was the only one who remained calm, collected, and efficient. "The delicate, fragile-looking Clemmie was showing nerves of iron . . . The war might have ended in 1915 and millions of lives saved but Winston could not force Kitchener and Fisher to plunge."

One month later, on December 20, 1915, Jennie wrote to Leonie again: "I see that the Dardanelles is being evacuated. It is sad to think of all the lives lost for nothing . . . the Government will be shown up at the end of the war when the papers are published and the public will realise how easy it would have been to get to Constantinople had men only been sent when they were asked for . . . Meanwhile Winston has been offered a battalion which will be in the fighting line. It is quite true that his orderly was killed near him the other day."

Jennie continued to rage, while Clementine remained "heroically calm." She knew there had been no mistakes at the admiralty while Winston was in charge. The problems had come from Kitchener's war office, and also from Fisher, who—the government now decided—had literally gone mad.

CHAPTER EIGHTEEN

WINSTON IN THE FRONT LINE

ONE OF THE REMARKABLE CULTURAL SITUATIONS at the opening of the war, and for several years afterwards, was a lack of initiative at the gradual realization that Britain had been awakened to an unexpected and more brutal war for which leadership was lacking and neither the troops nor the tactics were properly prepared. Consequently, when soldiers arrived for battle, they did not seem to know what to expect, or what was expected of them. It seemed to be true also of the Allies and sometimes even of the Germans, despite the fact that a German military cast had planned the war. Britain had bravely responded. But no one was prepared for it. The Kaiser evidently thought that all that was necessary to win were new technologies, using traditional tactics. When it came to fighting each other, a miasma of incomprehension, uncertainty, and incompetence settled like a heavy fog over the activities on the battlefields. By the time anyone began to realize the dangers, it was already too late.

Winston had plenty of time to reflect on those problems during the period he was in disgrace. Casting his mind back to his visits to Antwerp and to the Dardanelles fiasco, and attempting to analyze the causes of confusion and inertia, he attributed them to a lack of "design and decision." More familiar words today might be failure in strategic planning, leadership, and training. What could have been going on in the minds of the admirals and generals and other senior officers who simply could not get things right at Gallipoli? The soldiers who arrived too late to take up the best positions hesitated before seeking cover, giving the enemy time to surround them instead, so that they were forced into hand-to-hand combat to their own disadvantage.

From everything that history tells us of the events, it should have been fairly easy to take Constantinople from the Turks and end the war in 1915 or

1916. But it needed the will. Winston put it slightly differently when he said the leaders of the armed forces were twenty-five years out of date and fighting the wrong war. They also appear not to have been sufficiently well motivated to put aside personal jealousies, insecurities, biases, crass ambitions, or feuds.

Before leaving for the front, Winston wrote a letter to be given to Clementine if he was killed. After reassuring her about their financial situation, he appointed her his literary executor and told her how to obtain admiralty records which proved what really happened with the Dardanelles campaign.

Winston's feelings that something very strange had been happening in the tardiness of the landings on the Peninsula and the feebleness of Army support, which he attributed to Kitchener at the War Office, seems to be confirmed in a sentence written by military historian Liddell Hart, who wrote, "When, instead, Hamilton was given command of the Gallipoli expedition, Wilson used all his influence with [Sir John] French and the French to deprive it of adequate resources. Thus did personal animosities fatefully mar national purposes. If as a commander Hamilton did not rise to the full height of his apparent opportunity, the malevolent limitation of that opportunity would seem more responsible than any of his own limitations."[1]

Wilson was General Sir Henry Wilson, a controversial figure in the British Army. Sir Ian Hamilton was a friend of Winston's who had been twice recommended for the VC but passed over the first time because he was too young, and the second because he was too senior. It seems that obstacles were continually placed in his way because he wanted to reform the Army, whereas its high-ranking officers did not want to change.[2]

One of the factors which had swept away Winston's obsessive fixation on the core of the disaster and lightened his mood had been an introduction to watercolor painting by Lady Hazel Lavery, who was an ardent and accomplished artist herself. His depression lifted as he became absorbed in interpreting the landscape before him in thin background washes of watery paint and more striking foreground figures of trees or bushes. "The spell was broken," he said incredulously. He became distracted from his former misery. The change was so positive from his former abject self that Kitchener asked him to visit the Dardanelles and report on conditions. Asquith and Balfour approved. But when he saw how aghast were the leading Conservative ministers who were intent on blackening Churchill's name, he declined the offer.

In fact, he did obtain what amounted almost to first-hand experience, from his brother Jack who served in the Army there, and from his friend Sir Ian Hamilton who commanded troops there. The new landings were situated on Suvla Bay, but the Army never reached its objective. Despite virtually no Turkish opposition when they arrived, the British Army officers hesitated as if they had no idea what to do next, instead of leading their men to capture the ridge. Undecided, they waited patiently for the Turkish defenders to arrive, as if planning to toss a coin in the air and decide who should take the better side of the field for a football match. As a result, they were entangled in fierce close combat for four days. His brother Jack had seen it.

"The generals seemed apathetic," Jack said. And their apathy spread to the men. "They landed and advanced a mile & thought they had done something wonderful," Jack explained. They were unready for war. They had been taught fair play at school, so they generously gave the field to their enemies to win.

Despite their training—such as it was—they failed to understand that they had to kill the enemy before the enemy killed them. They didn't want to. After the exuberance at an opportunity for adventure overseas and a swift return home for Christmas in front of a friendly coal fire, the novelty of war had begun to wear off. They would much rather have been friends with the Turks and the Germans. It was how those nice, polite young men had been brought up by their loving mothers. Bemused by the unexpected situation, they had offered themselves up to the enemy. They were not, after all, anything like the soldiers of Napoleon's *Grand Armée* who had rampaged across Europe and done whatever had been necessary to earn the bread that the Emperor put on their tables, without which they would have starved to death. The young men who had volunteered for the British Army did not possess the killer instinct. Despite their own bayonet practice as cadets, they must have been surprised and amazed when the reality of the cold steel of the enemy bayonets being thrust into their bodies left them bleeding to death on the battlefields.

The Fall of Winston Churchill

Asquith's daughter Violet was among the guests at a farewell luncheon at 41 Cromwell Road, when Winston readied himself to depart for France to join his regiment in November. Clemmie, she said, was admirably calm and brave.

Eddie Marsh blinked back his tears. The rest of them hid their leaden hearts. Winston was the most cheerful and at his best. He was now a Major in the Queen's Own Oxfordshire Hussars.

He departed from London in his officer's uniform on the 18th and headed for the Western Front, having heard of the government's decision to evacuate the Dardanelles. Two days later, he joined the 2nd Battalion of the Grenadier Guards, just in time for its spell in the trenches at the front line. He spent the first night north of Neuve Chapelle in a much-battered farmhouse, where a dead Grenadier was laid out for burial. The men were very suspicious of him at first because of his celebrity and the accusations against him. But after settling in to the customary conditions of army life at the front, he found himself in good company. They moved to a dugout in one of the forward trenches on the second day. There was filth and rubbish everywhere and graves built into the defenses.

He quickly became used to the water and muck everywhere and to cold feet in the trenches, and to the squadrons of large bats swooping and gliding in the cold moonlight. Naturally enough, there were incessant rifle shots and machine-gun fire and, as he wrote to Clemmie, the "venomous whining and whirring of the bullets which pass overhead." The effect of it all on Churchill was as might be expected; in war he was at peace, as he knew he would be: "I have found happiness & content," he wrote, "such as I have not known for many months."[3]

Back in London, Maurice Hankey (Secretary of the War Cabinet) wrote in his diary, "Since Churchill left the Cabinet and the War Council we have lacked courage more than ever." But the embarrassment to the Asquith Government of all the incompetence and failure required a useful scapegoat, and Winston was it. Nevertheless, back in his natural element as a soldier and a war correspondent, he was more likely to be observing the war dispassionately and planning how to use the new material to describe it. Writers always look for good copy, and Churchill was no different. He wrote to Jennie on November 24, "Do you know I am quite young again."

Two days later he was annoyed to be taken out of the trenches which had become his home, by an order to pick up a car which would wait for him behind the lines, to be driven to meet his Corps Commander. He left as the Germans began shelling the trenches, and had to walk for an hour in rain and wind, across a soaking wet field among falling rifle bullets, to a crossroads where the vehicle was supposed to be waiting for him. But the driver had been alarmed by the shelling, and had fled. It turned out to be a wasted trip, since the general had only wanted to introduce himself.

But, as Winston explained to Clementine, on returning to the trench, he found a shell had burst a few feet from where he'd been sitting and killed one man out of the three. So his walk had been a fortunate escape after all. Now you see how vain it is to worry about things, he remarked to Clementine. He himself never sought to throw himself on the ground under attack or shelter to avoid danger, as many others did: he took the shelling and bombing in his stride.

Finding a young soldier asleep on sentry duty reminded him that the Army still considered it a crime and would condemn the young lad to death for it, if they knew, or imprison him for two years. It was a time when justice could still not be found and institutions were often even more cruel to their own people than to the enemy.

Much of Winston's forty-fourth birthday was spent on the wet mud floor of a dugout only two feet and six inches high. There was a good deal of shelling, he wrote to Clementine, about two shells a minute for about three hours. He enjoyed the entertainment. Then, after eight days out of the line, he returned to St. Omer, where General French's headquarters were situated, referring to himself for laughs as "the escaped scapegoat."

While there on December 1, he wrote a note to F. E. Smith about the considerable advantage of an armored vehicle on caterpillar treads that could cross obstacles, like ditches and even trenches. It would have to be huge to do so. He recommended arming it with two or three Maxim guns and flame-throwing apparatus. Nothing, he thought, but a direct hit from a field gun would stop it from advancing on the enemy trenches with machine-guns mounted behind armored shields.

Don't Play the Fool!

Despite Winston's composure—and he really did seem to be enjoying himself—Jennie and Clementine feared for his life at the front. Clementine cautioned him to be extra careful or, they would say he sought death out of grief or guilt for the failure of the Dardanelles. And Jennie warned him to consider that he'd had ten years of a sedentary life, so don't "play the fool!" He should remember he was destined for greater things.[4] But he refused to be tragic. To reassure them of his safe and comfortable life, he explained that he was writing from between clean sheets after a glorious hot bath at the St. Omer headquarters, where he was resting after dinner.

Although the Grenadiers had been given no choice but to receive him, they were all smiles by now with invitations to return whenever he felt like it. He had also lunched twice at Lord Cavan, the Commander of the Division, about his future command. Four days later he visited the French front line near Arras with a young captain named Louis Spears, whom he'd befriended at headquarters. A French general at Arras gave him a French steel helmet that he thought so good that he continued to wear it. They also drove to La Panne on the Belgian coast where the trenches ran into the sea.

Spears made a note of their discussions, and of Winston's plan to shorten the war by attacking the Germans through Holland or at Borkum. He was also interested in the idea of firing torpedoes from seaplanes. Then, after a letter from the Conservative Statesman Lord Curzon, he said he might have to leave for London. But next morning he decided it was not a good idea to go back at this juncture after all.

On December 9 he had orders to take command of the 56th Brigade as its Brigadier-General. But first he had to spend a few days preparing by studying the supply chain "from base to trenches." Meanwhile, he had received a comfortable sleeping bag from Clementine. But he had been away for only four weeks, and there would be months to follow. He would have to sit them out in the trenches until the time came for him to stand up in Parliament again and "procure the dismissal of Asquith and Kitchener."

Meanwhile, in London, Asquith knew he would be questioned in the House of Commons by Conservative MPs who were out for his blood about Churchill's treatment. He dodged them by clamping down on Winston's authority and promotion.

Sir John French's last day after dismissal as commander-in-chief, before handing the responsibility over to Sir Douglas Haig, came on December 18, when he took a picnic lunch with Winston—after which French told Haig that although Winston had been vetoed for a big brigade by Asquith, he should at least be given a battalion. Haig said he had no objection since they were short of battalion COs and Winston had done good work in the trenches. He saw Winston afterwards and treated him with great courtesy. Winston agreed to take a battalion.

Winston felt that French did not deserve dismissal, but he knew that Asquith would throw anyone to the wolves to keep himself in office. But it was not always easy to be philosophically detached from what was going on in London. He continued to observe the insipid, directionless, and incompetent policy of the government while considering what they should be doing instead, and yet admitting to himself that it was pointless to fret about it. [5]

Since no battalion had been allocated to him by Christmas, he returned to London, where F. E. Smith was now Attorney General in the government. He dined with Lloyd George, who was now the real power center, isolated from Asquith and ready to "smash the government." He lunched with the editor of the *Observer,* who sought to patch up the relationship between his friend Fisher and Winston.

Back again at St. Omer, he found Max Aitken had been appointed as a "Canadian Eye-Witness at the Front." They became firm friends. Meanwhile, Lloyd George was having lunch with Clementine at 41 Cromwell Road. He told her, "We must get Winston back."

Winston was visiting parts of the front line for the first time—Neuve Chapelle and Vimy Ridge. The French line ran from there. It was where, as Winston wrote to Clementine, "You cannot show a whisker without grave risk of death." He learned in the New Year of 1916 that he would command the 6th Royal Scots Fusiliers. It was a battalion of the Ninth Division. He dined with them that night and found officers he had served with before, or knew at Harrow or Sandhurst, and even Malakand. His own battalion had suffered heavy losses at Loos, leaving only an eighteen-year-old officer as the last regular soldier in it, who had only a few months' experience. All the other officers were volunteers without any experience of trench warfare at all. He would have only two months to train them with his second-in-command, Archibald Sinclair.

Command

He was looking forward to taking command of his new battalion with the rank of lieutenant-colonel. To strike what he considered to be an appropriate chord between them, he asked Clementine to send him a copy of the complete edition of the poetry of Robert Burns. He greatly admired the Scots, and had of course been close to his Scottish constituents in Dundee.

His battalion was stationed temporarily in reserve billets in a little village ten miles behind the lines called Moolenacker. Its attitude was mutinous at the prospect of being led by a disgraced politician. But that afternoon, he called his officers together and gave them an enthusiastic lecture on lice and its effect among troops that was so informative it left them fascinated. He then formed a committee to take measures to exterminate all the lice in the battalion. He had vats brought in for collective delousing.

The success of his first project as commander was momentarily forgotten when he read in *The Times* that Asquith had refused to introduce conscription. Churchill fretted at the shortage of troops to finish the war and the lack of action. Nevertheless, it was far more important to train his own men to get back to the trenches on active service. The other officers, as he explained to Clementine, were all good and brave middle-class Scotsmen who were intelligent and willing, but were all new to soldiering, since all the older and experienced ones and the professionals had been killed at Ypres. He felt that he had at least raised their morale by the end of two weeks. He also made sure they were comfortable and well-disciplined. One of his officers wrote later that Churchill worked hard to inspire confidence, and gained confidence himself.

It turned out that after marching and drilling, trench discipline and inspections, gas-mask training, and rifle and grenade practice, there was an extra week in reserve. Although he was impatient, the men were more than pleased. He made a point of organizing entertainments, like sports days and concerts, which not only kept his men happy but also contributed to comradeship and conviviality.

When he watched German aircraft in combat in the sky all morning above their billets, he was reminded of his initiatives in forming the naval air force, and felt again that there was no excuse for not having air superiority. But their last day at Moolenacker came on January 23, and the next day they moved closer to the front at a village named La Crèche. It was the anniversary of Lord Randolph's death, and Winston felt close to his father, whose respect and love he had always craved.

Their orders were to hold a sector of the front at a Belgian village from January 27. They had six-day spells in the trenches. He gave last-minute instructions to his officers, which included "Laugh a little and teach your men to laugh . . . War is a game that is played with a smile." His frontline headquarters was not far from trenches that had already suffered from numerous bombardments. His first day in them was spent largely in listing needed improvements to the dugouts. This was to be their home for some time and there was always a risk of sudden death or injuries, and from continual shelling of one of their own gun batteries close by. Due to poor accuracy of the German gunners, they were more likely to be killed by accident than by intention.

He wrote encouragingly to Jennie, "We have only to persevere to conquer." His policy, he told her, was to fight on. But while he was good at witty one-liners and quick rejoinders, inventing slogans and maxims, neither the Government nor the War Office or the Admiralty were much good at carrying them out.

Lloyd George, Bonar Law, and F. E. Smith visited Max Aitken's headquarters at St. Omer, and Winston met them there. They appeared to be in total agreement that Asquith had to be got rid of at all costs. Lloyd George wanted to be Secretary of State for War.

Back at the front line, Winston could not resist going through the barbed wire into no-man's-land after dark. The battalions' forward posts were situated in shell craters between the two opposing armies that faced each other in trenches, which they would dive into the moment machine-gun fire opened up, often to find corpses already lying there ahead of them.

When he was visited by an old friend from Bangalore days, Hugh Tudor, who had recently fought at Loos as an officer, he heard the same stories of mistake after mistake as he had seen and heard of elsewhere. He watched Tudor's artillery at work against the Germans, and the enemy retaliation. It was the first direct fire he had been under so far.[6] The Germans also fired trench mortars as well as shells. Captain Tudor was as cool and calculating under fire as Winston. He had previously fought in the Second Boer War. He was one of several young officers with a professional eye and mind and an expert tactician whom Winston knew at the Front.

By February 13, Winston found that his political career in the House and his career at the Admiralty had receded from his mind, as if his younger days as a second-lieutenant in South Africa had simply developed in a direct line to his present position in the army. It seemed to him that he'd always thought of himself as a soldier first. And he found it exciting. When the nearby farm was shelled again by the enemy, they removed all their stores of food—eggs and bacon, bread, and marmalade—and took it to the dugout, while a wounded officer had his open wounds bandaged by a doctor only a few feet away.

He was excited to receive news that day of the development and first trials of the tanks he'd imagined long ago. But everything took too much time. He seethed at how easy it was for people to do nothing, how hard it was to achieve anything. He knew he was impatient with lazy-mindedness, but somebody had to be, or nothing would ever get done. Two of his men were killed at the end of February from British shells falling short, and three more from German shells hitting their target.

He had seven days leave due from March 2, and traveled to Boulogne, from where he took a destroyer to Dover. He was home by nightfall—where he heard that Balfour was due to present the Navy Estimates to the House in five days. He immediately began to prepare a speech. On March 4, Clementine was appalled to have to entertain Fisher for lunch, since Winston had decided to invite him. He told her that Fisher needed him [Churchill] to manage him—he'd be a disaster without him [Churchill].

He tried out his speech on Fisher the next day, and the old admiral was impressed. He particularly liked it when Winston intended to call for Fisher to be reinstated at the Admiralty. Winston's aim was to warn Parliament of imminent danger and get rid of the Asquith Government and its complacency. In his speech, he railed against the dangers from enemy submarines, the need to bomb zeppelin sheds in Germany, and the passivity in 1916 when the Admiralty and the Army had already been modernized and mechanized with new technologies that were not being exploited to the full. He added that the Admiralty in which he and Fisher had served would never have been content with the passive way the war was being run. Finally, he warned the House that the times were crucial, the issue momentous, that Britain's existence depended on the Fleet. And he suggested that Fisher be recalled.

The response in the house was not what he had hoped for—it was amazed and aghast.[7] One Conservative MP sprang up and said, "We all wish him [Churchill] a great deal of success in France, and we hope he will stay there."

Stunned and disappointed though he was, Winston decided to continue his attacks on the Government instead of returning to his battalion in France.

Clementine disagreed heartily. After his speech requesting the reinstatement of Fisher, she felt he would not obtain any support in Parliament. But Winston was so sure that he could get military, naval, and air deficiencies solved by influencing Parliament that he was no longer interested in commanding a battalion or an army, and asked Kitchener to relieve him of his military command. Kitchener turned to Asquith for advice, and Asquith nodded.

When Winston met with the Prime Minister later that day, Asquith solemnly reminded him how his father had thrown away his political career through poor judgment and one impulsive action. It was a historic incident that could easily be repeated by Winston Churchill's impetuosity, his crusading zeal, and his impatience to lead.

CHAPTER NINETEEN

ANGUISH AND TORMENT

WINSTON'S TIME IN THE TRENCHES WAS now over. All that was left was to resettle his battalion and return to London on May 7, 1916. He had no prospects in sight as a Parliamentarian, but he still had his constituents in Dundee. Everyone else had abandoned him as a pariah. Two days after parting from his old comrades, he spoke in the House on the desperate need for more men. Britain was outnumbered and its resources ill-used. But, after attempting to dissuade both parties from becoming embroiled in Ireland's problems, for the far more urgent concern was to concentrate on winning the war in Europe, an Irish nationalist shouted out, "What about the Dardanelles?" The implied accusation would ring in his ears for years to come and continue to cast doubts on all his judgments.

He did his best to persuade Asquith to publish the truth about the Dardanelles fiasco, and Asquith agreed. It was now a year since Winston had left the admiralty. Now he began to assemble the documents that should exonerate him from the failure of Gallipoli. Feeling encouraged, he wrote to Fisher, "Don't lose heart. I am convinced destiny has not done with you." As it would turn out, he was wrong: the future was clouded with the vagaries and ineptitude of bad politics.

Three days after attempting to encourage Fisher, he spoke at the Air Board debate on May 17 and described how he had set up the new air defenses of Britain as soon as war had erupted. He presented facts and figures to counter the erroneous claims of his neglect. They had lost the air superiority England built up at the beginning of the war, he told the House—but England can recover it. He spoke again in the Army Estimate debate. He argued against the unfairness of placing all the action on the soldiers in the trenches, while others were not being used at all. "What is going on while we sit here, while we go away to dinner or home to bed?" Every twenty-four hours, nearly a thousand of our men were knocked into bundles of bloody rags and thrown into hasty graves or field ambulances. He warned against futile offensives without plan or justifications, and pleaded for more men to defeat the enemy.

He wanted the ministerial power to fulfill all those objectives, but all he was allowed to do was talk in anguish as a Member of Parliament. And he was alone—only he spoke of the shortcomings and lack of will of the government, of failure to use the nation's resources strategically, since no one wanted to be seen to be associated with him.

On May 31, Admiral Sir John Beatty of the British fleet in the North Sea spotted an armada of German battleships. The total number in both of the fleets added up to 250 ships. The British Navy engaged Vice-Admiral Franz Hipper's battle cruisers in the first stage of the Battle of Jutland. It was an attempt by the Kaiser's modern fleet to dominate the seas. Ironically, it was the only time that the expensive German fleet was used in the entire war. Admiral Sir John Jellicoe lost three battle cruisers in the first stage—apparently through faulty technology that resulted in unexpected explosions. After the second engagement in the evening, the German Navy turned tail under cover of darkness. Both sides claimed victory, but 6,094 British sailors were killed, to 2,551 Germans. Britain lost fourteen ships to eleven in the German fleet.

Balfour asked Winston to write an uplifting article for the press that would encourage the British public, who viewed it as an awful defeat and had become very depressed. But that was all he was asked to do. Meanwhile, he and Sir Ian Hamilton studied the Admiralty documents that he knew would exonerate him—particularly those involving Kitchener's mishandling of the war.

Kitchener left Britain by sea for Russia on June 5, where the Allied campaign was not going well. Meanwhile, Winston and his old friend Hamilton were still sorting through Admiralty documents to prepare evidence for the Royal Commission on the Dardanelles—including Kitchener's telegrams to Ian Hamilton—to make sure that nothing was excluded that showed Kitchener's hesitations, uncertainties, changes of mind, and neglect of the Army when it had landed on the Peninsular. Kitchener had appointed Sir

Ian Hamilton to take command of the operation, and then apparently held back resources needed for victory, or someone had. Hamilton felt he might have been betrayed by Wilson, who appeared to have a personal grudge against him, or a double agenda. Hamilton had watched the landings from aboard the HMS *Queen Elizabeth* and wondered at the reason for the delays; watched the shells flying overhead; and landed with the Army, wondering why nothing ever happened according to plan. It seemed that both Wilson and Kitchener had an alternative agenda for which the Gallipoli landings had suffered.[1]

They were examining the papers in Winston's study overlooking Cromwell Road when they heard shouting in the street beneath the window. Hamilton described the scene later on: "We jumped up and Winston threw the windows open." A newsvendor was hovering outside with a bundle of newspapers beneath his arm, calling out, "Kitchener drowned! No survivors!"

As Hamilton wrote later, the fact that Kitchener vanished when he had questions to answer in a case against him was one of the coincidences that Kitchener's career was crowded with. He was not going to answer a charge that he may not have wished Gallipoli to succeed in case it enhanced Ian Hamilton's reputation and stature. But Winston's reputation would remain blackened unless Asquith spoke up. And Asquith did not want all the documents published because, although they might clear Winston, they could discredit Asquith. Asquith told the House of Commons on June 26 that "A considerable period must elapse before these papers are likely to be ready."

When Lloyd George became Secretary of State for War on July 7, Winston requested publication on the grounds that the nation had a right to know the truth. But now the Government preferred to sweep away the residue of past failures. Then, on July 20, Winston heard that the Admiralty objected to publication of their documents, too, including the crucial naval telegrams. Asquith wrote to him that the Government had since decided not to publish the Dardanelles documents at all.[2] Winston remained deep in thought but powerless to act. Meanwhile, Asquith, of whom it had always been said he had a great future, had already eaten it all up and looked bloated. He had fallen in love with a woman far younger than him in the summer of 1914— Venetia Stanley—and wrote her love letters every day to tell her how much he loved her.

Picardy

The sole offensive effort of the Anglo-French Allies' part on the Western Front had so far been a series of partial actions in Picardy from July 1. The two armies appeared to be exhausted after the overlong defensive actions of Verdun, which represented "the glory and the graveyard of Kitchener's Army. This was the loss of many of those citizen volunteers who, instantly answering the call in 1914, had formed the first national army of Britain."[3]

Previous Allied failures were attributed by Joffre to bad weather conditions or shortages of ammunition. Now the French general envisaged his troops attacking with forty divisions on a twenty-five mile front from Lassigny to the Somme, and the British attacking with twenty-five divisions. His sole reason appears to have been that the British "would be bound to take part in it."[4]

In the little British Army which originally took the field, personality had for a time more scope. And much was to depend on it. Unfortunately, the issue was to suggest that the process of selection had not succeeded in bringing to the fore the officers best fitted for leadership. It is significant that, on the way out to France, Haig spoke to Charteris (his military secretary and future chief intelligence officer) of his qualms concerning the Commander-in-Chief, Sir John French, whose right hand he had been in South Africa:

> "D.H. unburdened himself today. He is greatly concerned about the composition of British G.H.Q. He thinks French quite unfit for high command in time of crisis . . . He says French's military ideas are not sound; that he has never studied war; that he is obstinate, and will not keep with him men who point out even obvious errors. He gives him credit for good tactical powers, great courage and determination. He does not think Murray will dare to do anything but agree with every-thing French suggests. In any case he thinks that French would not listen to Murray but rely on Wilson, which is far worse. D.H. thinks Wilson is a politician, and not a soldier, and 'politician' with Douglas Haig is synonymous with crooked dealing and wrong sense of values."

This judgment is similar to that of another general, eminent as a military historian: "There could hardly have been worse selected G.H.Q's than those with which we began the South African War and 1914."[5]

The Battle of Loos

The Battle of Loos on September 15 would be another failure. General Haig had been against it from the start: "It will cost us dearly, and we shall not get very far." General Robertson agreed with him. But Joffre was for it and would not accept any arguments. General Joffre was backed solidly by Wilson, who "was a devout believer in the infallibility of French military judgment."[6]

French and Wilson simply excluded their critics or opponents from discussions, even from their personal mess, so that they could ignore them. Most surprisingly, Lord Kitchener had added his weight to the argument when he had visited Sir John French in August, saying, "We must do our utmost to help France in this offensive, even though by so doing we may suffer very heavy losses."[7] It was a reversal of his previous attitude, perhaps born out of despair at all the other failures he was involved in, like the Dardanelles, Verdun, and the Russian Front—and a gambler's desperation that something, anything, might work and recoup his losses.

Joffre's draft plan had been sent to French, the British commander-in-chief, on June 4, when Haig was still French's subordinate. Haig visited the area and claimed it was not favorable for an attack. He was right: "The ground, for the most part bare and open, would be so swept by machine-gun and rifle fire both from the German front trenches and from the numerous fortified villages immediately behind them, that a rapid advance would be impossible."[8] But Joffre dismissed the reality of the situation in preference for his delusion of a proposed victorious offensive. Like Wilson, he believed in his infallibility, against which reason or reality did not figure.

The official history, after the event, stated that "Under pressure from Lord Kitchener at home, due to the general position of the Allies, and from Generals Joffre and Foch in France, due to the local situation in France, the British commander-in-chief was therefore compelled to undertake operations before he was ready, over ground that was most unfavorable, against the better judgment of himself and of General Haig, and, with no more than a quarter of the troops, nine divisions, instead of thirty-six, that he considered necessary for a successful attack."[9]

Historian Liddell Hart's interpretation was entirely different. It was that the appointment of a Supreme Commander of the Entente forces was under consideration and Kitchener may have anticipated a call to this post, and a timely concession to the French over Loos was likely to make them more receptive to his appointment later on.[10]

Whatever the real reason—and there appear to be no rational ones—the decision had been taken to attack Loos, and the artillery bombardment began on September 21. Meanwhile, the Germans had strengthened their defenses. British casualties amounted to 60,392. The Germans lost 20,000. French losses were 191,797 officers and men.[11]

The Somme Offensive

To facilitate the main Anglo-French blow, Joffre had persuaded the British Army to make an initial attack north of the Somme in April, and a second one in May. Haig preferred one overwhelming blow with every force available to ensure collapse. He was justified, in the circumstances, but Joffre had history on his side—and this war had already demonstrated that decisive offenses failed unless an enemy's reserves had already been weakened or diverted elsewhere first. But one overwhelming attack did not appeal to Joffre, who preferred a war of attrition from Britain, Russia, France, and even Italy.

The British Army agreed to do its share, while cautioning President Poincaré that "we cannot cope with the politicians, who, after the Germans, are our worst enemies."

But hesitation and organizational delays gave the advantage to the Germans with their attack at Verdun from February 21 onwards, which impaired the entire Allied campaign of 1916. When Joffre requested help, Haig sought to relieve the French Tenth Army near Arras. Allenby's Third Army moved north. With Rawlinson's Fourth Army, British forces now held an eighty-mile front from Ypres to the Somme. Since French forces had been depleted at Verdun, their contribution shrank at the Somme, to less than half in the original plan, covering only an eight-mile front (instead of twenty-five miles). As a result, British forces bore the main weight of the campaign on the Western Front: so that "July 1st, 1916 [became] a landmark in the history of the war." Haig failed to readjust his goal to his shrinking resources.[12]

The main thrust was left to Rawlinson's Fourth Army, but Haig also provided him with two cavalry divisions, led by General Gough, and another two in reserve. He had 1,537 guns, of which 467 were heavy ones. It gave him a concentration of one piece of artillery to every twenty yards of front. The French possessed 900 heavy guns on a far shorter front, providing them with greater concentration. The problem was that they were, in effect, "storming a fortress," for which their artillery was deficient—a factor which General Headquarters were blind to. As usual, they were thinking in pre-war terms, "under the influence of General Sir Henry Wilson," who chose rather to "follow French ideas," instead of using more accurate information from the British Intelligence Branch.

By the time of Verdun, there was considerable anti-war feeling from all sides. There were anti-war protests in Germany, which were continuing to grow as a result of the Allied blockade of food. Around 88,232 German deaths from starvation were attributed to the British naval blockade. The number of deaths from starvation rose in 1916 to 121,114. Food riots erupted in more than thirty German cities. Karl Liebknecht, the anti-war member of the Reichstag, was sentenced to two years of hard labor for urging soldiers not to fight—increased to four years soon after, to discourage mutiny.

German attitudes were divided between the war-making Junker landlord class and the average German who did not want war. Much the same situation applied to Russia, except for the far larger number of opponents to war, who were suppressed by secret police and the military, but would finally get their way through the Bolshevik Revolution. France had its own sporadic mutinies.

The balance of incompetence, fear, blind courage, lack of training, and inept leadership, as well as the bravery of young officers and men from either side competing with the other, was shown by taking ground and losing it, retaking it and losing it again. Any experience gained would count on either side, so that "On the Italian Front, a third of the Austrian advances made during the Trentino Offensive were steadily recovered, despite a terrifying Austrian bombardment on the night of June 28, when hydro-cyanide gas shells were fired, causing grave injury to more than 6,000 sleeping Italians. On the next day, however, the Italians retook the trenches they had been forced to abandon, helped by the blowing back of the gas on the Austrian troops, more than a thousand of whom were injured, and took 416 Austrian prisoners. On the Russian front the Austrians were mauled at the Battle of Kolomea, when the Russians took more than 10,000 prisoners . . ."[13]

The Battle of the Somme was an attempt to break through the German lines with a massive infantry assault. The British soldiers sang as they marched to the battlefield. What did they know? They were aged from eighteen to about twenty-three, some even younger who had lied about their age to get in to the army—partly for some imagined adventure, partly because jobs were scarce and they found the boredom intolerable, and partly because they had been led to believe in a myth of comradeship that would actually last for too short a time to be meaningful.

The battle had begun on July 1, with nearly a quarter of a million shells fired in just over an hour at German positions. The barrage was so intense that it was heard on Hampstead Heath, a north-western suburb of London.

The weight of the Tommies' equipment was so heavy they could barely climb out of a trench, and were so slow in moving that they made excellent targets for German gunners. They carried about "sixty-six pounds' weight of equipment: a rifle, ammunition, grenades, rations, a waterproof cape, four empty sandbags, a steel helmet, two gas helmets, a pair of goggles against tear gas, a field dressing, a pick or a shovel, a full water bottle and a mess tin."[14] Not surprisingly, less than half came back.

A hundred German machine-guns, hidden in armored positions, opened fire on the British infantry. Many were killed before they could even get out from their own barbed wire. Two German-held villages were taken that day, and a strongpoint known as "the Leipzig Redoubt." The cost was "over a thousand British officers and more than 20,000 men . . . and 25,000 seriously wounded."[15] The cost in human life on that day was greater than on any other day of battle in the war. And yet, the first-hand reports of the young men showed extraordinary cheerfulness, courage, and exuberance at still being alive afterwards—like winning a hundred-yard dash at school and being cheered for it.

The Dardanelles Commission

Winston wrote four articles for the *Sunday Pictorial* that summer. The final one dealt with the changed public attitudes to war after Loos and the Somme. The initial excitement had been overtaken by the deaths. Enthusiasm had been overcome by endurance at the long drawn-out battles of attrition and hydro-cyanide gas hovering like an autumn mist over the battlefields. Sorrow had become numbed from the thudding of the guns. He spoke in the House as the soldiers' friend, appealing for a fairer system and better conditions for them, quicker promotions, and more recognition for bravery. He expressed doubt that people at home understood what soldiers endured in the frontline trenches.

Young men writing home or returning on leave had no wish to burden their families with descriptions of the horrors of war, of killing strangers and being killed. They were inhibited by good manners and compassion from sharing their suffering with their wives, their mothers, or their children. Most pretended it was an adventure, a bit of a change, or just a bit of fun. Their families were kept in ignorance of the reality and believed them. Only those who returned blind, or without limbs, or suffering from shell-shock, demonstrated that they were lying. Even so, who could imagine the squalor or what they were required to do unless they had been there themselves?

F. E. Smith circulated a memorandum from Winston to the Cabinet which pointed out how the troops were being worn down more and more with every new offensive on the Western Front. Lloyd George invited Winston to meet with him to offer his views, which he would discuss with others at the War Office. The Conservative Lord Derby, who was now Director General of Recruiting, told him that it would be distasteful for everyone in the War Office to have Churchill there—they would not work with him because he was too untrustworthy. But Winston refused to look shamefaced or apologize for what he had not done.

When he heard that the caterpillar tanks were about to be used in battle, he called on Asquith to ask him not to allow them to be used unless they were in large enough numbers to be effective. There was at least an opportunity for one big surprise where a huge victory could be achieved. But it turned out that fifteen had already been used on the Somme, and the element of surprise was already lost.

He carried on preparing his case for the Dardanelles Commission of Enquiry, but was thwarted in his intentions without being able to use Admiralty documents and War Council minutes to clear his name. He had also intended to be present to answer anyone's charges, but was told that the inquiry would be in secret, and only the witnesses for that day would be admitted. He submitted his documents and listed five questions he thought required discussion at the inquiry: 1. Was there complete authority? 2. Was there a reasonable prospect of success? 3. Were greater interests compromised? 4. Was all possible care and forethought given to preparations? 5. Was vigor and determination shown in execution?

His preparations and paperwork were considerable. He hoped to publish his evidence when the commission concluded its findings. He had already begun to write three articles for the *London Magazine.* He wrote to Clementine's brother about how the war was so little understood by the general public and how frustrated he felt at being unable to guide them. He had felt too limited at the Front, whereas he evidently had a following at home, to judge from the growing circulation figures for the *Sunday Pictorial* and the *London Magazine,* where his articles had appeared.

But the Conservative newspapers continued to attack him, using the old Dardanelle accusations. The *Daily Mail* of October 13 wrote of "the contemptible fiasco of Antwerp and the ghastly blundering of Gallipoli." He protested at once to the Commission, of bias without evidence, and gave his own evidence again. He knew he had to publish his own evidence if he was ever to work in the Government again. But the Government agreed only to publish a general report. Since his pen was the only weapon he had left, he wrote a full account of the Antwerp expedition for the *Sunday Pictorial.*

Meanwhile, Lloyd George and Bonar Law were conspiring to replace Asquith. They finally succeeded when they and Lord Curzon resigned from the Government. Asquith was obliged to resign the same evening. And the King asked Bonar Law to form the next new Government.

During a dinner to which Winston was invited, Lloyd George, Aitken, and F. E. Smith discussed the new administration. Lloyd George had to leave, and asked Aitken to drop a hint to Churchill that pressure was being placed on them to exclude him from any new government. He told Aitken that he himself could not offer Churchill a Cabinet position. Aitken did as he'd been asked, and Winston flew into a rage and marched out.

Lloyd George became Prime Minister when not enough MPs would support Bonar Law, and informed Winston that he might be able to offer him Chairmanship of the Air Board. But it would have to await publication of the Dardanelles Commission Report. Winston replied that he would take whatever position he was offered to serve his country. But the Conservatives had other ideas.

Winston spent Christmas and the New Year holidays at Blenheim with his family. Then, speaking at the Army Estimates on March 5, 1917, he begged the Government not to allow another campaign like the Somme.

When the Dardanelle Commission was finally ready to publish their report, Lloyd George gave Winston a draft copy of the Admiralty section beforehand. Churchill was not blamed for anything. On the contrary, the report showed that when de Roebeck halted the naval attack on March 18, only three rounds of ammunition remained in the guns of the Turkish fortress, and the British Army was within minutes of success. But they had been ordered to stop. And Kitchener had failed to give the War Council enough details of his military plans.[16]

Nevertheless, Winston was disappointed at the generality of the report—it failed to answer a lot of specific questions regarding the war, or the stalemate of the trench warfare. And a general coverup had misrepresented the Somme battle as a series of victories. "Contemporaries have condemned the men who tried to force the Dardanelles," he was at least able to write. But "History will condemn those who did not aid them."

His trials were not yet over, since Winston still had to defend himself in the House.

CHAPTER TWENTY

MUTINY

BY THE MIDDLE OF MARCH IN 1917, most people involved in the war had grown tired of what they saw as a pointless and even stupid enterprise that seemed endless and costly in lives, and achieved nothing. Nevertheless, Douglas Haig's troops had advanced much further than any Allied Army had since trench warfare had begun two and a half years earlier. It seemed that either the German troops had lost their spirit—which would be entirely understandable—or Haig was an outstanding general who knew what he was doing. Even so, they had taken only sixty-one square miles of territory from the Germans, 20,000 prisoners, and 252 heavy guns, in little more than a month. But one contributing factor differed from previous battles, in that tanks had been used as a tactical weapon. They had now become a regular feature of infantry equipment.

The technology which had previously pinned down troops in trenches facing each other across no-man's land, so that they dared not advance over the top without instantly losing their lives, was the Maxim machine-gun. Churchill saw the possibility of the tank as an armor-plated, moving fortress against which machine-gun bullets were useless. They bounced off. Infantry soldiers could follow behind and take potshots at machine-gun emplacements without danger, while their moving fort advanced relentlessly with its own cannons and machine-guns. But it had taken two and a half years for that concept to be designed, produced in several different prototypes, and then manufactured with the right specifications for use on the battlefields.

Trials for a German tank began on May 14 at Mainz, with a number of other crucial incidents that affected each of the Allies and their enemies. But the first tank had been used at the front about eight months previously at the Somme offensive on September 15, 1916. The tank brought movement back to warfare as a killing machine on land, in much the same way that battleships had at sea, when moving and firing and being provided with armored protection at the same time. What had been famous for its powers of annihilation before the machine-gun entered the equation was the cavalry charge, as Winston had experienced it at Khartoum against the Dervishes. Hiram Maxim's invention of the machine-gun had made the cavalry obsolete.

The concept of a tank came to the mind of Colonel Ernest Swinton while visiting London on October 20, when he met with Colonel Maurice Hankey, Secretary of the Committee for Imperial Defense, and described the type of creature to beat the machine-gun: it was a machine-gun destroyer. Hankey took the matter higher up the line of command at the War Office. Swinton followed suit in France, where he found with no interest. Hankey's approach to Kitchener received the same negative treatment. So he submitted a memorandum to Prime Minister Asquith. It was from Asquith that Winston Churchill first heard of the concept, which he instantly realized was exactly what was needed to break the deadlock in frontline trenches. Asked for his opinion, he wrote back enthusiastically to Asquith. Asquith sent his letter on to Kitchener and, again, nothing further happened.

In the absence of imagination, which Kitchener did not possess, it required specifications to be finally coordinated with the making of a prototype model named "Little Willie" (since everyone liked to poke fun at Kaiser Wilhelm). Swinton rejected the model as unsuitable for the required military tactics. They then showed him a full-size wooden model of a different design that could climb a five-foot-high wall and cross a trench eight feet wide. It was first named "Mother" and "Big Willie," and given a trial at Hatfield on February 2, 1916. The results were so good that the War Office ordered forty tanks to be made. They were big and heavy.

General Joffre had approved something similar two months previously in France, with a difference that they were smaller and the French Army had ordered four hundred. They soon doubled that number.

The training of tank crews took place in Thetford, Norfolk. Its nicknames were dropped and it was referred to from then on as a tank. But, as Churchill feared, they failed to surprise the enemy by using it in big enough numbers, and put it into the field when not quite ready. In fact, Haig agreed with those tactical principles but was pressured when the Battle of the Somme came to a standstill and he needed something to give the Allies an advantage over the enemy: so he used only sixty at the Front. But the new tanks were used as intended at Cambrai in November, and they triumphed. With tanks protecting the infantry from enemy machine-gun fire, they could get out of their dugouts, and the war could move forward.

Mutiny

At the very same time as Britain showed signs of war-weariness, and Lloyd George was considering a separate peace with Austria and Bulgaria, which he hoped the German Kaiser would follow, French troops on the Western Front were exhausted. And military discipline had broken down on the Eastern Front in Russia.

Frontline Russian cavalry were issued with live ammunition to protect themselves from the ranks and prevent mutiny. As Georgi Zhukov would recall many years later, there was a demonstration on February 7 with red banners. After returning to his regimental headquarters, a cavalryman explained to them that "the working class, peasants and soldiers no longer recognized the Tsar."[1] They wanted peace, land, and liberty. According to Zhukov (who would become perhaps the greatest General of the Second World War), there was no command, but the soldiers knew what they must do.

Demands for bread and looting of food shops began that evening. Ninety thousand factory workers were out on strike. Martial law was announced in Petrograd by the Petrograd Soviet Workers. Forty-eight hours later, the Tsar returned to the capital city from the Front, where he had foolishly taken command of the war without knowing anything about it. Soldiers from the garrison joined the crowds demonstrating in the streets against him. Soldiers had already begun murdering their officers. Some officers advised the Tsar to abdicate. General Russky was persuasive when he visited him, and Tsar Nicholas II abdicated under pressure from his uncle. The Romanov dynasty was over.

The Petrograd Soviet called for "peace without annexations or indemnities" on May 15. But the provisional government of Russia rejected all such calls, and the Minister of Justice, Alexander Kerensky, was appointed war minister on that same day. He was determined to continue the war with Germany.

The German government was aghast at this, since they had engineered a situation whereby Russia would drop out of the war, leaving German forces on the Eastern Front to be transferred to the Western Front and overwhelm British and French troops. This move should have been doubly effective since the French troops were exhausted and the number of deserters from the French army was growing.

Meanwhile, the leader of the Bolshevik Party in exile, Vladimir Lenin, returned to Petrograd in April. Leon Trotsky, who had been interned in Canada, now also arrived in Petrograd to stir up either the Menshevik or Bolshevik faction. Stalin also played a key role in the revolution. But Kerensky intended to halt the slide into peace and anarchy, in which 30,000 Russian soldiers were deserting from the Front each day. The calendar of events proved to be against Kerensky in the end. The Bolsheviks won out over the Mensheviks in June. Kerensky was appointed Prime Minister of the Duma in July. Trotsky was appointed Chairman of the Petrograd Soviets in September. In the same month, the Russian government declared that Russia was now a republic, after which revolution took over on the Eastern Front with a clash between the provisional government and the Bolshevik Revolutionary Committee. Kerensky's provisional government ordered Russian troops to the front, and the Bolsheviks told them not to go.

After only six months in office, the provisional government disappeared under the force of the revolution, while four million copies of a peace decree were distributed to Russian troops at the Front. The Kerensky government was overthrown in November—known as the "October Revolution" in Russia, because of their different calendar. Perhaps the most sinister action in their political schedule was Lenin's creation of the secret police, called the Cheka, which was run with ruthless efficiency from then until his death by Feliks Dzherzinsky.

In a very short period of about eight months, from May to December, Russia had gone from an oppressive police state ruled by an emperor, to another oppressive police state ruled by a dictator. One of the more prudent acts of the Bolsheviks, which they attempted to undertake in secrecy, was the shooting to death of Tsar Nicholas and his immediate family in order to avoid a split in the nation.

Desertions

An enormous demonstration for peace was staged in Petrograd on July 1. Six thousand sailors from the Kronstad naval base joined the revolt. But Lenin thought it was premature. It was the same day that the victorious General Brusilov launched an offensive in Eastern Galicia. He led thirty-one Russian divisions on a fifty-mile front with 1,328 heavy guns. Lemberg, which was his objective, was defended by German and Austrian forces. The Russians captured 10,000 of them as prisoners of war in the first thrust of the offensive.

A Czech Brigade fought alongside the Russians. There were also Czechs fighting against them with an Austrian Division. Some Czechs called on their enemy kinfolk to desert. A few mutineers threw down their rifles with relief. It was followed by a similar reaction among Russian troops who refused to advance any further. The mutiny soon spread as one soldier after another threw down their weapons or stood immovably with folded arms and grim, provocative expressions before their officers, who attempted to cajole them into carrying on. In some cases, the officers, seeing they were outnumbered by undisciplined men, turned on their heels contemptuously, to resume fighting without them. Others were murdered by the rank and file.

In another offensive to the south, General Kornilov took 7,000 Austrian prisoners. The collapse of troops on that front was prevented by German reserves arriving. Even so, Kornilov pushed on to cross the Dniester, taking Halich and Kalush in his drive through the passes of the Carpathian Mountains and across the Hungarian border.

As the Austrians began an advance on July 23, Polish troops behind the German lines refused to swear an oath of loyalty to the Kaiser. Over 5,000 were arrested in that month alone and interned for the rest of the war. When General von Beseler pleaded with the leader of the Polish Legions, Josef Pilsudski, to cooperate with German troops, he replied, in effect, "Your Excellency, do you imagine for one moment that you will win our confidence while your hands are throttling Poland?" Piludski was imprisoned and his troops were interned in camps in Germany.

As had been the case with the conflicting variety of ethnic, religious, and cultural language groups in the peacetime Austro-Hungarian Empire, nationalist sentiments of each region or group now saw opportunities for independence instead of being ruled by the Emperor Franz Joseph's Austrians and Hungarians. Every possible racial group appeared to be determined to break away on their own. There were Poles against Germans, Arabs against Turks, and Turks against Armenians and Kurds, as old scores were settled.

On July 6, 2,500 Arabs surrounded 300 Turkish soldiers defending the port of Akaba on the Red Sea. The Arab forces were now within 130 miles of the British front in the Sinai, where General Allenby waited for the planned Arab rebellion to distract the Turks while Allenby's troops took the forts from inland. All the Turkish cannons pointed away from the British troops and were fixed to fire only at invaders from the sea. It was why Allenby attacked from the interior.

He had been ordered by the war cabinet to reach Jerusalem by year-end. Colonel T. E. Lawrence crossed the Sinai desert and managed to avoid Turkish patrols before meeting with Allenby in Cairo on July 10. He was given a monthly payroll for the Arabs of £200,000 in gold, and they would receive a bonus of £16,000 if they took Akaba.

At the same time in England, a Women's Auxiliary Army Corps was formed for the first time, to send women to France as clerks, cooks, telephonists, waitresses, and instructors. The objective was to release more men for active service at the front. Women had worked for several years on the home front, and were enjoying relative independence. But it came at a cost of long hours and dangers. Eleven thousand women worked in the cordite factory at Gretna in Scotland. Over a third of them had previously been domestic servants. Those working with TNT explosives developed yellow skins from TNT poisoning. Sixty-one died from it. Eighty-one died from other work accidents. Seventy-one were killed in a factory explosion at Gretna, sixty-nine at Silverton in London's East End. The Silverton explosion ruined a square mile of property.

Meanwhile, German High Command had become more convinced than ever that their U-boat campaign against unarmed British merchant ships would spell victory over the Allies. The rising monthly figures of torpedoed Allied merchant ships carrying food to Britain gave General Ludendorff satisfaction that the British would soon run out of vessels. Foreign Minister Walter Rathenau thought otherwise, and warned him that the British were manufacturing new vessels quicker than they were being sunk by German U-boats.

Mustard gas, another innovation of the First World War, was used first by the German Army against British troops at Ypres. Using 50,000 gas shells, eighty-seven British soldiers were killed and 2,000 had to be removed from the front when they were incapacitated. Over the next three weeks, the enemy increased the number of gas shells to a million and killed another 500 soldiers while also taking several thousand out of the front line. In a tit-for-tat attack on July 17, the British Army retaliated with poison gas against German troops.

On September 5, a British private was executed for desertion. He had served in the Army for over six years, in Gallipoli and on the Western Front, and had been buried in the trenches by a German shell. Nevertheless, British Army justice when it came to its own troops was swift and harsh. His friend was one of the members of the firing squad. The twenty-six-year-old private was still alive after the volley of rifle shots left him helplessly squirming on the ground, and the officer in charge was supposed to finish him off in accordance with Army protocol, but he couldn't do it. Instead, he passed his service revolver to the victim's friend and commanded him to shoot his friend in the head. The friend never forgot the experience, and recalled it to mind seventy-two years later at his own death. It had tortured him all his life.

The mental conditions of British troops assumed importance almost as soon as the war started, and shell-shock cases accelerated with the Battle of the Somme and Verdun in 1916. Special hospital centers were established in the following year to study and deal with their cases. But no one seemed to understand the symptoms or their cause, or how to treat them. They were all described either as shell-shock cases or hysteria. A significant aspect of the mental and often physical condition was the repeated reoccurrence of the shock that the brain cells had registered and retained, and played back intermittently with visual flashbacks. Patients were generally sent back home. But it was viewed as only a temporary condition for about a third of the cases. For most, it would be a lifelong mental and often physical aberration that they would never forget.

The Third Battle of Ypres on September 26, 1917 showed significantly more German than Allied losses. General Haig was comforted by territorial gains of "a hundred yards here, a hundred yards there." He justified Allied losses by jotting down in his diary, "The enemy is tottering."

One tragedy that had a depressing effect on the British public was an explosion on board the battleship *Vanguard* at Scapa Flow, in which 804 sailors died.

Despite the continual carnage, efforts at making peace failed. Greek-born Sir Basil Zaharoff, who was one of the richest men in the world from trading in arms and ammunition, had several times been used by SIS because of his high-level contacts all over the world. He met with the Turkish Minister of War, Enver Pasha, with an offer of one and a half million dollars in gold to repudiate the Germans and join his Turkish troops to the Allied forces. Enver Pasha refused the offer, probably worth about $15 million in today's currency.

Meanwhile, tens of thousands of Russian soldiers continued to throw away their rifles and desert from the front, and hundreds of officers were murdered by their men when they tried to stop them.

CHAPTER TWENTY-ONE

"THE YANKS ARE COMING"

NOW THAT RUSSIA WAS OUT OF the war, Germany could move its forces from the Eastern Front to the Western Front, where American troops began to move in behind the lines of the French sector. The difference was that, whereas the German troops were war-weary, the Americans were inexperienced in action at the Front. They were still being trained in October, and the American General Pershing was unimpressed with his officers; writing to the US Secretary for War on October 2, they "have neither the experience, the energy, nor the aggressive spirit to prepare their units or to handle them under battle conditions as they exist today."[1]

But apparently they were considered ready for the battlefront by November 2, when an American infantry battalion took over from the French at Barthelémont in Lorraine, and were outnumbered by four to one by a German raiding party which took twelve American prisoners and killed three others. It was the first American experience of fighting on the Western Front. Pershing wept.[2] An inquiry decided that American troops should be removed from the Front for more training.

In addition, there was growing mutiny among the French troops in this sector. Thirty thousand French soldiers left their trenches, and other French troops in four towns behind the lines refused to go to the Front and took over buildings which they defended. Some mutineers attempted to travel to Paris by train, but were stopped. Two days later, another two hundred refused to go forward to frontline trenches to support French-Moroccan troops in the line. In one place, at Missy-aux-Bois, a French infantry regiment took over the entire town and set up an anti-war government.

French military authorities made mass arrests of deserters and mutineers, and 23,385 were found guilty in French courts-martial. Mutiny was punishable by death. More than 400 were sentenced, of which fifty were shot by firing squads. The other 350 were sent to penal servitude in French colonies. Some had fought for their country in the trenches for three years.

Pétain made immediate improvements for the rest, with longer leave time, more home leave, and improved food rations. The French mutinies were finished in six weeks. Nevertheless, the mutineers who were left to continue the war made it clear that, while they agreed to continue to return to the line, they would not go over the top. That put an added burden on British troops and increased their losses in battles that attempted to distract the attention of German troops from the weaker French sectors.

Other mutinies and desertions took place, most of them hushed up after a swift execution by a firing squad. A German stoker in Wilhelmshaven took 400 sailors into town. Imagining he could confront the authorities, he shared his thoughts with his comrades: "Down with the war! We no longer want to fight this war!" Seventy-five sailors were arrested and imprisoned. The stoker was shot to death by a firing squad. One of the rebels claimed during his trial in court, "Nobody wanted a revolution, we just wanted to be treated more like human beings." The stoker had previously written home about the curse of the German militant state.[3]

As for the anticipated American troops, it was assumed that their effect on the war would not be felt for at least a year. As mutinous French troops in Paris talked of peace, the French minister of war became alarmingly aware that there were now only two dependable French divisions between the front and Paris—a distance of only seventy miles. In view of the shortage of dependable troops for protection, the French government called for Polish volunteers.

Socialists in England held anti-war meetings. Ramsay MacDonald, the leader of the socialist Labour Party, congratulated the Russians on their revolution. In England, there were only about a thousand pacifists, and they were already in prison. The intellectual Bertrand Russell claimed it was now possible for individuals to defy the power of the state by refusing military service and maintaining the dignity of man.

On the Western Front, General Haig was convinced that it was only a matter of time before the German population reached a breaking point, perhaps even that year. Meanwhile, British sappers placed land mines in tunnels they dug beneath the German lines and blew them up. It had taken six months for British, Canadians, and Australians to dig shafts and tunnels as long as two thousand feet. An estimated 10,000 German soldiers were killed or buried alive by the mines. Others were stunned or dazed by the impact of the explosions. Future Prime Minister Anthony Eden, serving at the front as a young officer, carried with him in his mind the noise of the explosions, the guns and the screams of the victims, and the sight of one of his own soldiers dying on the ground, sixty years later, as a flash-bulb memory, caused—as neuroscientists describe it today—when brain cells that wire together fire together; a factor which may result in the repetitive symptoms typical of shell-shock.

But, as Churchill had declared, most people at home had no conception of front-line conditions, or what their sons and husbands were enduring.

"Over There"

There have always been two different sides to war—the fantasy and the reality. What all war propaganda for recruiting adventurous and energetic young men had concentrated on was the romantic fantasy. Perhaps it was the vigorous and cheerful new song, "The Yanks are Coming," that revealed the dramatic difference between the fantasy world of Britain's and America's home front and with the very different realities of the battlefronts. George M. Cohan wrote a song entitled "Over There," when Europe was still a long, long way from North America by ocean liner, and few young men could afford to pay for the trip. It was right after the United States declared war on Germany in April 1917, as a consequence of German submarines torpedoing the British Royal Mail Ship *Lusitania* on May 7, 1915, off the Irish coast. One thousand one hundred and ninety-five passengers and crew were killed in the incident, including 128 American passengers. A number of American ships were sunk by German U-boats soon afterwards.

It may seem surprising today to hear how shocked and appalled President Wilson had been about the behavior of the German military and navy, because of today's communications and transport systems which have shortened time,

brought everyone closer together, and bombarded us with incessant information. But most Americans at that time had no idea what was going on outside
of North America, nor were they much interested. "Abroad," or "overseas,"
were exotic places and cultures they knew nothing about and generally did
not want to know about, since they were the countries that they or their families had fled from because of religious hatreds, poverty, police or military
oppression, or revolutions. America's policies were devoted entirely to their
own self-interest. German militarism changed that.

Cohan's lyrics were masterly in featuring the main ingredients that entice
raw recruits to battlefronts—adventure, heroism, patriotism, the chance to
carry and use a gun, fighting for liberty, and courage. He was an accomplished
wordsmith who pressed all the right emotional buttons that made his song
popular and produced new recruits.

> Johnny, get your gun, get your gun, get your gun.
> Take it on the run, on the run, on the run.
> Hear them calling you and me,
> Every son of Liberty.
> Hurry right away, no delay, go today.
> Make your Daddy glad to have such a lad.
> Tell your sweetheart not to pine,
> To be proud her boy's in line.

> Johnny, get your gun, get your gun, get your gun.
> Johnny, show the "Hun" you're a son-of-a-gun.
> Hoist the flag and let her fly
> Yankee Doodle do or die.
> Pack your little kit, show your grit, do your bit.
> Yankee to the ranks from the towns and the tanks.
> Make your Mother proud of you
> And the old red-white-and-blue.

> *Chorus:* Over there, over there,
> Send the word, send the word over there
> That the Yanks are coming, the Yanks are coming

The drums rum-tumming everywhere.

So prepare, say a prayer,

Send the word, send the word to beware—

We'll be over, we're coming over,

And we won't come back till it's over, over there.

The American Expeditionary Force

US General John J. Pershing and his staff arrived in Liverpool on June 8, 1917, to lead the American Expeditionary Forces. He had already fought against the Spanish in Cuba and the Philippines. He had been an observer in the Russo-Japanese War; had fought against the revolutionary Pancho Villa in Mexico, and against the Sioux and the Apache Nations in North America. He had the confidence of two American presidents. He was considered to be a tough disciplinarian, known as "Black Jack." His first shock came when he saw the troops that were sent to him from the United States. Not only had the artillery units arrived without weapons, some "had no idea what those guns looked like or how they operated."[4]

Pershing established his headquarters in Paris at first, then moved to Chaumont. But only a small number of American soldiers had arrived so far on the Western Front, and they only filled menial jobs. Meanwhile, he organized a line of communications and created a General Purchasing Board by ordering 5,000 aircraft and 8,500 trucks for delivery in June 1918.

Although the public and the king were highly optimistic, as a result of unrealistic expectations about the power and riches of the United States, the Allied Generals did not expect that American troops would have any influence on the war for some time. There were only 14,000 US troops behind the lines in France by June, and they were untested in battlefront conditions. They would have to be trained, equipped, armed, and battle-hardened.

But the Allied appraisal turned out to be wrong. Whether the success of the small American forces was due to Pershing, or to quite different factors, is difficult to ascertain even now. For one thing, the German forces were already exhausted, demoralized, and almost ready to plead for peace. For another, tanks—which are generally thought to have been too few to make a difference—had already brought with them enormous changes by taking frontline troops out of the trenches. Tanks enabled them to undertake offensive actions instead of being limited to sitting out the war in defensive dugouts, suffering from trench foot and other debilitating illnesses and waiting to die. The tide was already turning even as American troops arrived, but they were welcome because the Allies had had enough of war.

Four hundred fifty-six tanks were used by the Allies on August 8 in the Somme area. General Ludendorff admitted afterwards that it was the black day of the German army in the whole war. As a result, he advised the Kaiser to seek peace terms, or it would get worse for them. Five of the Allied generals, at least, were formidable—Foch, Haig, Pétain, Rawlinson, and now Pershing. The German command had relinquished any hope of victory for the time being. And the Allies now focused on avoiding loss of life: Haig recommended "economy of force," and the other generals agreed. It was made possible only as a result of the introduction of tank warfare. For example:

> On November 19th, 1917, the German troops in front of Cambrai were contemplating with undisturbed minds the apparent normality and comparative tranquility of the British lines opposite them . . . On November 20th, 381 tanks, followed by a relatively small proportion of infantry rolled forward in the half-light upon the astonished Germans . . . On November 21st the bells of London rang out in joyous acclaim of a triumphant success that seemed a foretaste of victory, perhaps at no distant date. And Ludendorff, back at the German Supreme Command, was hurriedly preparing emergency instructions for a general retreat.[5]

That offensive was one of several stepping stones that led to the victorious warfare of 1918—"advance, hit, retire." It brought to mind the tactics of the Boer guerillas in the previous war in South Africa, but now using tanks instead of ponies. What had begun with the Allied generals being entirely indifferent to tanks, then pessimistic about using them, had turned into enthusiasm at the solution that would make all the difference to the outcome of the war.

And, by that time, on September 15, Allied Armies attacked the Bulgarian front, which collapsed almost immediately.

Fighting Together

Pershing got along well enough with everyone he met in England, whether it was the king, the other Allied generals, his own troops, or the other Allied troops, perhaps because the relationship between the British and Americans has always been a special one of competition, as between squabbling brothers. The younger one is anxious to prove how smart he is, while the older one wants to demonstrate how much more experience he has. They have boasted of their progress to each other ever since they left England and opened up new colonies in North America, and then fought a war for independence. Which is the strongest, which has more money, which is more modern, which has more initiative or drive, or which one has built an ideal democratic society, are all subjects of endless discourse between them. They mock each other and put each other down—the Limey and the Yank. But whenever they have any serious differences of opinion, they soon get over it. It is all part of their comradeship, and both are better off as a consequence of the friendly competition, in which one is the alter-ego of the other.

As for the French, on his arrival at the Front, Pershing met Pétain on June 16, and immediately noted the general's pessimism when he said, "I hope it is not too late."

The Americans had not brought over any of their own heavy equipment— it was supplied by the British government, whether artillery, munitions, tanks or airplanes. Pershing began by keeping his troops separate, while fighting alongside other Allied divisions. His almost instant successes brought about trust from both sides, and very soon he was mixing his troops with other Allied forces.

Despite the initial low expectations of the Allies, in recognition of the American troops having to be trained for combat and seasoned in battle, the US First Army confronted the German Army at the St. Mihiel Salient—which the enemy had been settled into for the past three years—and quickly beat them. The unusual mobility and speed indicated that their tanks played a significant role. Colonel George S. Patton Junior had already trained two tank battalions, using the revolutionary Renault FT light tanks, since Pershing recognized their importance.

Pershing then switched 600,000 American troops to the forests of the Argonne, which were heavily defended, and kept the enemy fighting for forty-seven days, this time alongside French troops. The Meuse-Argonne Offensive on September 26 in 1918 was the biggest military action in US history. It left 26,277 American soldiers dead. Pershing's intention was to occupy the whole of Germany and destroy German militarism permanently. But the American impact was so powerful that the German generals soon decided they wanted an armistice. Pershing wrote to the Allied Supreme Council to demand that no armistice should be considered; that they should press on with the war and force Germany to surrender unconditionally. But political policy was not one of his responsibilities and he was rebuked for it.

The outbreak of a naval mutiny in Germany and civil unrest with fighting in the streets, coupled with Pershing's victories, led to Germany seeking an armistice in the end.

There are two opposing assessments of Pershing as a commander; one is that he was an excellent soldier who produced evidential results. The other is that he "led from the rear." He didn't agree with generals leading troops into battle. If it suggests that he was old-fashioned, we have to recognize the times he lived in and the types of wars that were waged before this one. It was, after all, only within the lifetime of Winston Churchill that the most advanced weapons technologies were the saber and the spear, and the supreme tactic was the cavalry charge on horseback. All that had been replaced in one man's lifetime by machine-guns, heavy artillery, Howitzers, airplanes, and tanks. The fact remains that it was the entry of Pershing and his American troops which would give the enemy the knockout blow to finish the war.

The young Major Douglas MacArthur won a French award for bravery on the Western Front and was promoted to Colonel. Lieutenant Bernard Montgomery was so seriously wounded in battle at age twenty-six—a German rifle bullet went right through his chest—that they dug his grave in readiness for burial, since it didn't seem possible that he could remain alive. On the other side of the front, a young Lieutenant named Erwin Rommel showed his audacity and unconventional initiatives that took the Allies by surprise on several occasions.

Churchill's Enemies

Back in April, Winston had met Dr. Christopher Addison twice, at Lloyd George's suggestion. He was Minister of Munitions. The aim was to see if there might be a position for Winston to produce munitions. Addison suggested he should chair a committee within the ministry to develop the tank and any other mechanized inventions or innovations, but Lloyd George turned down the idea.

Winston considered it a waste of Allied lives to continue the failing offensives with massive carnage when the Allied troops required rest, recuperation, and new planning; they should be freed from inevitable slaughter until fresh American troops arrived. He put forward his ideas in a secret session on May 10, in which he also pointed out the purposelessness of fighting without numerical superiority, or artillery preponderance, or air superiority, which were necessary for a successful offensive. It would be better, he argued, to increase the number of Allied troops and train them in improved methods, "for a decisive effort in a later year." But Lloyd George was already committed to an offensive in 1917, ready or not.

Even so, according to Winston, he and Lloyd George became colleagues, repeatedly discussing all aspects of the war and using Winston as a sounding board. On May 26, for example, Winston left for France with a letter to the French Minister of War, who was asked to give him every facility to visit the French sector at the Front. As a consequence, he did a tour of the 1916 battlefields. All he saw was carnage and ruin. He met Sir Henry Wilson, who was then commander of the Fourth Corps. Wilson made notes in his diary revealing Churchill's recommendation that the Royal Navy should be fighting instead of doing nothing. One of his beliefs was optimal use of available resources, and that the Admiralty was being wasted and had simply become an expensive burden. He had plans to lay mines close to enemy ports to provoke them into fighting.

He was energized by being busy and full of ideas. But he had no authority to carry them out. On May 29, he wrote to Clementine that never "does the thought of this carnage and ruin escape my mind."

He was still keen to avoid the slaughter by waiting for the additional strength of fresh American troops. He put forward his argument again when he met General Haig at St. Omer on June 2. Haig noted it in his diary, but his opinion differed from Winston's. He told the War Cabinet that he wanted the summer offensive because he felt sure that Germany was within six months of total exhaustion. One more push, he believed, and the war could be won in 1917. General Smuts of South Africa agreed with him. Jan Smuts had returned from leading South African forces against the German Army in East Africa and had earned a fine reputation. Both he and Churchill respected each other. But Smuts was eager for an offensive, whereas Churchill was not. It was the often repeated argument that just one more blow was needed for the collapse of the German Army. Churchill explained that it would simply cause unnecessary loss of Allied lives, and they should rather wait for the next shipload of American troops. The wise Boer General was highly regarded, as were the fighting skills of the Boers, who had virtually invented movable trench warfare and hit-and-run tactics. So Lloyd George nodded to his experience.

The renewed offensive was to be bigger than the Battle of the Somme which had been fought only a year previously. It was planned to commence at the end of July. The anticipated carnage was exactly what Churchill wanted to avoid. Meanwhile, the Americans whom he hung his hopes on still required training, so they were not expected to have any effect on the offensive.

Although Winston was beginning to enjoy feelings of purpose and new ambitions, his enemies in the opposition and the conservative press conspired to prevent him from returning to politics. The *Sunday Times* of June 3 warned readers that any public appointment he filled would be a danger to both the Administration and the Empire. They insisted that he did not possess either a balanced judgment or the shrewd farsightedness required of an administrator. Lord Curzon wrote to Lloyd George to warn him of the danger of allowing Winston Churchill to be in Opposition. He also wrote to Bonar Law to remind him that the whole point of his being in the Coalition was to keep Winston Churchill out of it. Lord Derby made the same point to Lloyd George.

Lloyd George wanted to give Churchill the air board, but found too much opposition putting pressure on him to keep Winston out. But by July 16, he had decided to stick by his convictions, and invited Winston to join the government. Winston wanted to be in munitions. The moment his new responsibility was announced in the press, two days later, it launched storms of protest in the Conservative newspapers and among the opposition in the House. *The Morning Post* accused Churchill of conceit in imagining he was a Horatio Nelson at sea and a Napoleon Bonaparte on land.[6]

To those powerful Lords who objected to the appointment he had given Churchill, Lloyd George threatened to resign. Since they feared that someone more socialistic might take his place, they backed down.

Churchill's Aunt Cornelia was Lord Randolph's sister. She remembered only too well the tragedy that had ruined her brother's career and his life. She gave Winston a piece of advice: "Don't try to run the Government."

CHAPTER TWENTY-TWO

THE KILLING FIELDS

COLONEL MAURICE HANKEY JOINED WINSTON FOR tea at Lullenden, where he spent his first weekend in the countryside as Minister of Munitions. It was a Sunday, July 22, 1917. Hankey enjoyed strolling around the beautiful property that Winston had bought some time before. He noted in his diary that Winston was already informed of the current war policy. Hankey was Secretary of the War Cabinet, and thought it wrong that Winston had already read the report he had prepared himself only recently on war policy for Lloyd George. Winston had breakfasted with Lloyd George that morning and Lloyd George had given him Hankey's War Policy Report to study.

Winston responded to Lloyd George in writing that evening to persuade him not to give way to the military who wanted to renew the offensive on the Western Front. And he appealed to him to limit the consequences of such offensives that might have been planned beforehand. There had already been too much unnecessary bloodshed. At the same time, he suggested an amphibious landing against Turkey from Europe with five or six divisions that were presently idle. The aim would be to force Turkey to surrender. It would free Allied troops from Palestine for action in Italy or France instead. He added another plea for Lloyd George not to get himself torpedoed on his trip to France, or Winston would be at the mercy of his colleagues in the House who never ceased to discredit him.

Churchill's new office was near Trafalgar Square and the Admiralty. Dr. Christopher Addison introduced him to his colleagues on July 24. He was received "rather coldly." But when Winston shared with them his plans for faster production of munitions, they were impressed and considerably cheered at the challenge.

Nevertheless, the *Morning Post* continued its hostility to his appointment. Four days afterward, Winston faced his first challenge at the ministry with an industrial dispute which had been dragging on, so far, for eighteen months, and had halted the production of several munitions factories on the Clyde. Several strike leaders had been fired, arrested, and prevented from living in Glasgow. Winston invited one of the leaders to the ministry. Daniel Kirkwood expected the usual arrogance of the upper class, or an abrupt military bullying. But he got neither. Instead, he was invited in for tea and cake, with a genial smile, as if he were a guest. He immediately felt he had found a friend.

Kirkwood wanted the men reinstated, in return for which the factories would start up again. It seemed like a reasonable request between two reasonable people, and the factories were back at work again in three days. But the *Morning Post* was not at all happy with Churchill's hand of friendship to the workers. It seemed that class distinction was still more important in England than cooperation. Kirkwood organized a bonus scheme for the workers that increased productivity at his factory to the highest level of any munitions factory in Britain.

Winston presented his first Munitions of War Bill to the Commons on August 15, with the aims of increased productivity and industrial peace. Good faith was the key to his employee relations. Now, since the Royal Navy was not using its guns, Winston decided to transfer them to the Army which needed them. The First Lord of the Admiralty immediately objected. He and Lord Derby even threatened to resign.

Three days later, Winston described his plan for streamlining the ministry by economizing, tightening, and quickening the organization with shorter lines of communications and direction, and harmonizing methods. More effective organization followed. On September 4, he was able to point out the drawbacks of the Admiralty and the War Office. There are only two ways to win this war, he said—they are the Air Force and the Americans.

He wrote soon afterwards to Lloyd George, to say, "I am delighted with all these clever business people who are helping me to their utmost. It is very pleasant to work with competent people."[1]

Passchendaele

Now that he had a war plan, he found it easier to schedule factory productions to produce the required war material. He made his first visit to the war zone in France as Minister of Munitions on September 12, with Edward Marsh, while German shells were bursting loudly sixty yards away. The two of them headed for talks with Haig and his officers at the St. Omer headquarters. Haig had planned his next offensive in the Ypres Salient for a week's time. He would attack through the village of Passchendaele, then advance on to Bruges.

Winston drove further on for tea with his brother Jack, who was serving with the Australian and New Zealand Division. Some of the troops recognized him as they moved forward, and cheered and waved at him. He had another munitions conference to attend at Arras, before driving towards the shells bursting at the front, which seemed to exert an irresistible fascination on him. They got out of their vehicle, put on their steel helmets, and hung their gas masks over their shoulders, to head for the front line.

Winston reached Paris at midnight, where his room was already booked at the Ritz. He met the French minister of munitions and agreed to an inter-Allied Munitions Council, so that he could make joint proposals to the Americans that had already been agreed on. He had dinner in Amiens the same evening, before driving to a destroyer off the French coast that headed for Dover.

General Haig's planned offensive took place on September 20. After an initial softening-up barrage of 3,000 guns, nine British divisions and six French divisions advanced on a fifteen-mile front towards Passchendaele.

Haig sent Churchill urgent orders for Howitzer ammunition. The British Mission in Washington put the request through to the commissioner of the American War Industries Board, Bernard Baruch. They developed a close working relationship that blossomed into a personal one. Haig began his assault on Passchendaele on October 12. There followed twelve days of close combat with hand-to-hand fighting that stopped the advance.

On the same day, the Italian Army was defeated by a combined force of Germans and Austrians at Caporetto. Over a million Italian troops were in retreat.

When a visitor had complimented the Austrian emperor on an early victory, he had replied with timeless philosophical detachment, "Yes it is a victory, but that is the way my wars always begin, only to end in defeat. And this time it will be even worse. They will say that I am old and cannot cope any more, and that after that revolutions will break out and then it will end."

His visitor had replied hotly, "But that's surely not possible—the war we are fighting is a just one."

The Emperor Franz Joseph had smiled and tilted his head quixotically to one side as he eyed her. "Yes, one can see that you are very young, that you still believe in the victory of the just."[2]

The Habsburgs (wrote their biographers) had a habit of viewing as important matters that had no meaning to non-Habsburgs. The key to the Habsburg puzzle was their unshaken belief in their divine right to rule; that they were linked in some special way to God, and therefore transcended immediate time. It would all come right in the end, whatever it was; meanwhile, you just "muddled through."

The Austrian Emperor appears to have been playing the tragic role of the legendary Fisher King from the Celtic mythology of the Holy Grail, whose wounds turn the country into a barren wasteland. His kingdom suffers as he does. Franz Josef was a tragic figure who suffered from mental anguish and grief at his brother's death in front of a Mexican firing squad, the suicide of his son and heir—Rudolph in Mayerling—and the loss of his wife Elizabeth who was stabbed to death by an anarchist. Now his new heir had been assassinated in Sarajevo. We can almost see in his grief a Christ-like acceptance on the cross that it is all over—*Thy will be done!*

But perhaps it was the opposite—that, with the typical arrogance of empire, he had decided that Serbia was so insignificant that it deserved to be wiped from the surface of the earth, even though there was no evidence to show they had been responsible for the assassination. If so, he had failed to consider the unintended consequences of his actions.

If we wonder at the powerful influence of ancient legends, we have to remember that the Habsburg dynasty was descended from the eighth to ninth-century King of the Franks, the almost mythical Emperor Charlemagne. They were Holy Roman Emperors who had inherited their holiness from a romantic and mystical world of religion that was, nevertheless, more real to them than the everyday reality around them. Franz Joseph was detached from the world and had buried himself in the daily administrative work on his desk to avoid thinking about what was going on in the real world outside his palace. What we might call his fatalism was a longing to escape to an imaginary world, one that he and his ancestors had been tantalized with all their lives by the Church.

It was different from the situation in England, where Queen Victoria had turned away from the real world to mourn her husband, Albert the prince consort, since she did not cut herself off entirely from the world outside Balmoral. For example, she protested vigorously at the way the French military and the French law courts victimized Dreyfus at the turn of the new century by cancelling her usual holiday to France and encouraging 50,000 Britons to protest in Hyde Park against the mendacious French who, apparently, could not be trusted for their morals or their ethical values.

There was also something fatalistic about the German Kaiser who—immediately before war became inevitable—turned petulantly away from Moltke, his Chief of Staff, when he insisted to the emperor that the German armies could not avoid launching an attack on France, instead of turning away to attack Russia instead, as the Kaiser suggested.

"There has been a debate ever since over whether Moltke was right, that it was too late for Germany to go to war on one front alone. General Groener, head of the General Staff's Railway Department at the time, maintained afterwards that it would have been feasible . . ."[3] Moltke never really recovered from the psychological battering he received that day. When he returned home, recalled his wife, after the Kaiser's request for a partial mobilization, "I saw immediately that something terrible had happened here. He was purple in the face, his pulse hardly countable. I had a desperate man in front of me."[4]

Cambrai

Unlike the Austrian emperor, Lloyd George believed that Britain's fate depended on him, and in the here and now, and not in the timeless supernatural. The defeat of the Italians by the Austrians at Caporetto was crushing. And it was an Allied defeat. But "Europeans themselves had a stoicism and doggedness which could keep them fighting through the long years to come even as the terrible losses mounted."[5] Philosophical though he was about the long term, Winston did his best to encourage Lloyd George to send British and French troops to help Italy right away.

Then, on the same day, Winston turned to his first meeting with the Women's Trade Union Advisory Committee, which involved very nearly a million women. He had recently supported a move to give women the vote. Now their agenda was to demand fairer wages. Their case was presented by a trade union leader named Ernest Bevin.

It was then, on November 20, that the British army launched the tank offensive at Cambrai. Churchill was in Paris when the French lines were overrun and the Army regained over forty-two square miles in two weeks of fighting. On the first day of the offensive, he visited the Chamber of Deputies to hear the new Premier and Minister for War, Georges Clemenceau, shout out defiantly, "No more pacifist campaigns, no more German intrigues, neither treason nor half-treason—war, nothing but war."

Winston completed his plan for a British gun factory north of Paris, and an Anglo-American tank factory at Bordeaux to produce 1,500 large tanks a month and avoid delivering back and forth from Britain. He believed they would bring final victory. He would buy whatever war material was necessary and available for the American troops when they arrived in Europe, including 452 airplanes. It was his forty-fourth birthday.

The Battle of Cambrai had ended two days earlier and showed that only about 3 percent of men were killed as were lost in Flanders, at only about 7 percent of the cost, due to tank warfare.

But a new danger emerged, since Russia's new Bolshevik Government was about to make peace with Germany. It meant that German forces would vastly outnumber the Allies when they moved their troops to the Western Front. Churchill appealed to Lloyd George to make sure that the British army was brought up to its full strength immediately. He said the crisis would come before June. And if this went wrong, then everything would go wrong: "The Germans are a terrible foe, & their generals are better than ours."[6]

He made sure the air ministry prevented orders from falling below 4,000 aircraft engines every month. And he scheduled with the Allied commanders their needs for ammunition, tanks, and mustard gas. He drove north to Ypres, where the German artillery began to fire on the Menin Road, at a position known as "Hellfire Corner." Shells fired in the skies without anyone taking any notice, since it was a normal occurrence, and airplanes were constantly being shelled overhead. About 800,000 men had been killed or wounded here over three years of continuous fighting.

As soon as he returned to London, he asked the War Cabinet to plan for new offensive strategies in 1919, with aircraft and tanks dominating the battles. Sir Henry Wilson was now concerned that minefields would be set up to deter the tank. That, in turn, led Churchill to propose work to be done to enable tanks to cross minefields in safety. He offered several different suggestions. He organized a tank board in the Ministry, with a need for 4,459 tanks by April 1919, and double that number six months later. He also planned to double the number of aircraft. It seemed that Clemenceau had been right—it was nothing but war, war, and more war!

War Poets

The view that "History is one damn thing after another" was proposed by historian Arnold Toynbee. Lance-Corporal Francis Ledwidge—an Irish veteran of Gallipoli and Salonika—discovered it for himself as a young poet. He was twenty-six when he took a brief tea-break after laying wooden planks on a muddy lane to facilitate army vehicles. A German shell exploded nearby and killed him. A verse from one of his poems expressed his worldview;

> And now I'm drinking wine in France,
> The helpless child of circumstance.
> Tomorrow will be loud with war,
> How will I be accounted for?

The nearby cemetery accounts for him and 1,291 other British and Commonwealth soldiers found scattered across the local battlefields, who were, themselves, tested for courage in the face of death. Plenty of other war poets found themselves to be "The helpless child of circumstance." Among them were Wilfred Owen, Siegfried Sassoon, Robert Graves, and Rupert Brooke. Graves had been left for dead and thrown for burial on a pile of corpses before someone heard him groan.

Poets are acute observers of people and places, which they analyze, then write an encapsulation of what they see and feel, and attach it to their worldview. They aim at the heart—although some are more cerebral—in ways that a war correspondent or a novelist cannot achieve, however hard they try—with the possible distinction of Erich Maria von Remarque. But Remarque didn't write his famous anti-war best-seller, *All Quiet on the Western Front,* until 1929.[7]

The problem that Owen and Sassoon encountered was describing the ghastly realities of war to civilians back home, when most servicemen suppressed the experience so as not to upset or offend their families or girlfriends. Gallantry and old-world courtesy were qualities of the Edwardian era. War poetry that described anguished soldiers killing or waiting to die in a dugout, and many of the bizarre and grotesque feature of the front line, left most potential readers struck dumb with incomprehension. Those poems seemed so self-indulgent, as the poet tortured himself with cruel memories of the battlefront. It had nothing to do with the Home Front, which was relatively untouched by war and encouraged ignorance about it. The killing fields were in the front line, where 95 percent of the slaughter took place. The other 5 percent happened as civilian deaths in major cities like London, and were barely noticeable.

Rupert Brooke was an exception. He was established as a poet before the war. Now he was a beautiful young and charismatic man, young enough to be an idealist about human nature and the world. He looked heroic and sounded heroic in his poetry, some of the most memorable of which is redolent of romantic self-sacrifice. He went to Rugby, and was the son of one of its schoolteachers. He was known by his contemporaries—in the "Cambridge Apostles" and the "Bloomsbury Group"—for his homosexual affairs. Homosexuality in Britain then was a criminal and imprisonable offense against the morality of the time. Added to his sexual confusion was the fact that he was bisexual. The strain of one or the other, or both, ended in a nervous breakdown.

Rupert Brooke was "taken up" by Winston Churchill's Private Secretary, Edward Marsh, when Winston was First Lord of the Admiralty.[8] Brooke was commissioned in the Royal Navy as a temporary sub-lieutenant. The words of his poem, "The Soldier," reveal the Byronic self-sacrificing quality of a romantic idealist and a patriot.

> If I should die, think only this of me:
> That there's some corner of a foreign field

That is for ever England . . .

It is redolent of a characteristic possessed by many young poets, one that sits on a razor's edge between what Churchill called "jingoism" and patriotism. While Churchill was a romantic patriot, he could not wear his heart on his sleeve, and probably thought it vulgar to do so. The emotional feeling is associated with compassion, altruism, or self-sacrifice, and is probably the predominant characteristic of "the hero."

Nevertheless, Rupert Brooke is probably known more for a poem he wrote in 1912, before the war broke out, which uniquely recaptures the last sun-filled, leisurely days of the Edwardian era before the war changed everything in England for ever.

"The Old Vicarage, Grantchester" was written while he sat at a table in the Café des Westens in Berlin in May 1912, reflecting on all he loved in England, and thinking nostalgically of returning home.

> God! I will pack, and take a train,
> And get me to England once again!
> For England's the one land, I know,
> Where men with Splendid Hearts may go;

The final six lines of the comparatively longish poem express much of what idealistic young Englishmen thought represented their country and their culture. It was, after all, England that had made them.

> Say, is there Beauty yet to find?
> And Certainty? And Quiet kind?
> Deep meadows yet, for to forget
> The lies, and truths, and pain? . . . Oh! Yet
> Stands the Church clock at ten to three?
> And is there honey still for tea?

This, and all the emotions behind it, was what was lost when young Englishmen rushed off to war in 1914. There is a myth that it was the old men who ushered the young to the battlefields, but that was only in Germany and Austria.

It was the other way around in England: older people dreaded the war, while the young and idealistic couldn't wait for what they perceived as an exciting adventure, after which they'd be back in time for tea with honey at some leisurely inn in the countryside, like the Old Vicarage in Grantchester.

Perhaps the most touching war poem that must surely be repeated far more times than any other is "For the Fallen" by Laurence Binyon. It is likely to be the first choice for every Remembrance Day, because it says what it means simply and directly to the heart. The fourth verse is the most popular one.

> They shall not grow old, as we that are left grow old:
> Age shall not weary them, nor the years condemn.
> At the going down of the sun and in the morning
> We will remember them.

The Stamina and the Means

Winston visited St. Omer again on March 18, and learned that a major German offensive was thought to be imminent. The British army would be confronted by twice their number. He and his old friend Hugh Tudor inspected every part of the defenses together, from artillery emplacements to the trenches manned by the South Africans.

The following morning, he was woken by German land mines blowing up underneath British trenches. It was the beginning of the German offensive. British guns opening fire competed with German shells bursting on the Allied trenches. The noise was so great that it drowned the sounds of two hundred guns from much closer. It was the signal for the enemy to advance at six o'clock. The South African position was overrun. Tudor warned him he'd better leave or he'd never get out. Winston drove back to St. Omer. By the time he arrived, the road he'd come from was impassable.

As more roads were overrun, he returned to London. At 10 Downing Street, Lloyd George wanted to know how any Allied positions could be held under such a massive onslaught. Winston explained to him that every offensive loses its momentum as it advances. That evening, Lloyd George and Henry Wilson were his dinner guests at his home in 33 Eccleston Square. Wilson made notes in his diary of that evening, in which he described Winston as "a real gem in a crisis."

It *was* a crisis—*another* crisis. And since it was one crisis after another, top British military officers tended to take it in their stride as just another day of work. It was their job—a factor that Winston had always been wary of. For the French it was different—they were either buoyed up by victory or utterly defeated in defeat. Lloyd George felt the only way he could obtain dependable firsthand evidence as to whether or not the British and French Armies possessed the stamina and means to halt the imminent German offensive was to send Winston to the Front. The main question that Lloyd George wanted an answer to was, would the French—who had been relatively little involved in the German offensive—be prepared to launch a vigorous attack to relieve the British line? He telegraphed Prime Minister Clemenceau that Churchill was on the way.

As soon as Churchill's critics heard of his intended trip, they called on Lloyd George to protest at Churchill being sent on an official mission to the Premier of France. Feeling pressured, Lloyd George immediately sent a message to await Churchill at Folkestone, where he was taking ship to cross the Channel, to tell him not to stay at French headquarters; better to go straight to Clemenceau as a messenger and report back.

Churchill arrived in France without having received any message, and proceeded to Haig's new headquarters in Boulogne, where he found Haig out, taking his afternoon ride, and a complete absence of the activity he had expected in the face of an enemy offensive—from which he now learned that 100,000 British troops had been killed or captured with over a thousand guns. Worse still, the Germans were now on the march toward the northern sector of the line. Winston could see a possibility that the British could be pushed back to the Channel Coast. But no one at Haig's headquarters knew what the French Allies were about to do, if anything. Nor did they know what French forces would be available if needed in an emergency. He drove to Amiens and found it already under bombardment. It was only when he reached Paris that he was handed Lloyd George's message.

Churchill had encountered all types of half-heartedness throughout the war, and in the Boer War, when officers failed to recognize danger signals or neglected to seize opportunities. He had recognized it when, in the Admiralty, he watched opportunities of success transformed into defeat at the Dardanelles, as a result of officers not focusing on the main objective, but being diverted by lesser administrative goals. In spite of nearly three years of carnage, the same almost disinterested attitude prevailed.

Clemenceau sent him a message that he would take Winston to the battlefront tomorrow. Winston informed Lloyd George that the French Prime Minister seemed to be in good spirits. But when Lord Milner heard of the impending meeting, he insisted that it was *his* responsibility, as Minister Without Portfolio, to visit the French Premier. Milner was still Churchill's adversary, and chose to view the situation as a personal snub, since everything important appeared to Milner to be all about *him*.

Meanwhile, Clemenceau took Churchill to Beauvais, where Foch awaited them at the Town Hall. Foch was Chief of the French General Staff. He described the battle vigorously for them on a wall map, and explained how the momentum of the German attack had gradually slowed down on each of the following days after the offensive had begun. He insisted that the line would be stabilized soon.

They drove on to where General Rawlinson commanded the Fourth British Army, and Winston asked him, "Would the line hold?"

"No one can tell," Rawlinson informed him. They had hardly anything between them and the enemy but exhausted troops. The Fifth Army would be useless from lack of sleep. They must have rest. At this moment, they were slowly crawling backwards and utterly worn out.

When Haig asked Clemenceau for support, he immediately ordered two French Divisions to support the British forces.

As Churchill drove on with Clemenceau, they passed British soldiers walking, half asleep and as if in a dream, oblivious of everything around them. Driving further on towards the front line, as Clemenceau eagerly wanted, the French staff officers were anxious for the Premier's safety. Clemenceau reluctantly agreed to go back. He loved the noise and bustle of adventure that he found in the excitement of the front line and, like Churchill, was completely at home under fire. Churchill was encouraged to see Clemenceau in good form in his natural element of battle. On their return journey, the French General on Rawlinson's right said he could hold out for twenty-four hours until relieved.

They met with General Pétain, the Commander-in-Chief, on board his train at Beauvais. He described the situation: ammunition would arrive within four days, strengthened artillery would be ready in forty-eight hours. Pétain was full of energy, optimism, and efficiency. Churchill returned to Paris and telegraphed Lloyd George, warning him to send as many troops as possible to France—he should scour the entire military organization for idle troops, including the Navy.

Lloyd George wanted to send about 120,000 American troops a month to France. Together with Prime Minister Clemenceau, Churchill drafted an urgent telegram to US President Wilson. Clemenceau's words were to the effect that they would contest every inch of ground and were certain to stop the enemy. Then Churchill urged Lloyd George to come to France and meet Clemenceau to settle details of the Allied high command structure. Lloyd George met with General Wilson at Montreuil, where they agreed that Foch would be the Field Marshal in charge of all Allied forces.

The Bolsheviks

Churchill turned his attention to the Bolshevik Government in Russia, which was now at peace with Germany. He was convinced of a common cause between them and Britain. As he put it to the cabinet, "Let us never forget that Lenin and Trotsky are fighting with ropes around their necks. They will leave office for the grave." They could do nothing without foreign aid. In the long run, they would be hostile to Prussian militarism and could be drawn into the Allied sphere.[9]

So far, waging gas warfare with mustard gas shells had been ineffective on the Allied Front. The first success using gas that year came from the Germans, when they attacked the British sector at Armentières. It was overrun three days later, losing any gains achieved by the Third Battle of Ypres. The main armies were advancing and retreating, two or three times, and revisiting old battlefields. Now Winston warned Lloyd George of the danger of the German forces driving a wedge between British and French troops at Abbeville. In the meantime, he had been able to fulfill his orders to deliver war material to General Haig on April 21. It replaced guns, aircraft, and tanks lost in the last offensive action.

The new American Armies already in France were still mostly untrained and others had still not arrived in France.

Jennie

On June 1, Jennie married Montagu Porch of the Nigerian Civil Service. Her second husband, George Cornwallis-West, had long since left her in 1913 to marry the famous and flamboyant actress, Mrs. Patrick Campbell, in London. Porch was twenty-three years younger than Jennie, and three years younger than Winston. He had been born into a family of landed gentry and enjoyed a private income. When war broke out in 1914 he was an intelligence officer in Africa.

"Porchy," as he was called, had met Jennie originally at a wedding in 1913. He was in love with her from the first, but it took five years for him to gather enough courage to decide to propose to her. He obtained three weeks' leave from the foreign office in Nigeria and, after returning to England in 1918, offered to drive Jennie to Ireland to visit her sister Leonie at Glasborough. They were engaged by the time they drove back to London.

Jennie had been lonely without a man in her life as, at that time, it was improper for a lady to go anywhere in public without an escort. She had even made ironic comments to friends about the situation when she was obliged to take her domestic servant with her to the theater once or twice. But, being an independent woman all her life, she had to be sure she played the dominant role in marriage. On the other hand, she was not content just to be a grandmother; her buoyant personality demanded a busy social life. She had been involved in various charities and had written a few articles or handbooks, and a play with Mrs. Patrick Campbell in the lead at the Haymarket Theater, which flopped after an eleven-day tryout.

Although she accepted Porchy's proposal, she did not take his name, nor would she live in Nigeria. She explained her decision by saying, "He has a future and I have a past so we should be all right."

Jennie was content with him and very loving. Accounts of her age at that time vary from fifty-six, to sixty, and even sixty-seven. People remarked that she looked twenty years younger, but younger than what? In her own mind she appeared to still think of herself as of a marriageable age, like eighteen, when she had attracted Lord Randolph on the Isle of Wight. Certainly she looked youthful at her wedding to Porchy.

Winston was back in Paris two days after attending the wedding and had managed to spend a few hours with Clementine, who was now four months pregnant

The Germans launched another offensive. There was some fear now that Paris itself could be threatened by advancing German Armies. They broke through the French lines at the Aisne and the Marne. He wrote to Clementine on June 6 and told her of the air raid over Paris. German forces were now only forty-five miles away. Although he felt hopeful, the fate of Paris could go either way. Even so, he invited her to visit him there next time—if there was to be a "next time."

He visited the French front line on June 8, and found both the French Generals whom he met seriously confident and even hoping to be attacked. He found them calm and gallant and cheerful. So were the French soldiers who waited patiently for the next offensive. But by the following evening, all the territory over which they had led him with such confidence was in the hands of the German army. And most of the French whom he'd met and talked to, and found so courteous, were dead, or among the 60,000 prisoners of war that the German forces netted as they had swept resolutely forward.

Even so, the German Army failed to reach its goal. It was Compiégne. The French counter-attack began on June 11.

The Killer-Instinct

Ever since Lord Milner had been appointed Secretary of State for War, he was relentless in his pursuit of his main adversary, Winston Churchill. Churchill felt frustrated when the cabinet began taking men from manufacturing munitions to the front line. It had already led to a drop in the production of new tanks. It made him anxious about the possibility of winning the war in 1919. When the war cabinet announced proudly that Britain would not make any air raids on Germany on Corpus Christi Day, Churchill was appalled at their missing sense of survival and their lack of commitment to helping Britain to survive. He remarked to Lloyd George that it was pitiful: the British upper-classes were still playing at being gentlemen against an enemy which had no such finesse, but possessed instead a crueler and more brutal set of values, the foremost of which was motivated by a killer instinct that had prompted the Kaiser to describe his Germans as the notorious Huns.

A new danger to providing munitions for the Allied forces came from some of the factory owners who refused to discuss wage increases with the trade unions. A shop steward was sacked at an aircraft factory and production came to a standstill. Churchill's solution was to nationalize the factory for the Government and then reinstate the shop steward, who was within his rights. But a week later, there were more strikes at tank factories when workers protested at being transferred from one plant to another against their wishes. To avoid work stoppages and a shortage of tanks at the Front, Churchill proposed to withdraw their immunity from military service. Bonar Law immediately opposed him. But when another 300,000 munition workers threatened a strike in Leeds, Lloyd George finally intervened by making a statement from 10 Downing Street that all strikers would be sent to the Front unless they returned to work.

General Rawlinson's Fourth Army launched a new British offensive on August 8, with Canadian and Australian troops. The battle featured seventy-two tanks. Churchill couldn't resist flying to France to see them in action and assess their potency. The tanks broke through the German frontline trenches at nightfall, and the net result was that the British troops took some 22,000 German prisoners-of-war and captured 400 German guns. After sending a telegram to congratulate General Haig, Churchill received a reply which stated, "I shall always remember with gratitude the energy and foresight which you displayed as Minister of Munitions, and so rendered our success possible."[10]

Winston visited Rawlinson on August 9 at Flixecourt, then took his brother Jack to the front. He wrote to Clementine afterward that they passed about 5,000 German prisoners-of-war marching dispiritedly in long columns by the side of the road, with some officers penned up in cages. He went into the cages where 200 officers were penned, to study them. Some, he thought, looked very young. But they were well-fed and sturdy. He said that he couldn't help feeling sorry for them because they looked so dejected, but decided they were safer where they were.

Closer to the Front at Lamotte with Jack, he saw tank tracks inside the German lines. Two days later, the British advanced and took another 10,000 prisoners. "The tide has turned," he wrote to Clementine. He was convinced that the success was due largely to the tanks.

Even so, Winston was still planning ahead for 1919—they would need another 100,000 men by next June. On August 11, he was back in the battle zone. The Germans "were hardly firing at all," he wrote to Clementine. And he found more German dead here than in the other sector he'd visited. Dead cavalry horses lay across the landscape. He saw a British observation balloon shot down to burst into flames, while the observers managed to parachute safely out. After meeting with the inter-Allied Munitions Council to plan the schedules for 1919, Winston found Prime Minister Clemenceau anxious that Britain's commitment to manpower would be met, since the war council appeared not to be making any great effort.

Winston sought help in the design and manufacture of long-distance bombing aircraft in Paris, to increase the bomb-loads and carry the war into German territory, so that they could see the type of carnage and ruin they were making in France and Belgium. He spoke to several young pilots waiting to take off from an airfield near Verchocq for a night bombing raid on Germany. "People have no idea what those lads are going through," he remarked.

Reds

Churchill was in London when Bolshevik troops broke in to the British Embassy in Petrograd on August 31. The British Naval Attaché, Captain Cromie, shot three of them dead before being killed himself. Winston had known him personally since the beginning of the war. He wanted justice, since he considered Francis Cromie was a fine young man and a fine officer. The greatness of an organized state, he wrote, and one of its truest measures, is the extent it is prepared to go to protect its citizens from outrage. On September 4, the War Cabinet decided to send a telegram to the Soviet Government, "threatening reprisals" against Trotsky and Lenin, and other Bolshevik leaders, if British lives were not safeguarded.

Three days later, he managed to join Clementine and the children for a brief visit to the Devonshire seaside, before departing that evening for Verchocq. Arriving at Haig's headquarters on the next day, he found a mood of confidence that the war would end in 1918. The following day he visited the former

German positions which they had just captured, east of Vimy. He wrote to Clementine, "The ruin of the countryside was complete . . . Everywhere pain, & litter & squalor & the abomination of desolation." Most of the British dead were already buried.

He was more candid with Prime Minister Lloyd George on September 10 about what happened at Drocourt. Every German line was overrun. But where German troops had left a few holes through which to fire their machine-guns, advancing British troops who got beyond tank protection were mown down. Four hundred Canadians died in one such location. He wanted a far greater number of tanks to be targeted for production in 1919, and an increase in the number of tank crews. He also intended to facilitate the design of a much bigger and stronger tank. Meanwhile, after all the slaughter of the Allies, he could not resist writing to Clementine of the Germans, "their whining in defeat is very gratifying to hear."

The idea of German defeat after all that time struck an encouraging note of optimism, so that Winston found himself returning to their past in a love letter. "Ten years ago my dearest one we were sliding down to Blenheim in our special train. Do you remember? It is a long stage on life's road. Do you think we have been less happy or more happy than the average married couple?"[11]

He returned to Verchocq from Paris, after beginning to fulfill an order from the United States for 2,000 guns, which should arm about fifteen more divisions, or close to half a million men. He also bought two to three thousand aircraft engines in order to bomb the Huns. After he arrived back in England on September 17, British troops devastated the Hindenburg Line with gas bombardments lasting for three days.

The Bulgarian army had surrendered unconditionally on September 27. They were the first of Germany's Allies to give in and get out of the war. Meanwhile, British armies on the Western front under Haig captured 10,000 more German prisoners and 200 guns. Germany was finally exhausted and facing starvation from the Allied blockade at sea. The Germans requested an armistice. The stern and formidable American President Wilson turned down their request. British forces marched and drove into Lille on October 17. It had been occupied by German forces for four years. Now they were no longer powerful enough to hold the line against the Allies.

To curry favor with the Allies, the German Government promised to end the U-boat campaigns which had torpedoed unarmed merchant ships.

Clementine wrote wistfully to Winston, "Can't the men munition workers build lovely garden cities & pull down slums in places like Bethnal Green, Newcastle, Glasgow, Leeds, etc. & can't the women munition workers make all the lovely furniture for them, babies' cradles, cupboards etc. Do come home and arrange all this."

Chapter Twenty-three

SPIES OF "ROOM 40"

Britain was riddled with spies, just like all the other most powerful nations in Europe, stealing technological secrets or manipulating influential leaders in the country, even bribing or blackmailing some of them. One of the first spy networks that English history elaborates on is the one masterminded by spymaster Sir Henry Walsingham in the reign of Queen Elizabeth the First, when Protestant England was under threat from either Catholic France or Catholic Spain. Then, one of the first notable spies was the poet Christopher Marlowe, who was assassinated at the age of twenty-nine after an alleged brawl in a respectable inn in Deptford. Spies were essential to Britain.

The Germans were singularly inept at spying: they lacked finesse and were easily discovered. Eleven were captured soon after arriving in the British Isles, tried for treason and condemned to death, then shot at dawn by a firing squad in the Tower of London. Carl Hans Lody was the first, in November 1914. He was the first individual to be executed there for a hundred and fifty years. Most were identified through letters they sent home which were intercepted by Britain's Secret Service. Their method of using invisible ink was amateurish, initiating the spy fever that had gripped Britain totally unnecessarily. They were not all German, but also Dutch, Latvian, Swedish, Turkish, and South American.

Winston Churchill was no stranger to spies. He was on intimate terms with a number of British ones. And he is still remembered for the leading part he played in the murders committed in London's East End by a small group of anarchists and Bolsheviks who had planned a bank robbery to obtain funds for their gang.

But what *were* anarchists? Were they all Russians or Polish, or Italians? Poland was part of the Russian Empire in those days. The Italian masses were crushed by considerable poverty and hopelessness. The British public were perplexed, and so were the Metropolitan Police. The question gained even more significance when readers learned about Mensheviks and Bolsheviks at the time of the Russian Revolution. As to the difference of ideologies between Trotsky and Lenin, intellectuals discoursed on the subtleties and books began to be written about them, since the subject could have some bearing on the future of Britain and the Empire.

Politically naïve people in London thought that the genial Count Peter Kropotkin spoke on behalf of all anarchists, because he wrote several books on revolution and edited a newspaper called *La Révolte*. He was an enthusiastic conversationalist who would be described in the twenty-first century as a TV celebrity, ready and eager to be interviewed by the media.

Kropotkin had arrived in England after escaping from a Russian prison hospital. He settled in London—like Voltaire and other free-thinkers—because it was an intellectual hub for refugees, anarchists, revolutionaries, and counter-revolutionaries. He was a short and tubby man who resembled the twinkly-eyed Mr. Pickwick, except that he sported an enormously thick and wild beard *a la Russe*. His complexion was florid. His false teeth were inferior. The wire spectacles he wore on his button-nose made him appear Dickensian—although his benevolent and even saintly demeanor might have been be more suited to a Dostoevsky novel. Kropotkin patiently and good-naturedly explained to anyone who wished to listen that anarchists were not a political group of organized revolutionaries planning terrorism. On the contrary, they were essentially free-spirited individuals who detested organizations, bureaucrats, politicians, governments, and all forms of authority. So there was a mystery as to what they expected to achieve by blowing up buildings or statues, except for propaganda purposes. But what were they propagandizing other than their own personal opinion that authority was in the wrong hands?[1]

The Mensheviks disappeared from public discourse when the Bolsheviks took over the government of Soviet Russia. A chill of fear and anxiety spread through the propertied classes in Britain and across the continent of Europe; as well as in the far-distant United States of America which initiated a long-lasting search for Communists right from the outset. If the English aristocrats and ruling classes had feared the possibility of a revolution after the French Revolution left bloodstains all over Europe, now they and America's moneyed classes had an added fear of confiscation of all property by a political ideology known as International Communism, apparently espoused by Trotsky and already taking place in Soviet Russia.

Churchill, with his sharp imagination, its focus on any danger to the British Isles and the British Empire, and his experiences of the grittier side of humanity, was a rarity in British politics, since he took a particular interest in spies at home and abroad, and in Britain's own Secret Service. He thrived on learning secrets that gave him an insight into other people's minds and the policy of governments in other nations. In this, he was remarkably like the Elizabethan Walsingham.

As a former Home Secretary, he had supported the passing of the Official Secrets Act of 1911. He had also authorized the secret interception of the Royal Mail, in order to identify traitors who might disturb the peace of the realm with violence to British citizens.

Winston loved the means and the uses of different types of deception that suited each individual situation, its chosen objectives, and the personal characteristics involved, as he worked very closely with the Secret Service. It also conveniently kept his mind working busily to banish his horror of boredom even for five minutes. Some saw it as "schoolboy simplicity," like playing with a chemistry set or learning the party tricks of a stage magician deceiving an audience with his sleight of hand. There was no doubt that he enjoyed the art and the skills of deception and the thrill of achievement whenever it worked.

Today's perception of him as a conservative statesman is entirely incorrect. He thought of himself as a soldier protecting the British people. He had killed scores of men, some face-to-face with a Mauser or rifle, and would not hesitate to do so again if necessary for his country. What was particularly remarkable about Churchill was that although—like Darwin and Freud—he had no illusions about human beings, he remained an optimist: everything could always be improved.

"Room 40" was a section of the British Admiralty which was involved in cryptanalysis: breaking enemy codes in order to obtain secrets of their military policy and strategies, tactics, new technologies, and battle plans and movements of their armed forces. No one knew more than he what it could be aimed at in order to obtain top secret information and to counter terrorism. Unlike most politicians, who either could not grasp its importance or its scope or dismissed it as ungentlemanly "double-cross," Churchill may have obtained more useful information that led to the Allied victory than anyone else ever had.

The Art of Deception

Of all of the British spies and masters of deception, none has received more attention than Sidney Reilly (although not his real name), as a consequence of that moment when Bolshevik troops broke in to the British embassy in Petrograd on August 31, 1918, and the British Naval Attaché, Captain Francis Cromie, shot three of them dead before being shot to death himself. The incident was described by British diplomat Robert Bruce Lockhart's son, Robin, in a book, *Reilly, Ace of Spies*.[2]

Robin's father, R. H. Bruce Lockhart, was a British diplomat, author, and secret agent. He was the British Assistant Vice-Consul in Moscow when the Russian Revolution erupted in 1917. Prime Minister Lloyd George and Lord Milner encouraged him to return there as the first British envoy to the Bolsheviks after the "October Revolution." He also worked for SIS (Britain's Secret Intelligence Service). His objective was to assemble a network of secret agents in Russia to counter German influence. Lockhart, and his secret service agent colleague Sidney Reilly, were alleged by the Bolsheviks to have plotted the assassination of Lenin in 1918, and condemned them to death. Instead, Lockhart was exchanged for Russian secret agents. He would write about his experiences as a secret agent many years later.[3]

Not only was Reilly the pivotal figure of a book with his name on the cover and portrayed enthusiastically by its author as Britain's top spy, but a novelist would immortalize Reilly under another assumed name as "James Bond."[4]

One of the problems of describing the British Secret Service is that it *is* secret. Another is the Official Secrets Act that prevents top secret information from being published. Add to that the alleged stories about Sidney Reilly, and the fictional stories about a mythical James Bond, and it becomes impossible to sort fact from fiction. Then we have to consider the culture of spying, which is based on deception. It is often said that British novelists like Somerset Maugham, Graham Greene, Malcolm Muggeridge, and Ian Fleming, who were hired as

British agents, would be unlikely to be sure of the difference between fact and fiction after playing a duplicitous role for so long. The same situation applied to more longstanding agents, and particularly double-agents. All we really know for sure about Sidney Reilly is that he was born in 1874 in the Tsarist Russian Empire and died in November 1925 in Moscow, where he was thought to have been shot as a spy on the orders of Russia's Bolshevik Chief of Secret Police, Feliks Dzerzhinsky. But it is possible that he was not shot after all.

Perhaps the most important thing that Reilly taught the British Secret Service was to stop playing at being gentlemen by offering all sorts of courtesies to the enemy, and begin to understand that they were victims of forces who were not interested in good manners but were out to kill them. It took a long time, even in the deceitful world of the Secret Service. Some thick-headed politicians and Army and Navy officers would never learn it. Many had been born into the upper classes and educated at British public schools—like Eton for Lockhart—and if they had nothing else to recommend them, they had innate good manners and treated each other as gentlemen. Their problem was their insularity: they thought they were living in a gentlemanly world and automatically treated the enemy in the same way. They had not learned, as Winston had, that it was simply a matter of the evolutionary process—of kill or be killed.

Sidney Reilly was not a gentleman, he was a survivor. He had not been educated in a British public school, but had grown up and survived in the most oppressive police state in Europe. It could be said with a great deal of truth that by the time Reilly faced a Soviet firing squad, he had taught the British how to be efficient and successful secret agents. And it is highly likely that those adventurous agents, like Lockhart, who enjoyed the excitement and challenge of leading a double life, were the very best. Certainly neither the Germans nor the Austro-Hungarians were much good at it. But Communist Russia would turn out to be exceptional in obtaining useful information that strengthened and protected them. And they possessed the advantage that they did not mind how many millions of innocent people they murdered. As Stalin would say, one man's death is a tragedy, but millions are only statistics.[5]

So although the fictional "007" is intended to epitomize the cool and courageous British hero—at least in the entertainment world of movies and TV—James Bond is only an invented character of wish-fulfillment for less impulsive or adventurous readers and moviegoers to admire.

A question that still remains unanswered about Sidney Reilly is why, if he was so brilliant at subterfuge and deception, he fell into Feliks Dzerzhinsky's unforgiving hands by returning to Moscow at his invitation—because that was clearly what it was, although claiming to be a group of anti-Bolsheviks known as "The Trust." But evidently Dzerzhinsky knew the art of deception better even than Reilly, or his close friend Savinkov. It may be that because Reilly had spent his whole life in an invented world that he could no longer recognize the real one, and thought he could do a deal with Dzerzhinsky. He had always managed to manipulate everyone else. And he was a successful gambler who liked to play for high stakes. So perhaps he thought that, with Dzerzhinsky's help, he could win the jackpot and become the ruler of Russia. Why not, since it had been ruled by idiots before? Or perhaps his sense of self-preservation was failing him, since the Secret Police Chief was utterly ruthless. And perhaps Feliks Dzerzhinsky felt that, despite Reilly's self-aggrandizement, he too was only another statistic to be erased from his ledger of enemy spies.

Sidney Reilly

Reilly's father owned land in Russia and was in business as a contractor. He himself spoke four or five languages fluently, and possessed qualifications in chemistry. He left Odessa at the age of nineteen and appears to have spent some years in spying, perhaps for the Japanese government, but none of it is verified. He arrived in London in 1895 and married Margaret Callahan Thomas three years later. He became Sidney Reilly only in 1899, because he was hired by Britain's Secret Service to penetrate Irish Fenian terrorist circles.

Captain Henry Hozier, who was connected to the War Office intelligence branch, may have introduced him to the British Intelligence Service. He spent some years in the Far East, working for the Japanese and probably also for British Intelligence. Being an astute businessman and a gambler, he acquired a great deal of money. He made contact with the revolutionaries in Petrograd in 1906. It has been suggested that he might even have been working for the Tsarist regime at the same time. He certainly lived lavishly, was a member of at least one exclusive club, and had an impressive art collection. He was envied as a successful womanizer. Despite the most common portrait of him in books and magazines, taken when he looked older, he was good-looking when younger, and had a seductive charm that attracted women to him. He had plenty of mistresses. He also charmed business associates, which was one of the reasons he had been so successful.

He obtained work with a German naval shipbuilder and copied blueprints and specifications of new German constructions and innovations, which he passed to SIS in London. When war broke out, he left for New York as a war contractor buying munitions for Russia, meanwhile maintaining contact with Mansfield Smith-Cumming, who headed British Naval Intelligence and was known as "C," because of the way he signed his letters with that abbreviation in green ink.

He was in London in 1917, from where he was sent to Germany to find out how close the nation was to defeat. According to Sir George Nevile Bland, a British diplomat in the Foreign Office, Reilly had enormous courage. Although always cool in the face of danger, he was evidently motivated by the challenge of deceiving people. He did so with success in business, too, and made millions. Like all spies, he was a suave, confident trickster.

Reilly kept in touch with "C" through his contact in New York City, William Wiseman, who had been recruited by "C." Mansfield Smith-Cumming admired adventurous and resourceful mavericks like Wiseman and Sidney Reilly. He directed Wiseman to concentrate on counter-espionage, including investigating suspects about whom much more and deeper information was required. And, with the problems posed by Irish terrorism, the situation of who was funding the IRA in America had to be watched. Irish terrorists and Indian nationalism had been the top items on the Foreign Office agenda before the First World War suddenly erupted. Now, the most important intelligence to acquire at this stage of the war was if and when the United States would enter the war. Coupled with that was influencing American public opinion and the US government on the side of Britain and the Allies, and ascertaining the views of American policymakers.

In that regard, Wiseman was part of the infamous Zimmerman telegram scandal when, in January 1917, German Foreign Secretary Arthur Zimmerman sent a coded telegram to the German Ambassador in Mexico City, telling him to offer an alliance with Mexico if Germany went to war with the United States. It suggested that Germany and Japan would help

Mexico to recover their old colonial territories of Texas, Arizona, and New Mexico, which they had lost to the United States in 1848. It also expressed Germany's intention to commence submarine warfare against non-military merchant ships and passenger liners on February 1. A copy was provided for American President Woodrow Wilson on February 24. When leaked to the news media, the scandal caused a sensation that resulted in anti-German sentiments in America—a softening-up process necessary before an American president could take the irrevocable step of declaring war.

Although average in height and with a slender physique, Sidney Reilly had piercing, intelligent eyes which gave an impression of importance, power, and purpose. His appearance was always immaculate. And, with his intelligent and witty conversation, he was known as a pleasant companion. He joined the Royal Flying Corps (RFC) as a second lieutenant. Norman Thwaites introduced him to the future MI6 as an ideal agent for the Secret Service. His recommendation was passed on to Mansfield Smith-Cumming. "C" also heard that Reilly was untrustworthy and unsuitable, that he was a shrewd businessman without scruples, patriotism, or loyalty.

Nevertheless, Winston Churchill supported his recruitment into Britain's Secret Service. He admired Reilly's personal charisma, his flair for theater, and his social skills. He also respected the initiative of people who went straight to the jugular of their enemies with a killer instinct. "C" was also impressed by his adventurous spirit. Reilly was sent to Russia in April 1918. He was in a group that included Bruce Lockhart. Their objective was to cause the overthrow of the Bolshevik Government. Reilly was fixated on Russia as his corrupted homeland and hated the Communists who had destroyed the middle-classes: the leaders were criminals and murderers as far as he was concerned.

An essential part of the plan was to obtain the cooperation of the Latvian guards in the Bolshevik Army. There were only two well organized and disciplined military institutions in Soviet Russia—the Czechs and the Latvians. The Letts "guarded the Kremlin, gold bullion, and munitions." Although Lockhart and Reilly had passed over a considerable amount of money, for their contacts, it ended up in the hands of Feliks Dzerzhinsky, who was in charge of the Secret Police, the Cheka. With it went details of the British conspiracy to overthrow the Bolshevik Government.

Reilly had planned for discontented nationalist-minded Lett Army officers to arrest the Bolshevik leaders. But their plans were interrupted by an attempted assassination of Lenin by a young woman on August 31. Dora Kaplan had just spent eleven years in a Siberian prison camp. The assassination was her protest at the closing down by the Bolsheviks of the democratically elected Constituent Assembly. The "Red Terror" followed with hundreds of arrests and deaths by firing squads, beginning with the attack on the British Embassy, led by the Cheka.

According to Robin Bruce Lockhart's account, "The gallant Cromie had resisted to the last; with a Browning in each hand he had killed a commissar and wounded several Cheka thugs, before falling himself riddled with red bullets, kicked and trampled on, his body was thrown out of the second floor window."

Reilly arrived at the consulate after the incident occurred and managed to escape at the sight of the Cheka thugs and their vehicles outside. He paid to be smuggled out of Russia and arrived back in England with useful information. SIS wanted to send him back to Russia again, but news of the "Red Terror" discouraged him, knowing it was a critical time for the Bolsheviks, and they would stop at nothing to destroy any opposition, including himself.

Instead, Reilly contacted Churchill to recommend his friend Boris Savinkov as the best person to organize the overthrow of the Bolsheviks. Churchill met Reilly with Savinkov and agreed that he was the only man who might succeed. The Foreign Office, still maintaining their gentlemanly standards and not wanting to get their hands soiled, thought differently and claimed he was crooked. Nevertheless, "C" decided to send Reilly back to Russia. And Winston decided, for the moment at least, that he would have to deal directly with the Bolsheviks. It was just as well, since Savinkov disappeared into the maw of the the notorious secret police now named the OGPU.

Other leading agents in what was generally called the SIS at that time (before becoming MI5 and MI6) were Commander Ernest Boyce; Paul Dukes, who was knighted for freeing leading White Russians from prison and spiriting them across the Finnish border; Major Alley, who claimed he had been ordered to kill Stalin but had refused; and Captain George Hill. A serious problem that developed was to identify which of them was a double agent working also for Felix Dzerzhinsky's OGPU in Soviet Russia.

"Room 40"

As "Room 40" was the Naval Intelligence Division of the British Admiralty in the First World War, Winston Churchill would have known all about it when he was First Lord of the Admiralty. He even wrote the charter for it.[6]

But the problem of kept secrets is that it can be very difficult to know with certainty why some officers reached high ranks or obtained awards. They are obviously evidence of some kind of services to the country, but we are left to wonder what exactly they are. The famous "Blinker" Hall is an example of this. About all that is known about him with certainty is that he took over the direction of Room 40 in May 1917 from Alfred Ewing, who was Director of Naval Intelligence. "Blinker" Hall became Admiral Sir William Reginald Hall, and was bestowed with several honors from different nations. His nickname stemmed from an uncontrollable facial twitch. It may well be that at least one of his positions or awards can be attributed to the work that "Room 40" undertook so successfully with the scandal of the Zimmerman telegram.

Churchill had been President of the Board of Trade when the Secret Service came into being in 1909. When he became Home Secretary, he provided surveillance technology to find German spies attempting to steal the Royal Navy's secrets. On the same day the Austrians gave their ultimatum to the Serbs, he was at the Admiralty, jotting down a checklist of his priorities. Item 14 on his list was "Espionage."

It had been the Agadir Crisis in Morocco in 1911 that triggered the establishment of a specially focused British Secret Service, since Agadir was recognized as a symbol of the German Kaiser's plan to increase the size of Germany's fleet of battleships and modernize them to compete with the Royal Navy. Churchill naturally asked himself why a nation traditionally dedicated to its disciplined Prussian land army culture would want a Navy to dominate the seas. And even earlier, Lieutenant-Colonel John Spencer Ewart—who was Director of Operations and Intelligence at the War Office—was always conscious of the dangers of espionage, as far back as in 1906. He was well aware of German spies in Britain and deplored the lack of British spies on the other side of the Channel. He discussed the possibility of mobilization with Richard Burdon Haldane, the Secretary of State for War, and with the Committee of

Imperial Defense, introducing the possibility of enemy sabotage to Britain's naval centers by enemy agents as a prelude to war.

The alarm bell had not only been heard by them, but also by certain best-selling novelists who capitalized on the "spy fever" by writing up-to-the-minute fictions about foreign conspiracies. Some people thought it was a clever ruse by the French to wake England up to the dangers from German militarism, since France would need Britain's help as an ally. Those authors, in turn, began to stir the general public into awareness.

Churchill himself had looked around the crowds of passersby in the streets of London and observed that most of them would be incredulous if they had been told that we might be close to war.[7] There were, for example, allegations that railway union leaders were receiving payments from a German agent, and Churchill thought there might be some truth in it. One of his attributes was that he had no illusions about the corruptibility of anyone, and turned his attention to the dangers to Britain's essential resources, in particular coal, which was used to fuel the British fleet at the time.

What seems obvious about sabotage to anyone today had never before entered their minds because, for example, Churchill himself had only just bought one of the newly-invented motor cars. He began to imagine how such a vehicle could be used for sabotage, and how easily it could also be made useless by cutting off the fuel supply to the engine. It was a symbol for much larger vehicles in the modern age, like railway engines and battleships which were dependent on coal as fuel. He heard from the owners of the South Wales Coal-Owners Association that four gentlemanly Germans had been noticed in the Rhondda Valley, because they had Ordinance Survey maps on which they were making notes of the positions of collieries. He invited the Secret Service Bureau to discussions on surveillance of the railways as well as the coal mines, two years after the Agadir Crisis.

By arrangement with Churchill, Captain Vernon Kell of the War Office was keeping his eyes focused for other clues of war preparation by Germany. He noted that they were making large purchases of wheat; they were practicing war maneuvers close to the Belgian border; the price of flour had suddenly risen because of Germany's heavy purchases. What Kell's reports suggested—although much was wildly at fault—was that on one hand Germany was taking natural precautions, and on the other, they were also focusing their own intelligence searches on Britain. As usual with all intelligence, the value was in the analysis of the intelligence material that was gathered.

One result of the Agadir Crisis was that it initiated Prime Minister Asquith's decision to appoint Winston Churchill's to head the Admiralty. What Churchill found there was that just as Army officers had been resisting reforms to modernize the British Army, the Admirals had been resisting reforms in the Royal Navy. He would spend the next three years reforming and modernizing it.

German Spies

Gustave Steinhauser was the German spymaster in Britain. Massive in build, he was a previous naval officer and a former Pinkerton detective. He had chosen his agents from German nationals in towns and cities with naval installations. Fortunately for Britain, none was much good at spying. They reported largely on the comings and goings of ships and the type and amount of work going on in the docks. The first one to enter the glare of press publicity was Dr. Max Schultz when he appeared in court for attempting to bribe a local solicitor for information about Admiralty secrets for an annual fee of a thousand pounds. The solicitor had immediately reported him to the police. Schultz's ways of making contacts and obtaining information was much like some other foreign spies, by conspicuously throwing parties for local influential business or government individuals and assessing their weaknesses and possibilities for exploitation under the effects of alcohol.

Immediately after Schultz was sentenced to prison, along came Heinrich Grosse, who had persuaded a naval pensioner to supply him with information about coal supplies in Portsmouth naval barracks. Or he thought he had. But the result of his contact was the same—he too informed the police. But this time, Kell fed the spy with false information to send back to Germany. Grosse was imprisoned, too. Armgaard Karl Graves was caught in Glasgow where he was spying on an arms manufacturer making heavy guns for the new and improved dreadnought class of battleship. But he was apparently so clumsy that Kell was able to intercept his mail. A search of his premises produced incriminating evidence and he too was tried and imprisoned.

The only Englishman who was tried for espionage at this time was George Charles Parrot, a naval gunner. He had been lured by a honey trap, and an incriminating document was found in his possession. As a traitor to his country, he was sentenced to hard labor.

There were only two more cases before the outbreak of war in 1914. One was a dentist in Portsmouth with a German background and an assumed English name who offered to spy for the German Admiralty. They wanted to know about recent torpedo trials. He was trapped by a British agent and served five years' hard labor—an increase in sentence resulting from the so-called spy scare. Adolphus Schroder ran a pub under an assumed name and had been hired to pick up any gossip useful to Berlin. Kell had been watching him secretly. He was sentenced to six years with hard labor.

While Churchill was Home Secretary, and when First Lord of the Admiralty, he had access to all the files and read them avidly to obtain more and more information about the secret world of espionage. One of the causes of naval secrets slipping across the Channel, he found, was discontent in the Navy regarding poor pay and generally poor treatment, which he was able to improve as soon as he arrived at the Admiralty. There had often been past mutinies in the British navy for those very reasons. Treatment in the British navy had always been harsh and primitive, particularly in the lower decks when sailors had been treated like the scum of the earth, and often were. They were frequently flogged in front of the other men as punishment for trivial offenses. It was intended as a warning to the others, for mutiny on board a ship on the high seas could be a terrifying ordeal for young and inexperienced officers—so the brutes had to be kept down in case they became too impertinent to control.

Churchill's improvements came as a sign—small though it was—of a slight change in attitude towards the lower social and economic classes. And it probably came just in time, as later mutinies in the German and Russian fleets and the French army would show—for once they mutinied, they had to kill their officers.

Churchill appears to have kept the British Secret Service alert to every possible danger. But by 1913, he admitted to himself that as far as a possible sudden and unexpected invasion was concerned, British Intelligence was hardly able to detect it well enough in advance. His cry was "How are we going to get early intelligence?"[8] Two British agents sent across the channel for surveillance of a coastline had been arrested immediately, perhaps because that stretch of coast had been featured in a popular adventure novel called *The Riddle of the Sands*.[9] Consequently, their trial became an embarrassment to British Intelligence. (And, as it would turn out, the novelist's wife was a passionate supporter of the Irish revolutionaries, even to supplying them with arms.)

Churchill did not rely entirely on Kell (sometimes known as "K"), or Smith-Cumming, for his intelligence information. He had a personal contact he called "Captain Tupper." Tupper was a burly individual with a huge drooping moustache who had organized the National Seamen's and Fireman's Union in 1911. He had led a strike at Cardiff docks and also became a legend as the hero of the Bristol Channel Ports. It is typical of Winston that he could mix easily with an individual with such an unconventional and dubious reputation and do business with him. But Churchill enjoyed unconventional people, even if their imagination extended to telling tall stories about themselves. He admired their adventurous spirit. Among other extraordinary reminiscences, Tupper claimed to have been wounded twice when fighting as an irregular with the Boers in South Africa—a story that would have appealed to Churchill and was probably invented for that purpose.

Most of Tupper's tall stories turned out to be "Walter Mitty" fantasies to cover his lifetime failures. "Tupper was born in Worthing, Sussex, the son of a coachman turned publican who ran local meetings for the Conservative Primrose League."[10] He had begun his career as an errand-boy delivering groceries while claiming he owned the shop. Today, he would probably be encouraged for his imagination and initiative.

Churchill is likely to have marvelled at his imagination and applauded his initiative, since he was unconventional himself—whereas most self-important people working in a government department or institution in those days of false moralities would have been self-righteously shocked and ready in an instant to punish the young Tupper for his impertinence. Churchill, instead, recognized how effective he was. He had been impressed by him at the Tonypandy colliery riots, when the miners grew rebelliously ugly, and Churchill had been the Home Secretary with a difficult problem of whether to call in the army to quell their rioting. But he saw Tupper cajole them, and soon have them marching around happily singing Welsh hymns. Churchill had faith in him from then on.

To a broadminded individual like Churchill, Tupper was an "irresistible bounder" who could be useful to him. His faith in him was repaid when Tupper gave him a list of possible spies for Germany among the seamen in the union who had been "too nosey about naval vessels and guns" in the Hull docks.

As the irrepressible master spy and irresistible bounder himself, Sidney Reilly remarked to a friend about Churchill, "His ear would always be open to something sound."

Penetrating the Enemy's Future Intentions

Churchill had given the possibilities of the uses of intelligence information a great deal of thought by the time he decided that its major goal was to put together every link in the chain of the enemy's secrets in order to "penetrate their future intensions." And the means to do it was by intercepting their telegraph messages. Wireless had only recently been invented and not many people knew anything about the new technology. But they learned fast, and so did Churchill. At first he accepted the common view that "interception posed no threat to naval radio transmissions." And surely the messages between the armed forces would be in cipher? He wanted to know how it all worked. So he agreed heartily to the suggestion of setting up a new department in a room to find out. The result was SIGINT (or Signals Intelligence).

Immediately war was declared, he received a visit from Sir Henry Oliver and Sir Alfred Ewing, Director of Naval Intelligence. Ewing had two major interests at that time—one was radio telegraphy and the other was cryptography. As soon as war erupted, he was swamped with intercepts of German messages that had come by wireless, with no way to decipher them. But British Intelligence had broken Boer ciphers in the South African War. Now Room 40 became their interception room for the First World War.

One of the new inventions that the Royal Navy was worried about was the submarine. So Churchill used Room 40 to track German U-boats as soon as Germany announced it would no longer follow the traditional international convention of stopping to search unarmed enemy merchant ships: instead, they now felt free to torpedo them on sight. Each U-boat tracked was recorded with its position and number, and general comments about where it could be headed and its relationship with Allied convoys. It was in that way that they traced U-20. But they did not know that it planned to fire a single torpedo into a luxury passenger liner named the *Lusitania*.[11] The German press proudly admitted it as a victory, but, as well as the loss of around 2,300 lives, some 10 percent were American citizens. It was one of the early signs that Britain and America were treating the First World War like some previous ones in which there had been some kind of a gentlemen's agreement between enemies. But honor among gentlemen had already broken down. It had apparently not occurred to either nation that a Cunard passenger liner would automatically be treated by the German Navy in the same way as a cargo ship. The disaster left great scope for conspiracy theories, some of which have still not subsided.

Soon after the Bolshevik Revolution in Russia, labor unrest began in some of Britain's munition factories where some workers with socialist hopes undertook storm waves of sympathy. Communist subversion now joined German espionage. It was soon followed by sabotage that included arson by foreign agents working in munitions factories. Churchill did everything possible to improve and maintain his output of arms and armor and ammunition when he was appointed Minister of Munitions. He allowed nothing to stand in the way of British troops receiving deliveries of the weapons and ammunition they needed to prevent a German victory.

"As for the Bolsheviks," he informed the House, "they destroy wherever they exist."

CHAPTER TWENTY-FOUR

THE BEGINNING OF THE END

―――――――

IN THE FINAL WEEK OF NOVEMBER, a German officer wrote a report about the weak points of the British tanks. They were able to conquer ground, but they couldn't hold it. And they had no free field to fire in when limited by narrow streets or alleys where their movements were restricted on all sides. Now that the surprise element had gone from the new tanks, so had the fear. The German Army learned how to hunt tanks down and throw several hand grenades underneath them to blow them up. The Battle of Cambrai, which had begun so well, was ending in a whimper.

Prime Minister Lloyd George believed that the German army was planning a knockout blow to the Allies before the American Army was sufficiently trained for combat on the front line. They were needed urgently this summer. But Pershing resisted his pleas for battle-ready American soldiers, although he did agree to a few black regiments already in France, who would fight alongside Pétain's French division.

In the meantime the dissolution of Austria-Hungary had begun to look like a possibility as national aspirations grew, and different ethnic and religious groups, who had always been in conflict, saw an opportunity to split away from the Habsburg Empire. First the Czechs wanted independence for their territories in Bohemia and Moravia. Then the German-speakers in Sudetenland wanted their own province separated from other "foreign" people whom they found historically repellent.

US President Wilson addressed Congress with a fourteen-point program for peace in Europe. He called for openness in diplomacy and in making treaties. Freedom of navigation on the seas would be established for all.

Economic barriers must be removed, with equality of trading conditions. There would be a reduction in arms and armaments. The interests of the colonial peoples must have equal weight with the government (whose title would be determined). German forces must leave all Russian territory. German troops must leave Belgium, and the country and its economy must be restored. French territory must be freed from German occupation, and Alsace-Lorraine restored to it. Italian frontiers would be established in accordance with clear national lines, with South Tyrol going from Austrian rule to Italy. Austria-Hungary would be given an opportunity for autonomous development. In the Balkans, Romania, Serbia, and Montenegro would be restored to independence, and Serbia provided with sea access. Turkish parts of the Ottoman Empire should have secure sovereignty, and other nations in Turkey should be assured of autonomy. An independent and autonomous Polish state should be created with unrestricted sea access. And an association of nations must be formed in order to guarantee political independence and territorial integrity to all states.

Those fourteen points were intended to act as a counterweight to the growing mass appeal of Bolshevism. But the aspirations of the South Slavs for their own state were not mentioned, and many Czechs did not find anything in the language that would give them independence. Nor were the Croats or the Slovenes mentioned. And, two days after Wilson announced his fourteen points, a Finnish delegation arrived in London to obtain British support for their own independence. As with the Austro-Hungarian Empire, even in its heydays, no ethnic or religious group wanted to cooperate, or live with, or share anything with anyone else.

More lobbying took place with other small nations who sought independence by obtaining patronage from more powerful ones. Both the enemy powers and the Bolsheviks supported Ukrainian independence, while Latvia announced its independence from Russia in January. Lenin and Stalin declared support for Armenian self-determination. At the same time, Trotsky used all his wits and threats to limit any demands from Germany or Austria for any Russian territory. The Turks also sent a delegation to seek the recovery of their old lands in Eastern Anatolia.

Meanwhile, in Britain, Lord Balfour insisted that all the horrors of war were preferable to a German peace settlement. Britain had two million armed servicemen and planned to add another 420,000 or more. On the other hand, the German home front was beginning to show war-weariness and even resistance to war. Four hundred thousand workers went on strike in Berlin. The strike-fever spread to six other German cities. The German government declared martial law in Berlin and Hamburg, and drafted many of the strikers into the army. But hunger from the efficient and dogged British sea blockade left German civilians only with dogs and cats and rats to eat for meat, and bread was now made out of potato peel and sawdust.

Regardless, Austrian and German Government representatives showed no inclination to meet the conditions that the Allies insisted were essential for peace. "Isn't German mentality a depressing thing," remarked Edward Grey, the former British Foreign Secretary. His own solution was economic equality after the war was over. He added, "I do not see how there is to be peace with the people who still run Germany."

Germany supported independence in the Ukraine, but Lenin's forces invaded and declared it a Bolshevik state. Russian Bolsheviks and Ukrainian nationalists became embattled at Lutsk. Lenin's troops entered Kiev and Odessa, then transformed Russia into the USSR or Soviet Union. The creation of a Red Army and a Red Navy followed. More mutinies occurred at sea, where sailors raised the Red Flag and attacked their officers. There were bread shortages in France and looting by thousands of hungry people.

The First American Division

New American troops were arriving every day. The 1st American division appeared on the frontline on January 18 at the St. Mihiel Salient, to gain experience without taking any action. As soon as the Germans knew they were untrained and ineffective, they attempted to demoralize them in hit-and-run raids, by killing, wounding, or capturing them a few at a time. Meanwhile, the Kaiser announced in Bad Homburg, on February 10, that "War is a disciplinary action by God to educate mankind."[1] Three days later he complained that there was a conspiracy against Germany by the Bolsheviks, President Wilson, Jews, and Freemasons.

Peace discussions broke down a week later between Germany and the Bolsheviks who refused to accept their terms. General Hoffman wrote in his diary that evening, "Tomorrow we are going to start hostilities against the Bolsheviks . . . Otherwise these brutes will wipe up the Ukrainians, the Finns, and the Balts, and then quickly get together a new revolutionary army and turn the whole of Europe into a pig-sty."[2]

Fifty-two German divisions crossed the cease-fire line and continued the war. Lenin was overwhelmed. He realized he had no choice but to compromise, even agree to do whatever Germany wanted. "We must sign at once," he told Trotsky.

Hoffman received their telegram asking for peace on January 19. He was annoyed at their presumption that he would agree, and used delaying tactics while the German advance continued. He preferred to make war—it was his trade. The Germans rounded up 90,000 Russian soldiers in Minsk and imprisoned them. "There's no fight in them," Hoffman remarked on a page of his diary. "One German lieutenant with six men took 600 Cossacks to prison!"

"It's the most comical war I have ever known," he added later on, after another handful of Germans had taken more prisoners at the end of their guns. In the end, the Germans rejected Lenin's acceptance of their peace terms by demanding even harsher ones. The Germans could see that Russia was falling apart. But then the new figure of Joseph Stalin began to make its presence felt.

US troops went into action on the Western Front on February 23, at Chevregny in Champagne. Ten days after Chevregny, a small group of Americans offered to raid the German trenches alongside French troops. Although both actions were small and of little importance, it seemed to demonstrate that some American troops, at least, had been properly trained for the Front. Three and a half years after the war had begun, American troops were finally participating with the Allies.

There was such a burst of optimism that the Americans could turn the tide of war in favor of the Allies that Pershing hurriedly objected to the exaggerated claims. But when Lenin and Trotsky finally signed a peace settlement with Germany on March 3, the German High Command was relieved, because they wanted to turn all their military might against the Allies on the Western Front, and the British did not have sufficient numbers of troops to withstand such an onslaught.

The continual German successes on the Eastern Front led to patriotic fervor among Germans to continue the war. The March 3 peace treaty between Germany and the Russian Bolsheviks meant that Russia would have to give up any claims to Poland, White Russia, Finland, the Baltic provinces, Bessarabia, the Ukraine, and the Caucasus. Those territorial losses amounted to about a third of Russia's prewar population and a third of its agricultural land. It was only part of the Treaty of Brest-Litovsk—Russia would also lose its naval bases, and its warships were taken away.

On the Western Front, the situation of the Allies was discouraging, too. But Churchill assured Lloyd George that he would produce 4,000 tanks by April 1919, since victory could only be achieved when Britain and France had stronger and better armies than Germany.

The German offensive began on March 9, as usual with a series of bombardments by their artillery. Until now, the main initiatives had been taken by the Allies—at the Battles of the Somme, Ypres, Passchendaele, and Cambrai— where they were all halted by superior fortifications and defense lines. Now the Germans would attempt to break through the Allied trenches. And this time they used half a million mustard gas and phosgene shells. They were betting as much as they could on their biggest gamble ever. Ten days later the British retaliated near St. Quentin. Only two days after that, on March 21, the Germans began their greatest ever offensive. Their objective was to drive the Allies from the Somme and the Aisne, and occupy Paris.

Ludendorff's offensive against the British Fifth Army took them by surprise, since he had given an impression that he would attack further south. Haig and his staff were not ready for it, and the French Army too, were unready and in the wrong position, waiting for a non-existent attack on the Southern Sector. And they were under strength.

The German bombardment on March 21, from 6,000 heavy guns, lasted for five hours, starting at 4:40 a.m. Added to their massive firing strength were 3,000 mortars. And 326 fighter planes hovered overhead where they confronted 261 British pilots. It took only two and a half hours for the German infantry to arrive and attack the British line; advancing four and a half miles and taking 21,000 Allied prisoners. Winston had been visiting the front line, but managed to leave the battlefield just before the German troops arrived. The momentum and their sheer weight were too much for the Fifth Army to halt and repel, although one British regiment fought unyieldingly to the last bullet and the last man.

The Germans advanced further next day. Twenty-five British tanks met them in a counter-attack, and sixteen were destroyed. Another thirty British planes went down. In one location, two British divisions were pushed back after holding out all day. Another one fought stubbornly for two days, until surrounded and bombarded from the air, and overrun. More than 1,200 British infantrymen were killed.

On the following day, March 23, Paris was bombarded by a specially made gun from Krupp, aimed at its target seventy-four miles away. It took about four minutes for each of its shells to travel the distance, and killed 256 Parisians.

The speed and mass of the advance was impossible to stop. The Allies needed more troops, but the Americans were still not ready. Prime Minister Lloyd George sent an urgent telegram to Lord Reading, the British Ambassador in Washington, instructing him to explain to President Wilson that Britain's manpower shortage was critical and they were being overwhelmed. When the President asked what he could do to help, Reading asked him to order General Pershing to mix American troops in France with British and French troops in the front line.

German forces crossed the Somme on March 24. Haig and Pétain argued about sending more French troops to the front. But Pétain feared a separate German attack and needed them. German troops broke through the next day, and about 45,000 Allied soldiers were taken prisoner. Three thousand more were assembled to hold the Allied lines, including 500 US Army engineers.

Meanwhile, discussions took place in the War Cabinet in London as to whether British forces should retreat to the Channel ports, since it was clear that the Germans intended to reach Amiens and cut off British troops from escaping through Rouen and Le Havre.

General Gough happened to meet a wounded British General on March 26, whose division had been reduced to an exhausted brigade. "Well," the General told Gough, "we have won the war!" What he meant was that the Allied resistance had been so great that the German Army was running out of zeal and purpose. They had advanced swiftly because of their numerical superiority, but were now dispirited by the implacable Allied defense. He was right—French troops stopped the German advance on March 27, and the German forces began to back off. The British took 800 German prisoners on the Somme.

General Gough stonewalled the heavy German offensive for as long as two weeks. But—perhaps because the British Government did not want to let the public know of the shortage of troops—Gough was ordered home and made to look like a coward who did not fight to the finish with the last bullet and the last man. The situation was so critical that, apparently, they needed to set an example of those who preferred to live, in order to encourage the others to die. As Lloyd George observed thoughtfully the next day, "The last man may count."

March 30 was the date of the Allied counter-attack from British, Australian, and Canadian troops that turned the tide against Germany. Doctors and nurses were hastily patching up the 60,000 wounded French soldiers and officers and sending them back into battle as quickly as possible. They were largely eighteen- and nineteen-year-old lads who had never been in battle before. Now Lord Reading's request to President Wilson resulted in 120,000 American troops arriving in France each month. General Pershing reluctantly agreed to mix American soldiers with Allied Armies at the front. But he was stubbornly fixated on having solely American divisions fighting under American commanders in future.

Churchill was still in France. He sent a message to Lloyd George to apprise him of what the French generals and politicians believed—that the Germans would continue the battles through the summer months towards a final conclusion. And, on April 4, the Germans launched another attack with twice the number of men than the British had. But General Ludendorff—after assessing the German losses—called off the Somme offensive the following day.

The position of the Allies was so critical that Britain's conscription now included Ireland. On the other hand, anti-war sentiment in Canada reduced the number of men who had been conscripted there, and there were riots in the province of Québec. On April 11, General Haig issued a special order: "There is no course open to us but to fight it out. Every position must be held to the last man: there must be no retirement. With our backs to the wall and believing in the justice of our cause, each one of us must fight to the end."[3]

A few days later, the cry was, "Here are the Americans!" Three thousand American troops had arrived behind the French lines. But before they could move forward to the front line, Allied troops were pushed back further, burned-out and exhausted. More than a thousand New Zealanders were taken prisoner on April 16. Despite their own exhaustion, the Germans launched another bombardment of gas shells. Over 8,000 British soldiers were gassed, although only forty died from it. Meanwhile, almost continuous air battles took place overhead.

On April 20, 1918, Americans fought at the St. Mihiel Salient against German "shock troops" who outnumbered them four to one. The Americans retreated with heavy losses. Pershing was disappointed with his officers for their poor generalship.

Holding Cantigny

For the remainder of April, Allied troops and enemy forces moved back and forth, each one taking a position and then losing it—a hill, or a village, or a strategic house. Both sides seemed fairly evenly matched, and both were burdened with fatigue and unable to hold any position for long. Meanwhile, they inflicted brutal carnage on the enemy and themselves. Ludendorff halted the German offensive on April 29, since in the past three weeks alone they had lost 30,000 men to 20,000 Allied soldiers. And there was a question of German morale. Many frontline soldiers were suffering from exhaustion and depression. They had long forgotten why they were fighting or why the war continued without end, as they focused only on surviving for one day at a time.

It was now nearly four years since the assassination in Sarajevo of the Archduke, heir to the aging Emperor Franz Joseph on the throne of Austria and Hungary. Now it began to look as if there would no longer be any Austria or Hungary. As for the assassin himself, Gavrilo Princip had been literally rotting in prison, and was now dying in the hospital from tuberculosis at age twenty-two. Millions had already died to avenge his rebellious act. In this month alone, more than a hundred merchant ships were sunk by U-Boats with 488 lives lost at sea. It was hard to believe that Austrian pride had to be assuaged with so many deaths. But that was no longer the objective of all the fighting—it resulted from the unintended consequences of one action after another.

Winston continued to work hard to provide arms and armor for the American troops. He loved being in the middle of the action. He had just ordered 225 heavy guns that summer and another fifty in November. More than three million US servicemen were expected in France by the summer of 1919, and part of the British "Plan 1919" was for up to 5,000 Allied tanks to make a breakthrough on the Western Front.

To double-check the reality of the plan, Clemenceau asked General Pershing if he had reconsidered his stubborn insistence on waiting until he had trained and equipped US divisions who would fight only under an American commander. Pershing refused to change his mind, either for the French Premier or the British Prime Minister, or Marshal Foch who was the Commander-in-Chief of all Allied forces. As Pershing put it, he did not want American forces to be at the disposal of French or British commanders. And he was prepared to wait for "the time when we have our own army."[4] Lloyd George agreed with Pershing as far as policy was concerned, but argued that they were presently engaged in what might be the decisive battle of the war: "Can't you see the war will be lost unless we get this support?"

Foch was angry: "You are willing to risk our being driven back to the Loire?"

Pétain was almost speechless with disbelief. But Pershing was adamant. "Gentlemen," he said. "I have thought this program over very deliberately and will not be coerced."[5]

The question of which would have the final say was left to Britain's Prime Minister and General Pershing at a conference in Abbeville on May 2. Lloyd George declared that perhaps the enemy's objective would have succeeded if the United States didn't come to Britain's aid. But if Britain had to yield to Germany, her defeat at least would be honorable, since she would have fought to the last man, while the United States would have been forced to halt without having put into the line more troops than Belgium.

Pershing repeated that the Americans had declared war independently of the Allies and must confront it with a powerful army. Their morale depended on fighting under their own flag. But Lloyd George's point apparently hit home, since Pershing finally agreed to a compromise—the 130,000 American infantry and machine-gunners already on the way to France by British ships, and a further 150,000 in June, could join the Allied forces. He would not commit himself to July. Clemenceau and Lloyd George had no choice but to agree. Meanwhile, the daily number of Allied soldiers who were slaughtered on the battlefields continued.

About a week later that month, the intoxicating drug of nationalism brought mutiny to the heartland of Austria, where an infantry platoon of mostly Slovenes took over their barracks and the munitions, looted the food stores, and destroyed the telegraph lines. "Let's go home, comrades!" cried the ringleader. "The war must be ended now . . ." Six of the mutineers were executed. But other mutinies developed. They were crushed. A fourth mutiny by Czech troops arose four days later. Their arguments mostly focused on lack of decent food or not being paid properly; they appeared to be able to put up with the hardships, and may even have enjoyed the life. But there was the ever-present lure of Bolshevism which, in their minds, seemed to translate into taking whatever they wanted from the middle and upper classes. To complicate the ethnic problem further, some Czechs found other Czechs fighting against them with the enemy.

Meanwhile, German bombing raids of large cities like Paris and London and munitions dumps and railways continued. But their scale was small. Ludendorff made another attempt to gain territory and reach Paris on May 27, and the Third Battle of the Aisne began. German troops reached the Aisne within only six hours, but a British battalion and a field battery stubbornly refused to withdraw. They fought it out with the German Army "until every man was killed or captured."[6]

On the other hand, at Contigny on the Somme, in the first American offensive of the war, their full brigade of 4,000 US troops swiftly overran the German position, after softening it up with a two-hour artillery barrage. Their flame-throwers took the German machine-gunners by surprise when flushed out of their holes where they had waited patiently to mow down the Americans.

The Americans took one hundred German prisoners at Contigny—but some they did not let live. Pershing now ordered them not to give back an inch of ground in German counter-attacks. According to their commander, after three days of action some men became "half crazy, temporarily insane." But the Americans held Contigny.[7]

When the French asked for 250,000 Americans to join the line in June, Pershing dumbfounded them by claiming that there were only that many left in the United States, and stood firm again. Foch kept repeating in amazement, "The battle, the battle, nothing else counts."

America's contribution of troops would not be ready until the end of 1918, possibly not even before 1919. When the British Prime Minister and the Commander of the Allied forces pressed him further, Pershing would only say he would not "surrender my prerogatives." However, he agreed to a small increase in future numbers, but insisted they would be trained in the United States.

The exhaustion of the German troops enabled the Americans to hold the line and even make small advances, which boosted French morale. On June 3, as a consequence of their victories, American confidence and persistence emerged during a German attack. Sergeant Dan Daly shouted to the US marine brigade: "Come on, you sons of bitches. Do you want to live forever?" One thousand eighty-seven marines were killed in battle. And when the question of withdrawing arose, an American officer was quoted as saying, "Retreat hell! We just got here."

Belleau Wood

The next big attack by German infantry took place at 4:30 a.m. on June 8. The customary artillery bombardment beforehand was more intense than previously, with three-quarters of a million rounds of mustard gas, phosgene, and diphenyl-chlorarsine. About 4,000 French soldiers were incapacitated by the gas, and the Germans took 8,000 prisoners. Churchill was in Paris, organizing and planning the munitions needs of the Allies. Ludendorff, too, ordered considerably more aircraft—300 planes a month—since it was evident that the Allies possessed air superiority, despite extraordinary German air aces like Manfred and Lowther von Richthofen, Ernst Udet, and Göring.

American troops were battling against enemy troops at Belleau Wood on June 17, when Marshal Foch asked Pershing for more American divisions to reinforce the French line: "People are asking, 'Where are the Americans?'" Pershing refused to be coaxed, insisting that American troops could do twice as much under their own leaders.

The issue continued to be critical four days later, when Canadian Prime Minister Robert Borden arrived in a convoy of ships bringing over 30,000

American troops to Britain. He wrote to Ottawa that the outcome of the war "may depend on the speed with which the American Army can be organised, trained and equipped."

Now that the Americans were on the front line, they began to be respected for their bravado, their stubbornness and persistence. US Marines, who adamantly refused to withdraw at Belleau Wood three weeks earlier, took it. The Germans were impressed, too. The Americans were serving under French and British commanders at this time.

At the beginning of the month, an influenza epidemic began to spread to Britain and India, and was expected to reach the Western Front soon. It would kill more Americans than the enemy did. Meanwhile the Americans took the village of Vaux with minimal losses on July 1. Three days later, they fought alongside the Australians and captured the village of Hamel. They were supplied with ammunition from the air for the very first time. Because of the spread of influenza among German troops, the German high command had postponed a renewed assault. But now they planned to go ahead with it. It was launched at midnight on July 14.

This time the German bombardment struck no troops—the French had left empty trenches in the locality they hit. The fully manned trenches were situated further in the rear and were barely touched by enemy fire. By the time that German infantry reached the French under continuous heavy fire, they were exhausted, confused, and disoriented.

East of Château-Thierry, Americans of the Third Division blew up the German pontoon bridges. As German troops swarmed to the river, American machine-gunners mowed them down, until the only Germans left were the dead. The French offensive was similarly successful, with some 30,000 German soldiers dead by the end of four days of battle. On July 19, British troops advanced on the Soissons Front, taking 3,300 German prisoners. A German lieutenant made a note in his diary about the extraordinary strength of character, morale, and physical endurance of young German soldiers.

When the Kaiser visited the German advanced headquarters on July 22, conversation was subdued. He was told of the failure of the German offensive and the successful Allied counter-attack. "I am a defeated War Lord," he remarked ruefully. The following day he recounted a dream he'd had the previous night of everyone he had known holding him up to ridicule. Meanwhile,

Colonel Mertz von Quirnheim watched General Ludendorff, who seemed to be sunk in a leaden introspective mood on August 7. Morale was low with a sense of failure and a loss of nerve. The Colonel jotted down what he thought in his diary: "We have lost the war if we cannot pull ourselves together."

Meanwhile, the carnage continued from one month to the next, and the German troops had not given up fighting on the Western Front. The first of Marshal Foch's "Liberating Attacks" began the next day. It was a turning point. The Kaiser told Ludendorff, "We have reached the limits of our capacity. The war must be ended." But the daily slaughter continued. Even when outnumbered, the Allies on the Somme fought with purpose and excitement now they felt they might be winning, as they overran and reoccupied ground they had lost in 1916. And the Germans continued to fall back.

As for the injustice of the shabby way General Gough had been treated, it motivated Sir Henry Wilson, then Chief of the Imperial Staff, to send a telegram to Haig, warning him that the War Cabinet would be upset at any harsh punishments being imposed on the Allies if the attack on the Hindenburg Line failed. But now that the Germans were turning tail, the Allied assaults on the enemy became fiercer. By the time Ludendorff gave the order to withdraw, the Allies had over 3,000 guns and 40,000 tons of ammunition for their attacks. More than 200,000 American soldiers with 48,000 French troops advanced in the pouring rain on a twelve-mile front, and fired 100,000 rounds of phosgene gas shells. Nine thousand Germans were incapacitated and fifty died. In the air above was the biggest number of aircraft ever seen in flying combats.

The Germans continued to pull back in the face of so many fresh and fit troops, while the Americans captured 13,000 prisoners and 200 guns. Their advance was so swift now that Ludendorff was overcome with emotion and barely able to make sense when he spoke. He had held on for years of slaughter in the constant hope that good fortune would weigh the balance in favor of a German victory. So had the Allies for an Allied victory. Now he believed that the German Army couldn't last for more than forty-eight hours. And he feared a revolution at the front and in Germany.

In spite of the Allied advance, some German troops continued to resist. MacArthur reported afterwards on "the ferocity of the fighting on October 16 1918 in an American battalion of 25 officers and 1450 men, led by Major

Ross." "Officers fell and sergeants leaped to the command . . . Companies dwindled to platoons and corporals took over. At the end, Major Ross had only 300 men and 6 officers left."[8]

Not only was German manpower being led to slaughter after slaughter, but German battle resources were fast coming to an end. Meanwhile, at a final discussion on whether Germany should carry on fighting, Ludendorff had a sudden change of mind in favor of continuing instead of seeking an immediate Armistice. He produced a plan to continue fighting into 1919 by withdrawing to Belgium. But the German war minister warned that if Romanian oil supplies were cut off, which was likely, German troops could only fight for another six weeks. Prince Rupprecht of Bavaria wrote the next day that "his troops, short of ammunition, artillery support, horses and officers, could not go on much longer." He urged the Kaiser to obtain peace before the enemy breaks into Germany.

The kingdoms of Austria and Hungary were breaking apart at the same time as the German Navy mutinied in Kiel and refused to take any further orders from the Kaiser. Dockyard workers in Kiel declared a general strike in support of them.

Soldiers were still fighting on the Front on November 7, but rumors spread of a German delegation signing an armistice, and an American journalist telegraphed the United Press offices in New York at 11:00 a.m. that American forces took Sedan that morning.

Many years later, looking back on the First World War, Churchill wrote, "It astonished me to read in these after years the diabolical schemes for killing men on a vast scale by machinery or chemistry to which we passionately devoted ourselves."

Surrender

The Austro-Hungarian Empire gave up fighting and formally surrendered to the Allies in London on November 3. Feeling optimistic about the outcome of the war, Churchill lunched with Prime Minister Lloyd George three days afterwards, in order to seek a policy-making position for himself in the postwar Government. Lloyd George had already made up his mind to appoint all Ministers of wartime departments to peacetime posts.

Next day, a German delegation requested an Armistice with the Allies in France. Lloyd George invited Winston to a special meeting of the cabinet to discuss negotiations, where they learned that the German Kaiser had fled to Holland. He had resisted abdicating for as long as he could, and only gave in to German entreaties when, on the evening of September 8, Admiral von Hintze called on him to say that the German Navy would not obey his orders anymore. Lloyd George felt that the Kaiser should be brought back for trial and shot.

Early next morning, Germany accepted the terms imposed by the Allies. Fighting must cease at 11:00 that morning, and German troops would leave France, Belgium, Luxemburg, Alsace, and Lorraine within fourteen days. They must also leave the Rhineland. American and Allied Forces would immediately occupy Germany west of the Rhine.

When the subject of Allied demobilization came up, the Government knew they would be unpopular if life in Britain did not return to normalcy as soon as possible. And Lloyd George's cabinet intended to remain in power. But Churchill saw the bigger picture in which some powerful nation would attempt to fill the vacuum created by a weakening of the balance of power in Europe, now that the Romanov Tsars were gone, the Hohenzollern dynasty in Germany was over, and the Austro-Hungarian Empire had collapsed. The only empire that remained was the British Empire. France was exhausted. And the United States would pull out of Europe to return to business as usual.

Winston warned the cabinet that Britain would now have to put Germany back in working order to prevent its economy from complete collapse. Otherwise there would be social unrest leading to the rise of Bolshevism. Churchill, with his broad sense of history, knew there was always another threat to Britain on the horizon. And the biggest danger now was the spread of Communism across Europe. One thing he insisted on before wartime budgets were cut in the relief of peace—Britain's Secret Service budget should be doubled in order to be able to know whenever new dangers threatened the British Isles or the Empire, and where they might come from, before Britain could be plunged into another war.

There were other problems to solve too, like selling off surplus munitions, and replacing production in munitions factories. What would three million munition workers make now to keep them employed? Guns, shells, tanks, and aircraft would no longer be needed. How would all those man-ufacturing plants be converted? Churchill thought about it while he stood by the windows in his hotel room by himself, overlooking Northumberland Avenue. "All the Kings and Emperors with whom we have warred were in flight or exile," he would write of that moment. "All their armies and fleets were destroyed or subdued." He felt confident that Britain had done her best from first to last.[9]

He heard the first stroke of eleven o'clock boom out from nearby Big Ben, and glanced down through the windows at the empty street below. As the second stroke sounded from Westminster, he noticed figures gesticulating with excitement and moving out of buildings into the street. Another stroke of Big Ben, and men and women began to pour out into the streets around his hotel until they were full of people. He could hear doors slamming, footsteps hurrying along corridors and down stairs, as everyone around him stopped whatever they were doing and ran out in the open with a renewed sense of freedom. Glancing towards Trafalgar Square, he saw more crowds surging in between the pedestals and columns, the statues of great men, and the huge implacable lions. Flags appeared miraculously as if out of nowhere as Big Ben announced the news with its eleventh stroke. Then cheers broke out among the waiting crowds.

Clementine arrived at the Hotel Metropole to be with her husband. She was expecting another child in four days. They decided to drive to 10 Downing Street to congratulate Prime Minister Lloyd George. It was a gloomy overcast day. But as soon as they were seated in their motor car, they were surrounded by happy and excited people who cheered and climbed onto the bonnet.

They finally reached the Prime Minister's official residence, where all the lights were on to cast out the gloom, and Lloyd George invited Winston to dinner that night. F. E. Smith and Sir Henry Wilson were guests, too. While they celebrated the peace, Winston's mind was already plunged into thoughts about what would be the consequences of the war and the future struggle to maintain peace. What would it take? Who would initiate it? And who would lead it? Where others were generally short-sighted, he always saw the long and broad view in historical perspective, in order to limit the type of mistakes the Western World had made in the past. He was well aware of the dangers of complacency. He would examine what unintended consequences could emerge from every judgment and action.

He and Clementine now had a new little daughter whom they called Marigold. He managed to spend several days with them before leaving London for his constituents in Dundee. Prime Minister Lloyd George had called for a General Election. Life was almost back to Winston's hectic normal pace.

Jennie generally had the last word in the Churchill family. She visited her sister on her sixtieth birthday, after a dinner party, and sat on Leonie's bed. "I shall never get used to not being the most beautiful woman in the room," she said "It was an intoxication to know every man had turned his head. It kept me in form."[10]

She would turn sixty-five in January 1919, when the peace of Europe and the whole world was discussed by heads of state, generals, politicians, and economists, in Paris. She was still filled with the joys of living, and her marriage to Montagu Porch continued to be completely happy. They remained in love to the end. And she continued to enjoy the company of Clementine and Winston and her grandchildren. Winston was still the most interesting man in her life: she was almost mesmerized by him and his sharply focused mind, his intense talk of affairs of State, and his dogged determination.

Even so, she never forgot her marriage to George; it reminded her of her lost youth. "Dear George," she wrote on June 17, 1919—long after he had left the famously volatile Mrs Patrick Campbell—"I heard about you from Clare . . . I am glad you wrote . . . and in your heart of hearts you must know that I never could have any but kindly feelings towards you. I never think of you but to remember all those happy days we spent together . . . I have forgotten everything else. I do wish you all that is best . . . Life is frightfully hard. Bless you, always your best friend, Jennie."[11]

George had his own version of Jennie, which he wrote down for posterity in an attempt to show what a remarkable woman he thought she was. He ended by saying, "Possessed of a great driving force in matters which interested her, she was a good organiser, as was proved by the success she made of the *Maine* hospital ship. Her greatest undertaking was the 'Shakespeare's England' exhibition at Earl's Court—for raising funds for a National Theater . . . Her extravagance was her only fault, and with her nature, the most understandable and therefore the most forgivable."[12]

The Cost of War

Peace came as a stunning anticlimax when many began to count the cost of war. It was not until 1926 that some people, at least, were able to recover enough to suppress "the tear in the voice." The invention of talking pictures on cinema screens created a welcome distraction from the harsh reality of what had happened and the emptiness that the dead had left behind them, to a movie fantasy world of skies that were always blue. Larger-than-life movie heroes and heroines and Hollywood songwriters like Irving Berlin put a smile on people's faces once again.

> Blue days
> All of them gone
> Nothing but blue skies
> From now on.

The artificial Hollywood-made dream-world was exactly what people wanted to believe in. And it began to lift the mist of mourning that still clung over their real world like a thin, gray, army blanket, sagging helplessly over the whole of Britain and some parts of the United States like a shroud.

The first full-length "talky" arrived a year later. It was a musical film called *The Jazz Singer*, with Al Jolson, who was described as "the man with a tear in his voice." His understanding of the pain of others in his emotional singing caused a catharsis that coaxed out people's anxiety and stress. It was an instant success. Audiences wanted more of it. Hollywood romances and musical extravaganzas would keep moviegoers entertained for the next decade or two. Then they woke up suddenly out of their trance-like happy fantasies to the bizarre symptoms of an emotional disease on the other side of the English Channel, once again, to be confronted by the outbreak of a Second World War.

Relative Strengths of Combatants:

	FRANCE	BRITAIN	AUSTRIA/H	GERMANY	RUSSIA	US
Population	40 M	45 M	50 M	65 M	164 M	92 M
Army	1.25 M	711,000	810,000	2.2 M	1.2 M	150,000
War Budget (1913/14)	185 M	250 M	110 M	300 M	335 M	150 M
Battleships	28	64	16	40	16	37
Cruisers	34	121	12	57	14	35
Submarines	73	64	6	23	29	25

	Enemy	Allies
Dead	4 M	5.4 M
Wounded	8.3 M	7 M

Source: *The Western Heritage.* Kagan, Ozment & Turner (Prentice Hall, NJ 2007), P. 850.

NOTE: The unintended consequences of Austria's declaration of war against Serbia included the collapse of the Austro-Hungarian Empire, the disappearance of the Ottoman Empire, the exile of the German Kaiser and loss of power by Prussia's Hohenzollern dynasty, and the end of Russia's Romanov dynasty, together with the murders of Tsar Nicolas and his wife and children by the Bolsheviks.

TOTAL CASUALTIES

Country	Dead	Wounded	Percentage of Population Killed
France	1,398,000	2,000,000	3.4
Belgium	38,000	44,700	0.5
Italy	578,000	947,000	1.6
British Empire	921,000	2,090,000	1.7
Romania	250,000	120,000	3.3
Serbia	278,000	133,000	5.7
Greece	26,000	21,000	0.5
Russia	1,811,000	1,450,000	1.1
Bulgaria	88,000	152,000	1.9
Germany	2,037,000	4,207,000	3.0
Austro-Hungary	1,100,000	3,620,000	1.9
Turkey	804,000	400,000	3.7
United States	114,000	206,000	0.1

Source: *The Pity of War.* Niall Ferguson (Basic Books, NY 1998).

ABOUT THE AUTHOR

John Harte is the author of the Skyhorse book *How Churchill Saved Civilization*, which examines Winston Churchill's role as leader of the free world during World War II.

Harte was born in London, England, between the two world wars. He absorbed the experiences and lessons of World War I while growing up in its aftermath and studying it at a time when magazines, books, and encyclopaedias were still puzzled and confused by it. He then observed the phenomenon of the growing dictatorships emerging on the Continent of Europe, which resulted in the outbreak of World War II. The fact that he was born when London was the center of the British Empire and the free world, politically, militarily, financially, socially, and culturally, invests his books about Churchill and England with particular significance, since he is one of the few left who can describe at first hand what it was really like.

He witnessed the bombing of London and the Battle of Britain from a high rooftop in the West End of London, and volunteered for the RAF while still underage. Stationed at the same aerodrome where Winston Churchill learned to fly, he was invalided out after hospitalization. Working in Hastings, he was able to observe the arrival of American troops for training inland on the southeast coast for the D-Day landings. Returning from time to time to London during the subsequent invasions by Hitler's so-called secret weapons, he experienced the effects of the enemy's V1 and V2 rockets launched from across the English Channel to destroy London and its population.

The author began his writing career as a freelance investigative journalist for leading publications in the UK, while as a playwright he had four of his plays produced in London and elsewhere. After moving to South Africa to work in the advertising industry with J. Walter Thompson, he also wrote freelance feature articles under his own byline for the two leading newspapers there, which were syndicated worldwide by Reuters. He also broadcast his own stories on the SABC. He now lives in Ottawa, Canada, where he writes books on history.

NOTES

<hr />

Preface:
1. *History of the First World War.* Liddell Hart (Cassell, London 1938). P. 18.
2. *The War that Ended Peace.* Margaret MacMillan (Lane, London 2013). P. xxv.
3. *Churchill: A Life.* Sir Martin Gilbert (Heinemann, London 1991).

1. Jennie:
1. So George Moore alleged.
2. Francis Younghusband. *India and Tibet* (John Murray, London 1910).
3. *Men, Mines and Animals in South Africa.* Lord Randolph Churchill (Appleton, NY 1892).
4. *Mrs. Randolph Churchill.* Anita Leslie (Scribner, NY 1969). P. 323.
5. *My Early Life.* Winston Churchill (Scribner, NY 1930). P. 12.
6. Ibid. P. 12
7. *Decline and Fall.* Evelyn Waugh (Kessinger, London 1928).
8. *The Audit of War.* Correlli Barnett (Macmillan, London 1986).

2. The Shot that Echoed Around the World:
1. Wheatcroft, Andrew. *The Habsburgs* (Viking, 1995).
2. *The Prisoner of Zenda.* Anthony Hope (Arrowsmith, London 1898).
3. Hamann, Brigitte. *Hitler's Vienna* (Oxford University Press, NY 1999).
4. Name changed from Princip to the Latin Bridge in 1993.
5. *The Habsburgs.* Andrew Wheatcroft (Viking, London 1995).
6. Rebecca West.
7. West, Rebecca. *Black Lamb and Grey Falcon* (Viking, NY 1941).
8. *DSM-IV. Diagnostic and Statistical Manual of Mental Disorders* (American Psychiatric Association, 1952).
9. In a recent poll in the UK to determine most people's main ambition, more people wanted to be an overnight celebrity than anything else.

10. We see his type in the role of the dim-witted army officer named Schlemiel every time we watch Offenbach's opera of *The Tales of Hoffman*. He appears from nowhere, gets in the way of Hoffman's sword, and dies stupidly for nothing.

11. Conrad, Joseph. *The Secret Agent* (Penguin London, 1907).

3. Prelude to War:

1. *History of the First World War*. Ibid. P. 18.
2. Michael Shelden. *Young Titan* (Simon & Schuster, NY 2013).
3. Michael Shelden. Ibid.
4. "The crowd symbol of the Germans was the *army* . . . it was the marching forest." *Crowds and Power*. Elias Canetti (*Masse und Macht*, Seabury, NY 1960). P. 173.
5. Mirabeau, 1788.

4. The Young Winston:

1. *Churchill: A Life*. Martin Gilbert (Heinemann, London 1991). P. 23.
2. *Churchill: A Life*. Ibid. P. 38.
3. *Churchill: A Life*. Ibid. P. 48.
4. *My Early Life*. Ibid. P. 60.
5. As described in Dostoyevsky's short story called "The Gambler," and the true case of Dreyfus who was victimized by the army in France to conceal the treachery of a fellow officer who had sold military secrets to pay his gambling debts.
6. *Churchill: A Life*. Ibid. P. 55.
7. *Churchill: A Life*. Ibid. P. 57.
8. *My Early Life*. Ibid. P. 96.

5. Cavalry Charge:

1. By Thomas Malory. Early fifteenth century.
2. Refined by Edmond Spenser into the longest such poem in the English language; *The Faerie Queene* (1590/6).
3. Thomas Malory. *Morte d'Arthur*.
4. Both spellings, Mordred and Modred, were acceptable in Old English, before standardized spelling became institutionalized.
5. *The Meditations*. Marcus Aurelius (AD 167).

6. The Victorians:

1. A curiously insightful impression of Post-Edwardian Englishness comes from a Russian anglophile nicknamed "The Englishman" by his friends. Naval architect Yevgeny Zamyatin lived in Newcastle for much of 1916/17, where he oversaw a number of new ice-breakers being constructed for Tsar Nicolas. He portrays what he considered to be typical Englishness (as paraphrased by book

reviewer Martin Amis) as "fastidious and fantastical, dogged and capricious, busy rationalizers of their abiding repressions . . . in thrall to a life of self-imposed timetables." He was impressed by the "human order and mechanical harmony," which must have seemed extraordinary after the chaos and resigned acceptance of a lack of time or purpose he must have been accustomed to in the vast and backward spaces between the isolated cities of the Russian Empire. (Martin Amis. Ibid. pp. 395-397.)

2. Played by actor Sam Jaffe in George Stevens' 1939 Hollywood film inspired by Kipling's poem. It featured Cary Grant, Victor McLaglen, and Douglas Fairbanks Jr., in which they crush an ISIS-like terrorist group intent on killing non-Hindus, known to history as the Thugees.
3. The ballad is longer, but abbreviated for this quotation.
4. Source: *The Telegraph,* April 20, 2014.

7. The Lady with the Lamp:

1. *It's No Use Raising a Shout.* W. H. Auden, 1929 (The Oxford Book of American Poetry).
2. In 1901.
3. Martin Amis on Northrop Frye's essay about Dickens and the Plautus-Terrence New Comedy tradition of grotesques. Ibid. P. 194.

8. The Flawed Human Condition:

1. Freud's concept was triggered by a patient, a young man who was afraid of horses with blinkers over their eyes. Freud's analysis discovered that the horse symbolized the boy's father, whom he viewed as a competitor for his mother's love.
2. *Berlin.* David Clay Large (Basic, NY 2000). P. 227.
3. *Fracture.* Philipp Blom (Harper, NY 2015). P. 256.
4. Hamann, Brigitte. *Hitler's Vienna* (Oxford University Press, NY 1999).
5. Jack the Ripper's real identity is explored in another book by John Harte, entitled *Addicted to Murders.*
6. Nead, Lynda. *Victorian Babylon* (Yale University Press, 2000).
7. Martin Amis.

9. Winston Under Fire:

1. *My Early Life.* Ibid. P. 232.

10. A Prisoner of War:

1. *My Early Life.* Ibid
2. *My Early Life.* Ibid
3. *The Killing Ground.* Tom Travers (Pen and Sword, 2009).
4. Tom Travers. Ibid.

5. *The War That Ended Peace.* Margaret MacMillan (Allen Lane, London 2013). P. 49.

11. Below the Poverty Line:
1. SAHO: South African History online.
2. The Fawcett Ladies Commission.
3. Times History.
4. *Churchill: A Life.* Ibid. P. 144.
5. *Poverty: A Study of Town Life.* Seebohm Rowntree (Macmillan, London 1901).

12. Winston's Rebellion:
1. Alexander MacCallum Scott.
2. *Churchill: A Life.* Ibid. P. 172.
3. *Churchill: A Life.* Ibid. P. 174.
4. *Churchill: A Life.* Ibid. P. 175.
5. *Churchill: A Life.* Ibid. P. 181.
6. *Churchill and the Jews.* Martin Gilbert (McClelland & Stewart, Toronto 2007). P. 1.
7. *Churchill: A Life.* Ibid. P. 183.
8. 1896-1909.
9. *Mrs. Randolph Churchill.* Ibid. P. 316.
10. *Mrs. Randolph Churchill.* Ibid. P. 318.
11. *Mrs. Randolph Churchill.* Ibid. P. 319.

13. Public and Private Lives:
1. As their daughter Mary would write in later life.

14. The Coming War:
1. *Churchill: A Life.* Ibid. P. 240.
2. *Churchill: A Life.* Ibid. P. 242.
3. The natural division between allies and enemies was racial more than religious, although both applied. Germanic races feared the enormous number of Slavs whom they thought of as barbarians, and vice-versa.
4. *Churchill: A Life.* Ibid. P. 248.
5. Captain Gilbert Lushington. *Churchill: A Life.* Ibid. P. 252.
6. Interest earned from Britain's shares in Anglo-Persian Oil would pay for the cost of all British battleships built after 1914.

15. "Kaiser Bill":
1. *Nietzsche and Antiquity.* Bishop (Camden House, 2004).
2. Lord Raglan's studies of the heroic profile were reinforced by psychologists Otto Rank and Jung's archetypes. They included such legendary heroes as

Odysseus, Achilles, Sampson, the Buddha, Mohammad, Jesus, Zeus, King Arthur, Moses, Krishna, and others.

3. To the *Daily Telegraph* on October 28, 1908.

4. *The Western Heritage.* Kagan, Ozment, Turner (Prentice Hall, NJ 2007). P. 485.

5. *Voltaire.* Theodore Besterman (Harcourt Brace, NY 1969). P. 409.

6. *The Western Heritage.* Ibid. P. 732/3.

7. Military historian Liddell Hart claimed it was fought for all three. *History of the First World War* (Cassel, 1930). P. 18.

8. *Through the Fog of War.* Liddell Hart (F&F London, 1938).

9. Liddell Hart. Ibid. P. 16.

10. Liddell Hart. Ibid. P. 17.

11. In 1938.

12. Marshal Saxe. Liddell Hart. Ibid. P. 17.

13. *The Anglo-Japanese Alliance.* Keith Neilson (Routledge, London). P. 49.

14. Margaret MacMillan. Ibid.

15. From *Outbreak of the World War: German Documents collected by Karl Kautsky.* Max Montgelas and Walther Schücking. No. 401 [1924]. Pp. 348-350. Trans. by Carnegie Endowment for International Peace.

16. Förster, "Im Reich des Absurden." 333

17. *The War that Ended Peace.* Margaret MacMillan (Lane, London 2013). P. 559.

18. Liddell Hart. Ibid.

19. Liddell Hart. Ibid. P. 20.

16. The First World War:

1. *Churchill: A Life.* Ibid. P. 267.

2. Lord Beaverbrook would later describe that fateful evening of August 1. "Winston rang for a servant, changed his dinner jacket for a lounge coat and left the room without speaking a word. He was not depressed. He was not elated; he was not surprised . . . He went straight out like a man going to a well-accustomed job. In fact he had foreseen everything that was going to happen so far that his temperament was in no way upset by the realisation of his forecast." *Mrs. Randolph Churchill.* Ibid. P. 346.

3. Private J. Parr. *The First World War.* Martin Gilbert (Weidenfeld London, 1994). P. 53.

4. *Churchill: A Life.* Ibid. P. 275.

5. *Mrs. Randolph Churchill.* Ibid. P. 347.

6. *History of the First World War.* Liddell Hart (Cassel 1930). P. 84.

7. General Haldane. September 3.

8. Eugene Gerrard, Spenser Grey, and Richard Bell Davies.

9. The British Lewis light machine-gun and the Stokes Mortar were marginally superior to the German guns. *British Fighting Methods in the Great War.* Paddy Griffith (Routledge, London 1996).

17. Winston in Disgrace:

1. Liddell Hart, Ibid. P. 83. Reducing Namur took six German divisions and five hundred guns August 20/5.
2. *Through the Fog of War.* Liddell Hart (Faber, London 1938). P. 21.
3. Liddell Hart. Ibid. P. 86.
4. Liddell Hart. Ibid. P. 93.
5. Captain Richmond.
6. *Churchill: A Life.* Ibid. P. 306.
7. *Churchill: A Life.* Ibid. P. 311.
8. *Churchill: A Life.* Ibid. P. 316.
9. *Mrs. Randolph Churchill.* Ibid. P. 355.
10. *Mrs. Randolph Churchill.* Ibid. P. 356.

18. Winston on the Front Line:

1. *Through the Fog of War.* Liddell Hart (Faber, London 1938). P. 108.
2. Sir Ian Hamilton was probably the last person from the Gallipoli affair who was still alive when Liddell Hart wrote about him in 1938.
3. *Churchill: A Life.* Ibid. P. 332.
4. *Churchill: A Life.* Ibid. P. 334.
5. *Churchill: A Life.* Ibid. P. 339.
6. Tudor was one of the first advocates of "predicted artillery fire." He rose to the rank of Major General and commanded the 9th Scottish Division.
7. *Churchill: A Life.* Ibid. P. 353.

19. Anguish and Torment:

1. Wilson ended the war with the rank of Field Marshal. He was assassinated on the doorstep of his home by two Irish nationalists.
2. *Churchill: A Life.* Ibid. P. 363.
3. *History of the First World War.* Ibid. P. 303.
4. *History of the First World War.* Ibid. P. 304.
5. *History of the First World War.* Ibid. pp. 58/9.
6. *History of the First World War.* Liddell Hart (Cassell, London 1930). P. 255.
7. *History of the First World War.* Ibid. P. 259.
8. *History of the First World War.* Liddell Hart. Ibid. P. 258.
9. *History of the First World War.* Ibid. P. 260.
10. *History of the First World War.* Ibid. pp. 259/60.

11. *History of the First World War.* Ibid. P. 268.
12. *History of the First World War.* Ibid. P. 305.
13. *First World War.* Gilbert Martin (W&N, London 1994). P. 256.
14. *First World War.* Ibid. P. 259.
15. *First World War.* Ibid. P. 260.
16. Kitchener was Commander-in-Chief of the Egyptian Army when he crushed the separatist Sudanese forces of "The Mahdi" at Omdurman and occupied the city of Khartoum in 1898 (when he became Lord Kitchener of Khartoum). He became Commander-in-Chief of the Boer War in 1900. Created a Viscount, he was appointed Commander-in-Chief of India. He ruled Egypt and the Sudan until 1914 when, (reluctantly) appointed Secretary of State for War, he enlisted vast numbers of volunteers in "Kitchener Armies." Although a public celebrity with his familiar portrait on recruiting posters, the War Cabinet did not worship him like the public did, since he was hopeless at teamwork and a poor delegator of responsibilities. He was drowned with 643 members of the crew of HMS *Hampshire* when it was sunk by a German mine on the way to Russia.

20. Mutiny:
1. *First World War.* Ibid. P. 313.

21. "The Yanks are Coming!"
1. *First World War.* Ibid. P. 365.
2. *First World War.* Ibid. P. 372.
3. *First World War.* Ibid. P. 355.
4. *First World War.* Ibid. P. 341.
5. *History of the First World War.* Ibid. P. 435.
6. *First World War.* Ibid. P. 374.

22. The Killing Fields:
1. *First World War.* Ibid. P. 378.
2. *The Habsburgs.* Ibid. P. 287.
3. Groener. *Lebenserinnerungen,* pp. 141-2. 145-6.
4. Mombauer. *Helmuth von Moltke.* Pp. 219-24. *The War that Ended Peace.* Margaret MacMillan (Lane, London 2013). P. 613.
5. *The War that Ended Peace.* Ibid. P. 634.
6. *Churchill: A Life.* Ibid. P. 382.
7. *All Quiet on the Western Front.* Erich Maria von Remarque (Ullstein, Berlin 1929).
8. Sir Edward Marsh, as he would become known in later life, became an art patron, a sponsor of poets, and a translator, as well as a civil servant. He was educated at Westminster School.

9. *Churchill: A Life.* Ibid. P. 390.
10. *Churchill: A Life.* Ibid. P. 393.
11. *Churchill: A Life.* Ibid. P. 397.

23. Spies of "Room 40":

1. *The Secret Agent.* Ibid.
2. *Reilly, Ace of Spies.* Robin Bruce Lockhart (Viking, London 1984).
3. *Memoirs of a British Agent.* (1932).
4. Ian Fleming, a former naval intelligence agent, would first write about the fictional James Bond in *Casino Royale,* after buying a publisher named Gilrose in London in 1953. He wrote twelve different novels featuring the mythical James Bond. Other authors wrote more after Fleming died.
5. Controversial and often misquoted.
6. *Churchill and Secret Service.* David Stafford (Murray, London 1997). P. 60.
7. David Stafford. Ibid. P. 41.
8. David Stafford. Ibid. P. 47.
9. By Erskine Childers. British agents arrested and imprisoned for four years were Lieutenant Brandon and Captain Trench.
10. David Stafford. Ibid. P. 49.
11. David Stafford. Ibid. P. 73.

24. The Beginning of the End:

1. *First World War.* Ibid. P. 398.
2. *First World War.* Ibid. P. 398.
3. *First World War.* Ibid. P. 414.
4. *First World War.* Ibid. P. 420.
5. *First World War.* Ibid. P. 420.
6. *First World War.* Ibid. P. 425.
7. *First World War.* Ibid. P. 426.
8. *A History of the Twentieth Century.* Martin Gilbert (Morrow, NY 1989). P. 516.
9. *Churchill: A Life.* Ibid. P. 401.
10. *Mrs. Randolph Churchill.* Ibid. P. 338.
11. *Lady Randolph Churchill.* Ibid. P. 378.
12. *American Jennie.* Anne Sebba (Norton, NY 2007).

INDEX